DEMOLISHING STRONGHOLDS

Demolishing Strongholds

Effective Strategies for Spiritual Warfare

DAVID DEVENISH

WORD PUBLISHING

WORD ENTERTAINMENT LTD
Milton Keynes, England

DEMOLISHING STRONGHOLDS

First published 2000 by Word Publishing,
9 Holdom Avenue, Bletchley, Milton Keynes, Bucks, MK1 1QR, UK.

ISBN 1 86024 371 1

Produced for Word Publishing by
Bookprint Creative Services, P.O. Box 827, BN21 3YJ, England.
Printed in Great Britain

CONTENTS

ACKNOWLEDGEMENTS

I want to thank Dennis Studd for preparing the first draft of this book from all my many tapes on the subject, and Stephanie Hedley for laboriously typing up many subsequent drafts. I am also grateful to Jane Sanders and Greg Haslam for their very helpful comments on the manuscript. They led me to think through more thoroughly many of the issues involved, though the responsibility for the final text is mine alone. Malcolm Down of Word Publishing originally encouraged me to write this book and has been very supportive throughout.

In particular, I want to acknowledge my gratitude to Scilla and our children, Tony, Neil, Justine and Sharon for their long-suffering and patience as I fought my way through the various issues of spiritual warfare identified in this book. My father, Roy Devenish, painstakingly put together and checked the references at the end of each chapter.

FOREWORD

Much that is said on the subject of Spiritual Warfare leaves many Christians uneasy because of its lack of biblical backing. Conclusions are drawn and assumptions made from the flimsiest of evidence. Christians and churches are encouraged to embrace methodology that is, at least, questionable, and sometimes unhelpful and misleading.

In great contrast to this recent preoccupation, it has been my pleasure to hear David Devenish preach with such helpfulness on the theme of 'Demolishing Strongholds'. I am delighted that he is now presenting this material to the wider Christian public in written form. David is a man of faith and action, as well as a man who has a great love for the Scriptures. He is also one who builds in local church life very wisely, bringing not only prophetic insight, but also pastoral wisdom.

Any who read this book will find themselves better equipped to face the challenges of a hostile world and culture, and satanic forces bent on destruction. Satanic opposition needs to be withstood in the light of Scripture and with the certainty of faith. David's book will help to fortify every believer intent on winning this battle. They will be the better armed for reading it.

Terry Virgo, New Frontiers International, April 2000

Chapter 1

PERSONAL EXPERIENCE
THE LEADING OF GOD INTO
SPIRITUAL WARFARE

Woodside Church was 'planted out' in a new housing estate in
Bedford during the late 1970s. We wanted to see people saved
and longed to see our new church grow. After two or three years,
exciting times began for us, as people on the estate responded
to our evangelism and a few were saved. Everything was going
quite well until I returned home one evening from my job in the
city to be met by frantic phone calls from a small group of
women, all of whom were new Christians. They had been listening to a tape about the gifts of the Holy Spirit. As they began
to pray afterwards, the power of God fell on them and they
began to prophesy and speak in tongues. They wanted to know
more, and they wanted me to explain what was going on.

This had to be from God, yet I had no personal experience
of such an occurrence. The congregation at the time, apart from
a few notable exceptions, could broadly be described as pre-
dominantly non-charismatic; it might even be true to say that
many were anti-charismatic. My wife Scilla and I, although
attracted by the apparent zeal of many charismatic believers,
were very suspicious. We had left the Exclusive Plymouth
Brethren in 1970 and during the next ten years or so were
involved in something of a spiritual journey. This was a time

11

when we were endeavouring to sort out our theological under-
standing and our experience of God in the context of the wider
Christian scene, that we had previously been taught was the
'Apostate Church'.

Still we had to respond to the phone calls, and so as leaders,
we agreed that the next thing to do was a Bible study. We
arranged to go to the house of one of these new Christians, and
do a study of 1 Corinthians chapters 12–14, to try to explain
what was going on. What none of us knew, however, was that
several of them had been involved in the occult before being
saved. Worse still, some had friends who were still involved. So
began a series of phone calls to me and the other leaders in the
church, telling us of strange happenings. In one house, a cross
was thrown off a wall, as if by an invisible hand. A friend of one
of the women was still involved in the occult and had 'prophesied' that the woman and her daughter would die. As if to prove
it, the daughter was rushed to hospital with an ectopic pregnancy. (That is a pregnancy where the baby develops outside the
womb, usually in the Fallopian tubes. It is quite dangerous; the
baby rarely survives and the mother's life can be at risk.)

Neither the other leaders nor I had any idea what was going
on. However, we agreed that, according to the Bible, demons
went when Jesus commanded them to leave and the important
thing for us, was that these people were experiencing demonic
manifestations; so we commanded the demons to leave. As we
started to do this, people were set free, peace returned to the
homes, and the hospital was able to help the woman with the
ectopic pregnancy so that she lived. We continued to pray about
the situation and another friend of the group whose death had
been 'prophesied' lived well beyond the date that he was supposed to die. This was our first recognisable experience of spiritual warfare. Until these situations began to arise, my
understanding of the Christian's battle against the powers of
darkness had been almost nil.

We were meeting in a local community centre while these things were happening, and it was not long before some of the local teenagers decided that they wanted to get to know us. They started coming to our services, generally making a nuisance of themselves and disrupting the services. Since they frequently outnumbered us, there was little we could do about it. It would have been easy to just push them out, but we tolerated their disruptiveness and a few of us tried to build relationships with them. One Sunday evening, we noticed that there were only a few of them instead of the usual crowd. We didn't take too much notice, and I didn't think of it any more until I got home. There, in my front garden, was a crowd of these 'hard' teenagers waiting for me. They were obviously upset, and some were crying. When I asked them what the trouble was, they told me that instead of coming to disrupt our meeting, a group of them had begun to use a ouija board. It had gone horribly wrong; an evil spirit had shown itself and had chased them down the stairs. At that point, they had run to my house.

As these sorts of situations grew, it was not long before we leaders were called before a meeting of the church. They had heard about the strange phenomena and demonic manifestations and because we were leaders in a church that was unsympathetic to the Charismatic Movement they wanted us to explain why we were allowing such things to happen.

As leaders we had come to the conclusion that if we were to plant an effective church, then we had to learn from the lessons that God had been teaching us. There were two issues that had to be considered immediately.

Firstly, although we had no training – and in many respects had no idea what we were doing – we began to recognise that the power and gifts of the Holy Spirit were essential if we were to reach out into that estate with the gospel, and set people free from demons and their effects and influences on people's lives.

Secondly, we realised that such outreach could provoke a demonic backlash, and that we would need to confront this, stand firm against it in our own lives, and set free people who were in bondage. We sought to explain this from Scripture during the meeting.

We were fortunate because a missionary member of our church, who was working with The Wycliffe Bible Translators, supported us. John Callow had come back to Bedford especially for this meeting, and told the church it was clear to him that the Holy Spirit was at work in the things we were experiencing. If we rejected this, said John, and resisted what God was teaching us, He would eventually remove the 'candle' of His presence from amongst us. I clearly remember getting home after that meeting and crying out to God in our spare bedroom, desperate that He would not remove the 'candle'. I wanted a church that would become well established and effectively reach the lost.

Sadly, a few of our members left us over the following months, but from then on we began to see spiritual gifts regularly manifested in the meetings. Most of the new people who were being saved were also being baptised in the Holy Spirit soon afterwards. We later became a part of the New Frontiers International family of churches (NFI) led by Terry Virgo.

A new understanding

The next stage in my journey on this issue was John Wimber's visit to this country. By this time, I had left my job as a senior manager in international banking, and had begun to be a 'full-time' leader in the church.

I confess to being cynical about John Wimber's teaching during the early seminars, and this was not helped by the physical manifestations that occurred every time he 'invited the Holy Spirit to come'. One morning as John was teaching on the Kingdom of God, I found myself repenting of my cynical, typically British, attitude. Although I didn't realise it at the time, I had begun to encounter a powerful stronghold of British culture that was affecting my life. As I repented of my attitude, the Holy Spirit came upon me, and I found myself sprawled across several seats, totally unable to move. This lasted well into the lunch break, and when I did eventually start to move, it was very unsteadily.

Through John's teaching at that conference I received a theological framework concerning the kingdom of God and its effects in terms of healing the sick and seeing people set free from demonic power. In many respects, this has helped to shape my ministry.

When I preached at our church the following Sunday, I was so obviously different that one of the members asked what had changed me during that week. As I began to reflect on John's teaching, I soon began to realise just how many Christians were in bondage to things in their past.

I started to pray about it. I prayed that issues which were hindering spiritual progress in people's lives might be brought to the surface. This was a very dangerous thing to pray, very dangerous indeed, because from that time on, all sorts of issues came to the surface and I began to get involved in praying for people. Many were set free, although as we were still seeking to learn how to handle these things, some were also left struggling.

I became so busy that I realised others would have to be trained to do the work. This is a biblical approach, so I spent a lot of time reading as much as possible in the area of Christian counselling, and eventually put together some training material for something I called a *Caring and Healing Course*.[1]

It was originally intended for a small group of people within our church and I did not think that it would be taught more than once or twice. The purpose of the course was simply to pass on the knowledge that I had gained, but God had other ideas. The course seemed to have an anointing on it that was equipping many people with skills that would enable them to set others free.

The course also sought to put the counselling ministry into a biblical framework, with the result that it has been taught now scores of times both in the UK and in other parts of the world.

Learning about cultural strongholds

So far, I had been seeing spiritual warfare in terms of individuals being set free, which is very important. I was soon going to learn more about what strongholds were at a corporate level.

In 1994, we began to hear reports of remarkable things happening in Toronto, Canada. What happened in Toronto brought a fresh move of the Spirit of God into our experience. For us, it began at a meeting where Terry Virgo and David Holden (leaders in NFI) shared their experiences of a conference they had just attended with Rodney Howard Browne. We all felt a new joy, a fresh sense of anointing and the tangible presence of God as the Holy Spirit came upon us in a remarkable way.

I had been booked to speak at a series of seminars at the forthcoming Stoneleigh Bible Week, organised by NFI. As I began to prepare for these seminars over the next few weeks, I asked God about what I should present and I realised that I should speak from Paul's second letter to the Corinthians on the subject of demolishing strongholds. As my studies came together, I began to experience more of the anointing of God's Holy Spirit. My choice of subject was later confirmed in the very pleasant lounge of a house in Cambridge where the group of leaders I was working with was meeting for prayer. The Holy Spirit came upon us again and I started marching around the room, stamping my feet. This is not the usual sort of thing that you do in such surroundings, but one of the other leaders began to prophesy that what I was doing was symbolic of my role in demolishing strongholds, so this underlined my belief that I should speak on this subject.

At Stoneleigh that year, there seemed to be an anointing on those seminars and many people were set free. I still hear from people whose lives were transformed at them. This was particularly true of the second seminar, where the screaming got so loud, it sounded as if half of hell was being driven out. People were being set free just by going to the time of prayer ministry. One pastor's wife, for example, knew that there was an issue in her life that needed sorting out and went along for the ministry time. (She had been attending another seminar with her husband). Without anybody specifically praying for her, God wonderfully delivered her from something that had held her in bondage for many years.

From these meetings, we realised that some of the issues we were having to deal with were not specifically individual issues, but were the result in people's lives of major cultural strongholds that needed to be confronted. We began to understand that evil spiritual forces were behind certain aspects of culture and, that as people were set free from their effects, their power would be overcome.

The difficulty here is that in many cases the church is also in bondage to strongholds in our various cultures. The church needs to be released in order to have an effective liberating ministry to unbelievers.

I began to question whether much of the effort that is put into spiritual warfare against principalities and powers might be somewhat misguided. It was not so much an issue of attacking these principalities and powers directly, but of setting people free from their influence so that the church can be more effective. These issues are dealt with in greater depth later in the book.

Strongholds conferences

Since that time, I have spoken at conferences about demolishing cultural strongholds in other nations, including India, South Africa, Mexico, France, the USA and the United Arab Emirates. As I travel to these conferences, I need to study the culture of the area I am going to visit. It is not possible, of course, to become an expert merely by reading books and talking to people about their culture, although those things do help. It seems that God has given me the ability to apply the principles of demolishing strongholds in ways that are relevant to the culture we find ourselves in.

An example of this occurred in Mexico, where the team and I spent the first two days with a senior secular anthropologist. He acted as a guide for us in Mexico City, and as he showed us around the various 'tourist' sites, he explained to us many of the principles of Mexican history and culture. This was very helpful in providing us with a number of living examples that could be applied in my teaching.

Enemy counter-attacks

As we have travelled on our spiritual journey, and especially as we have become involved in spiritual warfare, Scilla and I have endured many personal and vicious counter attacks from the enemy. A typical example occurred at the first session of the *Caring and Healing Course*. I had just gone 'full time' then, and immediately following that decision, the church had gone through a difficult period.

Many parents will know the sinking feeling of being called out during an evening meeting to answer a distress call from the baby-sitter who is looking after your children. This is what happened to us. Just as the first session began, someone came into the church building and called Scilla out. She did not come back, and I later discovered that Sharon, our youngest daughter, had started to cry as soon as I began to speak. She was with Ian, a reliable baby-sitter who she knew well, but nothing could be done, she simply would not stop crying.

When it happened again the second week, we began to realise that something was going on, especially since even Scilla could not quieten Sharon on the second occasion. As the time crept towards midnight, we decided that drastic action was necessary, and called out the other elders in the church to pray for her. From that time on, I could only teach the course if someone was praying in the house during the meeting.

When Sharon was about eighteen months old, I was called out to pray at a house that had been subjected to a form of voodoo called obeah. The next morning, as she tried to get out of bed, she was alarmed to find that she could not move. We eventually got her referred to a hospital where the problem was diagnosed as rheumatoid arthritis. They told us that she might grow out of it, but it could affect her for the rest of her life. So the church started to pray for her and a small group of women in particular prayed regularly. They focused their prayers both on physical healing and against the attacks of the enemy. They also felt that it was important to pray about some of the emotions that Scilla had experienced while Sharon was in her womb. After a few weeks, praise God, we saw real healing, and subsequent tests showed no sign of the rheumatoid factor in her blood.

On another occasion, while I was in India, teaching about matriarchal control and the spirit of Jezebel, my son was physically attacked by a young man at a church service. This man was not a regular visitor at the church, and did not know Neil; yet he said that the reason for the attack was that Neil was saying 'bad things about his mother'. This occurred at a time when many people in India were being set free from matriarchal domination. Many similar experiences could be quoted.

David Holden felt very strongly that we should be covered in prayer every time I spoke about cultural strongholds. At a gathering of the NFI pastors in our region, he spoke to them about sharing in this ministry, with the result that several churches are now praying supportively on such occasions. There is also a group of individuals who regularly support the work and I believe that it is essential for any leaders involved in pioneering work to have this level of prayer covering. The level of attack has actually gone down since so many people have supported us in prayer.

It is obvious to us now that those early encounters were not my first experiences of spiritual warfare. It was just that I had not realised at the time the implications of the situations that I found myself in.

When Scilla and I left the Exclusive Plymouth Brethren in 1970, it was because the international leader of that organisation had been found in bed with another man's wife and the organisation refused to discipline him, but continued to support his leadership. It might come as a surprise to other Christians that only a relatively small number of people left the Brethren after that incident. Many devout members still do not accept that their leader could do any wrong, even though they are godly in their own lives. They remain held fast by the legalistic doctrines of the movement.

It is obvious from situations like this that there can be strongholds in religious institutions as well as in the world. Christians can be deceived and believe lies even when they are genuinely seeking to follow Christ. If religious movements start to become exclusive or controlling, they can become prey to terrible deception. This is an issue of spiritual warfare. As I have begun to realise that strongholds can infect churches as well as cultures and individuals, I have started to minister into many of these situations.

My own journey has shown me that having an understanding of the enemy's strategies and a biblical model for dealing with them are essential for the progress of the church.

Indeed, for me, **Effective Strategy Number I** for pulling down strongholds is: Have a biblical model for understanding the enemy's strategies and dealing with them.

This book is written with the purpose of seeking to provide a biblical perspective on spiritual warfare and to equip Christians to set people free from strongholds of evil in their lives. As you read it, I ask that you seek to be open to God so that we can all be among those who set the oppressed free.

NOTES

[1] *Caring and Healing Course,* David Devenish (on video and cassette from New Frontiers International, 17 Clarendon Villas, Hove, East Sussex, BN3 3RE).

Chapter 2

THE REALITY AND IMPORTANCE OF SPIRITUAL WARFARE

When we read in the Bible about the advance of the Gospel of the Kingdom, there is a tendency to read it through the eyes of western rationalism and this can limit our understanding of the reality of spiritual warfare. We tend to treat what we cannot see as if it does not exist because of our so-called 'scientific' or 'rational' worldview – that is, our way of looking at the world – which in the West can often marginalise super-natural activity. However, there are many places in the world where the people have a different worldview and more readily understand demonic power. (It is not that demonic power is any more present there, just more obvious and recognised).

As you travel to preach the gospel and see people set free, you begin to realise the reality of the unseen spiritual world from a different perspective. For example, while in America, I spent time with a pastor who was leading a church in Haiti. This island in the Caribbean had been dedicated to Satan, although evangelical Christians have begun to make ground and have succeeded in stopping an annual rededication ceremony from being enacted. This pastor could fill a book with just some of his experiences, but here is one typical story.

The group that he leads wanted to build a new church

facility on a particular piece of land on the island. They bought the land and began to prepare the foundations where the building was to be constructed. They levelled off the ground to the size of building that they had planned and were just about to prepare the foundations when the pastor felt that God was telling him to dig further. So, they dug deeper, then levelled off the ground and started to prepare the foundations again. However, the pastor still felt that God was telling him to dig further. Now at this point, most people would begin to wonder whether it was God or their own insecurity that was telling them to dig. The pastor decided to be positive and believe for God; so they dug and dug and dug.

After digging really deep, their patience was beginning to run a bit thin and they were just about to give up when someone struck something hard and unyielding. They found to their amazement that they had dug up an old sacrificial altar that had been used for evil purposes. They cleared it out of the way, and God told them that they could now build. He did not want a building that was to be used for His purposes built on a foundation of something evil.

To western eyes, this whole story is a little bit weird. We might want to question what it means, what it is all about; but the pastor did as he was told, and they now have one of the few buildings on the island with a basement room. A happy side effect is, of course, that in such a hot country, the basement room is cooler for prayer meetings!

As a further illustration of differing ways of looking at things, I would like to mention something that happened to me in India. A Christian couple approached and asked me to pray for them, because they couldn't have children. Normally I don't tend to ask the details, but on this occasion I asked the wife what the problem was, half expecting a detailed gynaecological history. Her response was that when she was a teenager, she had killed a cobra, and because of that, she was now unable to have children. It had never occurred to me with my western perspective that in the superstitious traditions of that area, a girl in puberty must not kill a cobra (but must allow a man to do so on her behalf). Otherwise, it is believed, she will never have children.

So I prayed for her to be released from the influence of the powers of superstition in her life, and when I went back two years later she already had a baby, and there was another on the way. She and her husband are now small-group leaders in the church there. I will come back to this story later in the book.

There is a two-fold danger here. We can be influenced by a rationalist worldview into disbelieving spiritual warfare issues, or we can swing too far the other way and develop an unhealthy preoccupation with the demonic. The church often seems to fluctuate unhelpfully between these two extremes:

1. If the subject of spiritual warfare is ignored, the enemy gains the advantage that we are unaware of what he is doing and he is thus free to carry on.
2. If, on the other hand, we develop an unhealthy interest in the powers of darkness, we offer the enemy an opportunity to oppress us with fear, by shifting our focus away from the power and victory of God.

Definition of spiritual warfare

What do I mean by spiritual warfare? The definition I work with is as follows: '*The reality that the advance of the gospel and the building of the church involve us in attacking and experiencing counter-attack in relation to real cosmic forces of darkness under the control of Satan who is also described as the god of this world.*'

The implications of this definition will come out throughout this book but the important thing is that spiritual warfare is not some sort of specialist activity that people with special skills get involved with. It is rather what all of us will face as we advance the gospel and see the church built in our day.

Priority of spiritual warfare

What then is the biblical perspective? What priority should spiritual warfare have in our thinking?

It was very important in the ministry of Jesus. Jesus acknowledged Satan's existence and clearly faced up to him and to his influence in the earth. Immediately after He was anointed with the power of the Holy Spirit, and before He engaged in His public ministry, the Holy Spirit led Him into the desert for a confrontation with the enemy. He had to withstand and counter Satan's attacks on His integrity before He could attack the kingdom of darkness and set free those who were held captive.

(There are likely to be parallels in the lives of leaders in the church and, indeed, in all our lives if we are being are used to spread the gospel of the kingdom. There are likely to be issues the enemy will raise that will challenge our own integrity and will need to be fought with the Word of God.)

If we read about the things Jesus did as well as what He said, it is noticeable that a large proportion of His ministry involved setting people free from demonic power.

The context of the kingdom

Jesus saw His encounters with demonic powers in people as evidence of the kingdom of God having come. He said, 'But if I drive out demons by the finger of God then the kingdom of God has come to you'.[1] It is very important that we understand the basic theology of the kingdom of God when we are considering the issue of spiritual warfare.

In Scripture the word 'kingdom', which Jesus used frequently, did not mean a place you enter into – like the United Kingdom – but the 'ruling' of a king. In the gospels, it meant that wherever the rule of Jesus went, there was the kingdom. It is thus a dynamic, not a static concept. If the sick are healed, the kingdom extends. If those afflicted by demons are set free, if good news is preached to the poor, the kingdom comes. Wherever God is obeyed, His kingdom advances.

The kingdom rightfully belongs to God. He is sovereign, so ultimate authority totally belongs to Him. Man was appointed by God to fill the earth and rule it in accordance with God's will. However, because man sinned, Satan usurped man's authority and was allowed to become the 'Prince of this world',[2] dominating the affairs of man as an impostor.

When Jesus came preaching the kingdom and doing the works of the kingdom, He was invading Satan's rule with the rule of God. We must understand spiritual warfare in this context. Jesus then totally defeated the Prince of this world at the cross and in His resurrection and ascension. Because of man's fall, death had a right to all of Adam's offspring. Death had no rights to Jesus because Jesus was without sin in every way – both in His birth (from a virgin) and in His perfectly lived out life. Jesus took back the kingdom not by force, but justly through His defeat of Satan at the cross. Jesus therefore now rules the world even though we do not yet see everything totally under His authority. 'At present we do not see everything subject to Him. But we see Jesus who was made a little lower than the angels, now crowned with glory and honour.'[3] Jesus is now reigning until all His enemies are under His feet.[4]

We are to pray, as Jesus commanded us 'Your kingdom come, your will be done on earth as it is in heaven'.[5] This is warfare praying. We are actually saying, 'let the kingdom of God be demonstrated where previously Satan dominated'. This is really what spiritual warfare is all about. It is about Satan's resisting

God, and therefore attacking us because we are God's agents. We are seeking to advance God's kingdom into Satan's territory, where he rules as the usurping Prince of this world, or as Paul calls him, 'the ruler of the kingdom of the air'.[6]

Priority in the apostolic commission

Spiritual warfare was also a major part of Jesus' commission to His apostles. Mark describes this in chapter 3:14–15. Mark had a crisp, clear, assertive style and tended to write a summary of the events that he recorded. He reported that Jesus called His apostles together and told them that they were to be with Him, that they were to go out to preach and that they were to have authority in the spiritual realm.

Mark thus summarised the three important points in Jesus' commission to His apostles

- relationship with Him
- preaching the truth of the gospel
- demonstrating authority over demonic power.

While this is not all that there is to an apostolic ministry, these three areas are very important and can easily be overlooked in our consideration of apostolic ministry today.

Its importance in the life of the early church and the epistles

There was an abundance of power encounters with demonic forces as the gospel advanced. As Philip preached in Samaria, for example, there was a lot of screaming as demons left people.[7] When Paul went to Cyprus, he was confronted by a sorcerer as soon as he arrived.[8] At Philippi, he was confronted by a slave girl who told fortunes.[9] When he reached Ephesus, there were amazing power encounters that incidentally revealed that Paul's name was known even in the demonic world.[10]

In the book of Ephesians, Paul writes a lot about what he describes as 'heavenly places'[11] and 'principalities and powers'.[12] The term 'heavenly places' is not referring to our future home with Christ after we have died. It refers to the 'spiritual realm', a sphere which is just as real as the physical world but which we with a western worldview tend to regard as less real. This spiritual world is inhabited by spiritual beings such as angels and demons. Christ is described in Ephesians as having ascended above all evil forces in the spiritual realm, and we will talk more in a later chapter about the consequences of this for the believer's authority.

Paul also talks about principalities and powers existing in these heavenly places. Recently in theological circles, there has been a lot of debate about what these principalities and powers are. Some would argue that they refer to the human structures of government and social institutions. John Stott examines this perspective very thoroughly in his excellent commentary on Ephesians in *The Bible Speaks Today* series.[13] He makes the very important point that 'The Christian's spiritual warfare is specifically stated to be "not with flesh and blood but with principalities and powers", which has till recent days been universally understood as meaning "not with human but with demonic forces". The allusions to the "world rulers of this present darkness" and "the spiritual hosts of wickedness", together with the armour and weapons needed to withstand them, fits supernatural powers much more naturally, especially in the context that twice mentions the devil. . . . In fact, I have not come across a new theorist who takes into adequate account the fact that all three references to the principalities and powers in Ephesians also contain a reference to the heavenly places, that is the unseen world of spiritual reality.'[14] Paul is saying here that our battle is really against these principalities, powers and spiritual forces of evil in the heavenly realms and it is these we *wrestle* against – a very strong term.

In his letter to the Ephesians, Paul describes these principalities and powers. However, in Galatians and Colossians he talks about the 'elemental spirits' or 'basic principles'.[15] This is a similar idea and represents such things as legalistic principles that have a spiritual force behind them. Again, we will come back to this in later chapters.

Another reference by Paul to the reality of spiritual warfare is his concern that the enemy should not snatch people away. Paul had to leave the Thessalonian church in a rush and it seems that his emotions could stand the pressure no longer. He felt compelled to find news concerning the welfare of his new converts. So, he sent someone to enquire on his behalf. He says, 'For this reason, when I could stand it no longer, I sent [Timothy] to find out about your faith. I was afraid that in some way the tempter might have tempted you and our efforts might have been useless'.[16] Paul, afraid? Yes, this is what he says. It is a clear recognition of the reality of the struggle we face in seeing new converts established in the faith. Paul certainly saw the reality of spiritual warfare in the enemy's attempts to snatch new converts away.

Peter makes a similar reference, writing to more mature Christians with the same point. He says, 'Be self-controlled and alert. Your enemy the devil prowls round like a roaring lion looking for someone to devour'.[17] The idea of devouring means that we are taken out of the battle and are unable to continue our work for God.

The devil and all his works

All these circumstances have roots in the reality of the personal spiritual force of evil that we call the devil. We are told in the Scriptures that his purpose is destruction and it is his intention to lead the whole world astray. He prowls around, looking to see if he can devour this one or that one, and it is important that we are aware of this and that we don't underestimate him.

However, it's also important that we don't overestimate him either. He is not the opposite of God, but as C S Lewis said, is at best the opposite of the archangel Michael. So it is important that we neither underestimate nor overestimate his power.

The Old Testament prophets made some apparently mysterious comments about the devil, but before looking at an example of this, it is important that we understand how poetic prophecy often functioned in the Old Testament. The poet, or prophet would often describe something quite ordinary and then go on to expand what lay behind it, invariably a much larger picture.

A good example of this is shown in the description that Isaiah gives concerning the King of Babylon in Isaiah 14. He calls us to look at this king who will be attacking Israel. Then he begins to open out the picture. He calls the king 'Morning Star' and accuses him of wanting to ascend into heaven and raise his throne above God's stars. Then he says that, although the king once destroyed nations, he is now being cast down and he talks about him falling from heaven.[18] Although Isaiah is speaking of the human king of Babylon, as a parallel he is also talking about 'Lucifer',[19] called the Light Bearer and the Son of the Dawn or Satan, the devil. Isaiah states that it was actually Lucifer who wanted to ascend into heaven and to raise his throne above God's stars. This could not be a reference simply to a human king. Isaiah gives this as the reason why Lucifer was thrown out of heaven; in pride and rebellion, he rose up against God. It is Lucifer (Satan), who is behind the reality of what we know in Scripture and today as spiritual warfare.

The devil is spoken of in many ways in Scripture. He is the 'father of lies'.[20] He is out to deceive God's people, to make them mistrust God and His Word. He will lie to you to under-

mine your security in Christ. The strongholds of wrong thinking that are dealt with at length later in this book exist because
the devil is a deceiver.[21] He is described as 'the god of this
world',[22] 'the prince of this world'.[23] The Bible says, 'The whole
world lies in the power of the evil one'.[24] He has usurped
authority in this world through leading man into sin. We battle
against his wiles[25] and recognise that the world's system is based
on organisation that acts independently of God, and rejects
Him, His Word and His standards, whatever lip-service may be
paid to Christianity. He is a destroyer,[26] he is the thief who seeks
to cause harm to the flock, the people of God. Satan seeks to
destroy what he hates, that is anything which reminds him of his
Creator, with whom he tried to become equal. As a result, one
of the things he tries to do is to destroy the church, because it
is the body of Christ in this world. It is why the church is so
often made unattractive to Christian and non-Christian alike.
The enemy works to try and make the church quarrelsome on
the one hand or boring on the other (although we must
acknowledge that sinful Christians can play their part in doing
this as well!). The devil seeks to infiltrate the church with false
doctrine in order to undermine people's confidence in the Word
of God. Why do we so often experience troubles in church life?
It is because this is the express intention of the devil. We need
to recognise that and neither become disillusioned nor take it
out on one another. We must be on our guard, not ignorant of
his schemes[27] and advance against him to rescue people from
this present evil age.[28]

Overcoming

The priority of spiritual warfare is illustrated by the emphasis
given in Scripture to the issue of overcoming and being overcomers. We are all called to be overcomers. In chapters 2 and 3
of the book of Revelation, Jesus addresses seven churches, rep-

resentative of the church at that time and indeed all times, but also specifically relating to the seven churches individually addressed. In each case, issues of difficulty being faced by the church are pointed out by the Lord Jesus to John in a vision. Some of these are particular situations faced within the church, some relate to conditions prevailing in the cities where the churches are situated and which have affected the church. For example, the letter to the church in Pergamum refers to the fact that they live where 'Satan has his throne'.[29] Pergamum was the official centre of emperor worship in the province of Asia. Others relate to the persecution which authorities would bring against the Christians in some of the towns. In the case of Smyrna, this is specifically referred to as a work of the devil. It says, 'The devil will put some of you in prison to test you'.[30]

In each of these churches, there is a call to people to overcome. Sometimes it is a call to overcome sins or obstacles the devil has introduced into those churches. Sometimes it is the call to be faithful to Christ whatever the devil may bring externally.[31] Whatever is happening therefore, whether it is pressure from the world outside, or pressure because of the infiltration of false doctrines or practices into the church, our responsibility, each one of us, is to overcome. As we overcome, we find God gives us promises. There are particular blessings promised to the overcomers in each church. Would 'overcomer' be a fair description of you in your Christian life?

The idea of overcoming in Scripture is related to exhortations that encourage us to claim our inheritance. God makes specific promises to all of us as to what our inheritance is. It represents entering into everything God has promised for us. Our salvation is on the basis of God's sheer grace and our acceptance of it by faith. The particular promises over our life, though very much a gift of God's grace, nevertheless have to be fought for, by us, through overcoming faith. I do not believe that if we are a true believer in Jesus Christ, we can lose our eternal salvation. I do believe, however, that we can fail to enter into all the promises God has for us.

The concept of battling for our inheritance is set out as an example for us in the story of the people of Israel going through the wilderness and then facing the challenge of entering the promised land.[32] The land represented their inheritance – all that God had promised them. However, they failed to overcome. They believed a false report, rebelled and gave in to fear. They even expressed the desire to return to slavery in Egypt. They were not overcomers. On the other hand, Joshua and Caleb, who were the only ones of that generation to enter into the Promised Land, were overcomers. They refused to submit to the unbelief that failed to trust God to keep His promises. Later Joshua led the army of the next generation into the inheritance they were promised. Again, he had to battle.

Entering into the promises of God is described in the New Testament as 'entering into rest'. Rest here does not mean an absence of activity, but carries the concept of 'entering the promises of God'. The writer to the Hebrews deals with this in chapter 3:7–4:11. Entering into our inheritance requires faith. It requires us to encourage one another so that we do not become hardened by sin's deceitfulness.[33] It requires us to combine all that we hear from God with faith.[34] It requires overcoming faith and shapes us into people who will not give in to unbelief but rather keep going. This is spiritual warfare.

There is a particular call on young men to be overcomers.[35] However, it is not only for young men, it is for all of us. For some, it is to overcome sexual temptation, for others to resist giving in to worldly ambition. For others, it is to resist the lure of materialism. For others, it may be to overcome loneliness, disappointment, hurt or rejection. Some reading this book may be disappointed about the way their life has turned out or the way their hopes and aspirations have been dashed. You may have been hurt and disappointed because you have suffered a marriage breakdown, or because people have rejected you or not taken account of your genuine desires. You may be disappointed because church life has not yet turned out to be what you hoped. Spiritual warfare means that we are all called to overcome in these circumstances. We are called not to become cynical, hardened or disillusioned. We are to overcome and press on to God's purposes, forgetting what is behind and to keep on going.[36] The priority in our personal spiritual warfare is to overcome whatever circumstances we may find ourselves pulled down by. Let us overcome self-pity, let us overcome a negative attitude to life, and let us overcome a critical spirit. As you continue to read the rest of this book, be determined to have that attitude as we examine strongholds that need to be taken in the name of Jesus.

Effective Strategy Number 2: Recognise the high priority given to spiritual warfare in the ministry of Jesus and the early church, and give it a similar priority in our own lives, whatever our worldview has previously been.

NOTES

[1]Luke 11:20; [2]John 16:11; [3]Hebrews 2:8–9; [4]1 Corinthians 15:25; [5]Matthew 6:10; [6]Ephesians 2:2; [7]Acts 8:7; [8]Acts 13:6; [9]Acts 16:16; [10]Acts 19:15; [11]Ephesians 2:6 (RSV); [12]Ephesians 3:10 (RSV); [13]*The Message of Ephesians – God's New Society*, John R W Stott, page 267–275 (IVP, 38, De Montfort St, Leicester, LEI 7AP. Used with permission.); [14]Stott – page 273; [15]Galatians 4:3 and 9 (RSV/NIV), Colossians 2:20 (RSV/NIV); [16]1 Thessalonians 3:5; [17]1 Peter 5:8; [18]Isaiah 14:12; [19]Isaiah 14:12 (KJV); [20]John 8:44; [21]2 John 7; [22]2 Corinthians 4:4 (RSV); [23]John 16:11; [24]1 John 5:19; [25]Ephesians 6:11 (RSV); [26]Revelation 9:11; [27]2 Corinthians 2:11; [28]Galatians 1:4; [29]Revelation 2:13; [30]Revelation 2:10; [31]Revelation 2:10; [32]eg Numbers 13 and 14; [33]Hebrews 3:13; [34]Hebrews 4:2; [35]1 John 2:14; [36]Philippians 3:13.

Chapter 3

KEEPING IN BALANCE

It would be helpful to read James 3:9 – 4:8 in conjunction with this chapter.

Many books have been written on the subject of spiritual warfare, many conferences have been held, many ideas have infiltrated the minds and practices of Christians and in particular, many prayer meetings are focussed on what people understand to be 'spiritual warfare'. There is therefore a great need for balanced teaching on this subject, but the idea of 'balance' can sound a bit boring! People feel uncomfortable with the idea because it implies a sense of 'sitting on the fence', or 'taking the middle path', a view that involves compromise. However, that is not what I am saying here. Balance in this context is about not going to an extreme view on one aspect of biblical truth without considering other equally biblical teaching. It is to do with holding all aspects of truth on a given subject in tension without over-emphasising one in particular, even though at times the different aspects may seem paradoxical.

There are three clear factors that should be held in tension in considering any teaching on spiritual warfare.

1. God is sovereign

Our God is sovereign. All power and authority belongs to Him. We do *not* live in a dualistic universe, where equally matched powers of good and evil struggle for supremacy. It is not the case that if we fight long and hard enough, we may be able to tip the balance and overcome Satan and bring about victory for God. God is sovereign. His ultimate victory is not in any doubt. The devil cannot operate without God's sovereign permission, or exceed the parameters God allows him.

God is totally beyond us and infallible in all He does and says. So it is our responsibility as creatures to submit to Him and His Word even if there are times when we would really rather do something totally different, even when it offends 'human logic'. Adam and Eve were a particularly apt example of this in the Garden of Eden. The temptation they were given was to 'Be like God, knowing good and evil'.[1] Had they *submitted* to God instead, the outcome would have been very different.

Indeed the temptation to be autonomous as human beings, in charge of our own destiny, is still the essence of the warfare temptation we face from Satan. As we saw in the last chapter, it was the reason for his fall; he wanted to be equal with God. It was the temptation to which Adam and Eve succumbed. It was what caused the nations to fall and be scattered; they had wanted to build a tower to 'reach heaven'.[2] It is also the demonic power behind secular humanism today – the lie that man is sovereign, and in charge of his own destiny. The truth is that it is God who is sovereign.

2. We have personal responsibility

We fight against our flesh and the principles of this world. It is very easy to use demons or the devil as an excuse to abdicate responsibility, but we cannot blame them for everything.

Obviously, there are things that can be directly attributed to Satan, but as we will see later in this chapter, in many cases it is our own flesh that is actually the problem.

For example, if a wrong or lustful thought springs into our mind, it does not necessarily mean that a demon has intruded, or that Satan is attacking us. It is usually the result of sin at work in our flesh, the part of our life that has not been fully straightened out yet. Such thoughts are to be dealt with by thinking differently and renewing our mind.[3] This is one of the most common ways to resist the devil, not by casting out a demon, but by bringing my mind, thoughts and actions in submission to the Word of God. This is what it means to fight against our flesh or against the principles of this world.

It is no good blaming the devil if you cannot get up in the morning. You know the sort of thing: 'Oh the devil really had a go at me this morning; I just couldn't get up at all'. Then after this has been going on for a little while, you go for ministry. 'Lord, will you cast out the demon of sleep'. This may seem overstated, but such 'super-spirituality' is not unheard of. It is certainly not the way to deal with the problem. Maybe it is a case of having to deal with laziness, or maybe the solution is to go to bed earlier! *We are responsible for our actions; we must not blame the devil.*

3. *The reality of the devil and the demonic in our world*

The third factor we need to hold in balance with God's sovereignty and our responsibility perhaps seems obvious in view of what this book is about; it is the reality of the devil and the demonic in our world. I have already discussed this in Chapter 2 and so need not repeat it here. To summarise: the devil is real and powerful and is described as the god of this age. The Bible even says that the whole world is in the control of the Evil One.[4]

Holding this balance in the book of James

At the beginning of this chapter, I suggested you looked at a section in the book of James, which handles the issues of spiritual warfare in a way that, I believe, reflects this balance. James states things very clearly. He is not a very polite person, is he? When you read his epistle, you do not get the feeling that he is the sort of person who would call a spade a 'horticultural implement'! James tells it like it is, without any attempt to allow us to feel comfortable. He said that the people he was writing to did not have certain things because they did not ask, and even when they did ask, their motives were wrong. He was clear about our personal responsibility. He was not 'blaming the devil' for the lack of answers to prayer.

In Chapter 3, James talks about the power of the tongue. You can almost sense the amazement in his voice as he talks about the tongue being able to praise God one minute, then in the very next breath being able to curse someone. This is clearly an issue of our personal responsibility but then, in bringing in the idea of a 'curse', he is speaking of something that can have real spiritual effects.

Very often when I am praying for people, I see that they need to be set free from things people have said to them which have become a curse in their lives. This is particularly true when the words have been spoken by an authority figure such as a parent or teachers.

If you use words that are wrong, in whatever context, it is your flesh at work. If you say horrible things about someone, your words can bind them; the devil can bring power behind these words. That is the power of the tongue. James goes on to say that when we give in to the flesh we become friends with the world. Motives like envy and selfish ambition are principles of the world. James calls these 'unspiritual' and 'of the devil' and tells us that being friends with the world is like adultery.

He is not blaming the devil, but our friendship with the world
– our having given in to worldly principles. This is our responsibility, because friendship with the world is like hatred toward
God.

To put it in context, James was speaking specifically about
quarrelling and fighting in the church arising from envy and
self-interest. He even accused them of killing each other
(chapter 4:2), not with weapons, but with words and hatred.
Does that sound familiar sometimes? He recognises, however,
the evil spiritual dimension and points to the demonic origin
of their envy and selfishness (chapter 3:15). He also emphasises what God has done; how in His wonderful sovereign provision, He has furnished us with all we need in order to
overcome. He gives us wisdom that comes from Heaven and is
pure, peaceful, considerate, submissive and full of mercy. It is
full of good fruit and God gives us this by His grace to help
us live our lives.

Do you see how the three key truths are held in tension here?
We are clearly and personally responsible for the actions of our
flesh and for our adoption of the principles of the world.
However, there is a demonic aspect to it; this is equally recognised by James. But over all, God in His sovereignty has provided everything we need in order to overcome!

Submit to God, resist the devil

James also gives us here one of the classic spiritual warfare
statements, 'Resist the devil, and he will flee from you'.[5] The
context is specifically disagreement and conflict in the church.
He does not blame the enemy directly when there are quarrels
and fights among the members. He blames the people first,
holding them responsible because of their disobedience; then
he tells them to submit themselves to God, resist the devil and
he will flee away from them. Notice the order. Submit first, then

resist the devil and he will go. The first requirement is to submit to God. Only then will the devil flee when you resist him. Is the devil attacking you? Then submit to God, keep on doing the will of God. In that way, you resist the devil. This leads to a story with some relevance here.

On one occasion, while in India, where I had been preaching about a subject relevant to a cultural stronghold in the particular area, I was disturbed in my sleep by an evil, demonic being, that threatened to destroy my family if I continued to preach on this subject. The devil is a bully! By four o'clock that morning, I was in the lounge of the flat I was staying in, telling God that I would never preach on this subject again. Then I went back to bed. Twenty minutes later, I was repenting before God, and saying that I would continue to preach it, no matter what, and that I would preach it until He told me to stop. This was not bravado on my part. I sincerely believed that if I submitted to God, I would be able to resist the devil.

This has proved to be true, because since then things have become easier as I have travelled around preaching on this particular subject. Not only that, I have seen many people set free from this particular problem, and it seems that the more often I preach it, the more the devil runs away. The trouble is that many Christians do not do this. You hear them say 'Oh, I'm under attack again'; then they spend months in introspective self-pity. Before long they stop submitting to God's will, so they have stopped doing what He really wants them to do, and the devil is triumphant. What they should be doing instead is living kingdom life *more* as the devil attacks, submitting *more* to what God wants and pushing the kingdom further into areas of darkness. This particularly applies to those involved in pioneer work. They know what the principles of God's will are for them, so they should live them out. This is what drives the devil away and causes him to flee.

Further illustrations of this biblical balance

Here are some other illustrations from Scripture that should help to explain how these three truths are held in tension

- Adam and Eve sinned in the Garden; they were responsible but they were also misled by the devil into believing that they could become like God. God overruled it for good in that even in pronouncing the curse, He promised that the woman's descendant would crush the head of the serpent representing the devil. This looked forward to the redemption through Jesus Christ.

- This might be a difficult one to understand. During the life of King David, he once 'numbered the people'; in other words, he held a census to find out how many people he ruled at that time. David confessed that he sinned,[6] but it is said that Satan led him to do it.[7] However, God was still overruling; it says that God caused David to do it.[8] So here we have all three factors in tension: God's absolute sovereignty, David's work of the flesh and the devil's involvement in causing David to sin.

- Another example is King Saul. He was responsible for his own rebellion. Since rebellion is akin to the sin of witchcraft[9] and he did not repent, it says in the Bible that the Lord sent an evil spirit to trouble him, an aspect of God's judgement of Saul.[10] This is another situation that is hard to understand, that the Lord would send an evil spirit to trouble Saul. Again we have all three factors at work in a way our minds cannot fully understand but need to submit to. God was in control. Saul was responsible. An evil spirit began to work.

- Another mysterious example concerns the story about Ahab and the false prophets.[11] The false prophets were prophesying that Ahab, a wicked king in Israel, would secure victory in a battle. A godly prophet Micaiah said that God had permitted a lying spirit to deceive the false prophets.[12] It was the time when God's judgement would fall against the wicked king, Ahab. God had also sent Micaiah to describe accurately what would happen so Ahab was without excuse.

- Additionally, we must consider Job. His is the classic situation. Here we see Job, happily enjoying all God's favour and blessing without any idea what is about to happen. Somewhere far away, Satan has gone to talk to God. God turns to him and says, 'Do you see my servant Job? He is righteous and blameless, a man who fears me and turns away from evil.' Satan replies: 'Yes – of course he is good. You protect him and his household and all that he owns. You have blessed him and prospered him and he lacks for nothing. But stretch out your hand and strike everything he has, and he will surely curse you to your face.' The Lord, in reply, gives Satan permission to lay his hands on Job's family and possessions and, later, to harm Job himself, though not to take his life.[13] This is a tough one for us to understand, but it was even tougher for Job! We have the book and that makes it easier for us. We can look at the situation and maybe say 'Oh well, Job. It's obvious, isn't it? God just wanted to prove your faith by allowing Satan to attack you.' The trouble is, Job did not have the book. He did not know the reason. Job did not know what was going on behind his back; he just thought he was going through a tough time. The principle here is that Satan could not touch Job without God's absolute permission. Even then, God set a limit on what He would allow Satan to do; God insisted that Job's life must be spared.

- In a similar situation, Jesus once told Peter that Satan had asked God for the opportunity to sift Peter like wheat but that He had prayed that Peter's faith might not weaken. It is that same three-cornered principle again: Satan 'sifted' Peter, Peter himself was responsible for his own reaction to Satan's tempting and the Lord both gave permission for the onslaught and strengthened Peter's faith to overcome it.[14] Peter was still responsible for his actions in denying Jesus. He had to repent.

I want to speak personally to some of my readers. It may be that you are going through pressures that you do not understand. Satan is attacking you. All sorts of puzzling circumstances have befallen you. You are under intense pressure when all you were trying to do was to live for God. Maybe Satan has asked if he can sift you. Let people pray that your faith may not fail and make sure you submit to what you know is the will of God for you. Furthermore, be encouraged that, just as Jesus prayed for Peter, He is still interceding for you in heaven now.[15] The devil will eventually flee and your faith will become strong.

We must remember that we do not know in any detail how demonic principalities and powers operate or how they are organised. However, all that we do need to know has been revealed to us. There is a danger in speculating beyond what is taught in the Scriptures, and building a doctrine on that. Sadly there is often much speculation in the Christian church about the organisation of principalities and powers or about 'families' of demons. Some would teach that in order to deal with a demonic problem that has manifested itself, you need to trace back through related families of demons, to the 'strong man' behind them. All this detail has *not* been revealed to us. This is where the need for balance comes in, holding the three factors I have described in a dynamic tension. This is an important principle and any teaching that does not stress it should be treated with caution.

Effective Strategy Number 3: In our understanding of spiritual warfare, keep a balance between these three truths

- the reality of Satan and the demonic realm
- our responsibility for our actions
- the absolute sovereignty of God.

NOTES

[1]Genesis 3:5; [2]Genesis 11:4; [3]Romans 12:2; [4]1 John 5:19; [5]James 4:7; [6]1 Chronicles 21:8; [7]1 Chronicles 21:1; [8]2 Samuel 24:1; [9]1 Samuel 15:23 (KJV); [10]1 Samuel 18:10; [11]2 Chronicles 18:11; [12]2 Chronicles 18:22; [13]Job 1:12; [14]Luke 22:31–32; [15]Hebrews 7:25.

Chapter 4

TERRITORIAL SPIRITS AND 'STRATEGIC LEVEL SPIRITUAL WARFARE'

The issue of territorial spirits and what is called 'strategic level spiritual warfare' against them has been the subject of a large number of books that have been published recently. It is a practice that many evangelical believers are becoming increasingly involved with at the present time. I believe this involvement has come about because of the genuine desperation in all our hearts to see God move in revival power and for breakthrough evangelism into many areas of the world where there are so few born again Christians.

C Peter Wagner is probably the leading advocate of strategic level spiritual warfare and he has written a number of books on the subject.[1] Furthermore, exciting anecdotal 'evidence' of the effectiveness of these strategies has been coming out of Latin America, particularly Argentina, where there is quite obviously a mighty moving of God's Holy Spirit. The success of such powerful evangelists as Carlos Anacondia and Omar Cabrera is attributed by some to the practice of 'binding the strong man' over a city or an area before any major evangelistic thrust takes place.

What do its advocates mean by 'strategic level spiritual warfare'? Essentially, it involves three things:

- Discovering the name and nature of the particular territorial spirit over a city or region through such techniques as 'spiritual mapping'.
- Loosening such spirits' hold by dealing with the corporate sins that give them their authority through such practices as 'identificational repentance'.
- Binding and driving them out by aggressive warfare praying.

According to Wagner, there are three sorts of warfare in which we are to be engaged:

- 'Ground level spiritual warfare' – casting demons out of people, which is dealt with at some length later in this book.
- 'Occult level spiritual warfare' – confronting more powerful demonic beings that operate in those who practice witchcraft, shamanism, freemasonry, eastern religions etc.
- 'Strategic level spiritual warfare' – this is where the high level principalities and powers over cities, nations and people groups etc are confronted in the power of the name of Jesus.[2]

According to its advocates, we must see victory at this third level of spiritual warfare if we are to see breakthrough in world evangelisation.

In this chapter, I will be making my own contribution to this debate. For those that wish to study the issue further, I would commend the study in the book *Territorial Spirits and World Evangelisation?*[3] by Chuck Lowe. Also, Clinton Arnold in his book *Spiritual Warfare* has a very helpful section on this issue.[4] I am personally indebted as well, to my friend Greg Haslam, who presented a paper on this subject to us as leaders in the NFI family of churches. I was at that time researching for this book, and I found that Greg and I had come to similar conclusions. We now need to look at these issues in some more detail.

What about territorial spirits?

Are there such beings as 'territorial spirits'? The Bible does refer to higher levels of authority in the demonic world. It talks about 'principalities and powers',[5] about 'rulers and authorities'.[6] The Bible is very reticent, however, about how these beings are organised and operate. For example, one of the most frequent texts quoted in relation to these issues describes Daniel interceding and an angel trying to reach him with the answer, (Daniel 10).

It was explained to Daniel that God had answered his prayer at once, but that it took twenty-one days for the angel to reach Daniel with the answer because of a conflict in the spiritual world.[7] This conflict was with the 'Prince of Persia' who had resisted the angel.[8] The passage also talks about future conflict with the Prince of Greece.[9]

There are a number of points to note from this passage and it may be helpful for you to have it open as you read the rest of this section.

- Daniel does not deliberately engage in the battle. He simply prays earnestly, engages in a partial fast and responds involuntarily and physically to a dramatic vision that is revealed to him. Nowhere do we find Daniel joining the angel against the evil principalities.
- The 'princes' refer to two empires, one of which was already beginning to dominate the Middle East, the other of which, many years in the future (Greece) would expand right from Macedonia to India under Alexander the Great. It would be more accurate therefore to see the evil principalities, not as territorial but as inspiring these empires which expanded

over many territories. They were political or imperial rather than territorial spirits. Moreover, Daniel's prayer did not have immediate obvious effect – certainly not on the Prince of Greece; Alexander came centuries later. Perhaps it better illustrates the power and effectiveness of the fervent prayers and intercessions of the saints, not in preventing the growth of an empire, but in the preservation of God's people throughout all the political conflict. This is important – so let's pray!

• Some have suggested that the expression in Daniel 11 vs 1 'And in the first year of Darius the Mede, I took my stand to support and protect him' justifies direct involvement in the demonic conflict. However, the 'I' seems contextually to refer to the angel rather than to Daniel.

There is a further suggestion that demons operate territorially in the story of Legion.[10] Legion begged Jesus not to send them out of that region.[11] Notice however, that these demonic spirits do not float around in the air. Jesus casts them out of Legion and tells them to enter some pigs close by. Consequently, if these demons were operating territorially and were having a major effect on the people of that area, then Jesus dealt with them in a person by setting him free, not by combating them in the air.

It is also true that when Paul went into new situations, he frequently had encounters with the demonic before making further progress in that particular city. As soon as he arrived in Cyprus, for example, he was met by a magician who had a lot of authority in the area. So the demons were able to influence that whole area through him. A similar situation occurred at Philippi. In that circumstance, he was met by a slave girl with the ability to tell fortunes and cast horoscopes. There would have been a constant queue of people outside her door wanting to hear about their future, so she would have been very influential in that area. Again, the demons influencing her life

would have access to many of the people in the town and would
have been able to control them. I have heard of powerful effects
for the advance of the gospel when the church has prayed
against the power of a witchdoctor in a particular area who was
holding people in bondage. Sometimes through prayer, the
witchdoctor moved away or his power was nullified. The early
church prayed and Herod who had been attacking them succumbed to a terrible disease and died.[12]

However, in each of these situations, the demons were operating *in people* and, where appropriate, were cast out of those
people. This means that what Paul was engaging in was what
Wagner refers to as 'ground level spiritual warfare' or at best
'occult level spiritual warfare'. I am not sure that I would particularly distinguish between the two levels but I do agree that
as we advance the kingdom and preach the gospel, we will have
to encounter demonic power in new areas and deal with them
as Paul did in the book of Acts.

The example of Ephesus

Another interesting scenario is the situation at Ephesus.
Ephesus was evidently much given over to the occult and to the
worship of the goddess Diana. Paul had many power encounters in that city. There were extraordinary miracles of healing.[13]
His deliverance ministry was such that his reputation was
feared in the demonic world.[14] There was very effective preaching of the gospel so that the whole region heard the good
news.[15] The results were so far reaching, that even trade in idolatrous objects was undermined. But did Paul ever engage in
'strategic level spiritual warfare' to achieve these amazing
results? There is no record in Scripture of him having done so.
Scripture surely contains all we need to equip us thoroughly for
every good work.[16]

Peter Wagner recently held a prayer and praise event in

Ephesus. He felt that God had given a new assignment to the *International Spiritual Warfare Network* to deal with the highest levels of evil principalities and to confront the 'Queen of Heaven'. In his book *Confronting the Queen of Heaven*, written to prepare people for this event, Peter Wagner comments on this amazing effect of Paul's ministry. He writes, 'By the time Paul left Ephesus, Diana had been severely battered and weakened. But she wasn't yet out of the picture. Paul never confronted her one-on-one or entered her temple to do direct strategic level spiritual warfare. The silversmiths accused him of doing this, but they couldn't make their charges stick in court. Diana lost much power because of Paul's aggressive spiritual warfare on the ground level and on the occult level. . . . God chose the apostle John to do the final assault. Subsequent history, not the book of Acts, tells us that a few years after Paul left, John moved to Ephesus and finished his career there.'[17] Wagner then goes on to quote historians to the effect that John later went into the temple of Diana and engaged in direct spiritual warfare with the result that the altar of Diana split into many pieces and half the temple fell down.

The problem is that this justification for strategic level spiritual warfare is based not on events described in the Bible but on disputed history. Indeed, Clinton Arnold refers to the document on which this story is based as being condemned by the Nicene Council of 787, which stated that 'no-one is to copy this book; not only so, but we consider that it deserves to be consigned to the fire'![18]

Is there any further evidence for the existence of 'territorial spirits'? It is true that the people around Israel worshipped local 'gods'. Scripture does make clear that behind these idols are demonic powers,[19] but did they have territorial rights per se? It is more likely that they exercised influence there because of the idolatry of the people who worshipped them.

'Strategic Level Spiritual Warfare'

What other biblical evidence, then, is there for this practice of strategic level spiritual warfare? Commenting on Matthew 12, Wagner asserts that the strongman, Beelzebub, who is to be bound, is not Satan himself as most commentators in church history have assumed. He believes that Beelzebub is a minor territorial demon under the command of Satan and so is to be bound in order to release people from his power in that region. He justifies this by the fact that 'the consensus of written materials I have examined and of personal interviews I have conducted with experts about the occult lead me to that judgement'.[20] I would suggest that it is very dangerous to come to this conclusion on the basis of 'experts in the occult'. I believe that we would be safer to stand upon the consensus of many commentators that Beelzebub, 'the prince of demons'[21] is the devil himself.

Do we then have authority to engage these evil powers ourselves at all? In one sense, yes. The Bible states very clearly that our struggle in spiritual warfare is against these principalities and powers. In other words, we recognise that the source of our problems is not flesh and blood (ie other people)[22] but the principalities and powers that lie behind them. That is why we need a book on spiritual warfare! In that sense there is nothing wrong with rebuking the evil power at work in particular situations

On the other hand, in terms of coming directly against evil powers and rebuking them ourselves, I believe the Bible suggests not. The book of Jude, in an admittedly somewhat obscure allusion, refers to evil men who were engaged in that practice. Jude says that these men 'slander celestial beings'.[23] He then goes on to say, 'even the archangel Michael, when he was disputing with the devil about the body of Moses, did not dare to bring a slanderous accusation against him but said, "The Lord rebuke you!"'[24]

Of course, Jude was referring to the practices of evil men. I am not for one moment suggesting that those who believe in engaging in strategic level spiritual warfare are like that. However, I believe we are to follow Michael's example in engaging the enemy in prayer. If Michael considered it right to say 'The Lord rebuke you', I believe that is a helpful pattern for us and ensures that we do not exceed our authority. Some would argue that this is an Old Testament (or rather apocryphal) example and that in the New Testament, we do have such authority, but I would argue that Jude is writing for the benefit of New Testament readers. I get a bit nervous when I hear people talking about such things as 'booting the devil out of a situation'. I would much rather say, 'the Lord rebuke you, Satan'. It is God's prerogative to deal with the high-ranking spirits. Isaiah says 'In that day *the Lord* will punish the powers in the heavens above and in the earth below' (italics mine).[25]

John Paul Jackson, in his book *Needless Casualties of War*, even suggests that people can come to harm if they out step their authority in this way. I know there are those who have felt led to repent of exceeding their God-given authority when they have come to personal conviction about what is the appropriate form of spiritual warfare as described in Jude 9.

We need to beware of becoming either presumptuous about our authority or totally unrealistic about the effects of our praying. If we have engaged in so-called 'strategic level spiritual warfare' against principalities and powers over an area, how do we know when they have gone? If the people are still giving themselves to sin, then any evil powers linked with that sin would still have a hold. I would actually see things the other way round from those who advocate such warfare tactics. As people are set free through the power of the preaching of the gospel then the power of evil spirits is obviously undermined and dealt with as far as they are concerned. As God works on a large scale in a whole community through the preaching of the gospel and the works of the kingdom, communities can be transformed and evil principalities and powers have less effect.

Furthermore, the example of Scripture not only provides a caution to us not to exceed our authority, it also speaks of the awesome effectiveness when we engage the forces of darkness with the specific authority that God has given to us. Our call is to do the works of the kingdom, healing the sick, bringing good news to the poor and casting out demons. When the seventy-two disciples did this, as recorded in Luke's gospel, there were amazing spiritual effects. They saw demons submit to them in the name of Jesus.[26] When they reported this to the Lord, He reaffirmed their authority to 'trample on snakes and scorpions [a picture of demonic power] and to overcome all the power of the enemy'.[27] He also said that He had seen Satan falling like lightning from heaven, presumably as a result of the seventy-two disciples demonstrating the works of the kingdom.[28]

William Hendrickson makes the same point in his commentary on Luke's gospel, 'Jesus meant, while you were expelling the subordinates (the demons) I was seeing the master (Satan) fall. . . . One important item should be added to this interpretation: in all probability, the master's exalted language, "I was watching Satan fall from heaven like lightning", was not only a reference to this one event, namely, the success of the seventy-two, but rather to all similar events that would take place afterwards. In other words, Jesus viewed the triumph of these seventy-two as being symptomatic of ever so many victories over Satan through the course of the new dispensation; triumphs accomplished through the works of thousands of other missionaries. He was looking far into the future. He saw the ultimate discomfiture of the ugly dragon and all his minions.'[29]

In other words, it is not that we tear down the evil demonic forces from over an area so that we can do the works of the kingdom. It is rather that as we do the works of the kingdom,

Satan is seen to fall and thus his power and influence reduced so that society can be transformed through the gospel.

I believe that just like the seventy-two, we have authority given to us by Him, to cast out demons, to rebuke sicknesses or evil spirits that are affecting people, even, where appropriate, to rebuke physical manifestations stirred up by the devil as Jesus did for the storm.[30] However, when it comes to directly engaging higher demonic power, we are safest to follow Jude's advice.

So, what are we to conclude so far?

- I believe that there is a case for saying that demonic powers are behind the political, social and cultural conditions of the nations. They are given such authority to act because of the wrong choices of evil leaders and people. In this context such powers may operate territorially but they are given access there as people give themselves to evil.
- We do not have the authority to engage directly in warfare prayer against Satan or these 'higher' demonic forces. It is clear that sometimes there are demonic forces operating in evil people that can have an effect on a whole area or town. These can be rebuked as Paul did on the island of Cyprus and in Philippi. If those people respond to the gospel, then they can be set free too.
- What we are called to is the work of the kingdom. We are to preach the gospel, heal the sick and set people free from demons. As we do that, just as when the seventy-two and Paul did it, we can see Satan dislodged from his place of domination. God, through the power of the gospel, will then open eyes blinded by Satan to see the glorious riches of their salvation through Christ. This is powerful spiritual warfare.

Binding and loosing

The terms 'binding' and 'loosing' are often used in the context

of spiritual warfare and are applied by many to this concept of
territorial spirits. So we find people being told to bind the territorial spirits in an area by making a statement such as, 'I bind
the spirits over such and such a place'.

This concept of binding and loosing comes from Jesus' words
to Peter in Matthew 16. Peter is given the keys of the kingdom.[31]
Jesus then tells Peter that what he binds on earth will be bound
in heaven and what he looses on earth will be loosed in heaven.
I believe that these ideas of binding and loosing are frequently
misunderstood. Hendrickson, in his commentary on Matthew,
points out that the words are actually rabbinical terms for forbidding and permitting; they are legal terms for allowing and
disallowing.[32] Thus, in that context, as Peter has been given the
keys of the kingdom, he (and all of us) effectively permits or
releases people who respond to the gospel to enter its benefits.
On the other hand, those who refuse the gospel message are forbidden from enjoying its benefits. Jesus uses the terms again in
the context of church discipline.[33] He says that if a person won't
listen to us when he has committed a sin, then it is to be told to
the church. If he will not listen to the church then he is to be
excommunicated. Thus he and his actions are either permitted
or forbidden.[34]

What, therefore, in this context does Jesus' reference to
'binding the strong man' mean?[35] The Christian church has
usually seen this as referring to the victory of Christ over Satan
through His work on the cross, His resurrection and ascension.
Jesus in effect restricted the operation of Satan by His victory
over him at the cross. It is on that basis that Jesus can say, 'All
authority in heaven and earth is given to Me'.[36] It is because of
this authority that we are told to go into all the world and make
disciples of all nations.[37] We can do this because the power of
Satan has been limited, has been bound at the cross.

In the 'strong man' passage in Matthew 12, however, Jesus
seems to be referring to His own ministry of setting people free

from demons and explaining that He is able to rob the strong man's house because He has first bound the strong man.[38] Jesus was already setting people free from demons: how then, before His death and resurrection, had He bound Satan? I believe He did so by resisting him in the wilderness and then by doing the works of the kingdom.

The truth for us therefore is clear. Satan has been bound at the cross so we can go with the message of release to the captives throughout the world. We can also effectively prevent the enemy having a hold in us by not giving way to his temptations. We thereby restrict his power. Furthermore, as we do the works of the kingdom, so we further restrict the power of the evil one as we have already illustrated by Jesus' remarks to the seventy-two disciples in Luke's gospel.[39]

You see, in this respect, 'binding' is not a formula but an action. I do believe that the idea of forbidding and permitting can be extended into the spiritual realm. They are keys of the kingdom. They are powerful in their effects spiritually. I believe that when we are in authority in a situation or in a meeting, we can forbid or restrict the works of the enemy amongst us spiritually. I have no problem with that. I believe as a father I can pray authoritatively over my household, restricting the power of the enemy to get in and disturb. I believe, as an elder in our church, I can pray authoritatively to release, to permit good things to happen like an increase in prophetic words etc and also to restrict the activities of the enemy. I believe that as a church joins in united prayer there can be amazing spiritual effects in breaking the power of the forces of darkness.

However, I say again that I believe 'binding' is more than a statement or formula – it is an action. It is a description of what we are actually doing as we engage in the works of the kingdom. I recall John Wimber speaking about this and he compared it with somebody doing their ironing. He said that if you saw someone set up the ironing board, lay a shirt out on it, put the iron on the shirt and say to the shirt, 'I iron you, shirt!' without actually taking hold of the iron and using it, you would think that they were stupid. You can only iron a shirt by doing the action. Similarly, we can only restrict the efforts of the enemy by doing the things that restrict his activities, that is, the works of the kingdom to which I have already referred.

I recall speaking to some missionaries who had asked me about this. They had been puzzled because they had taken authority and 'bound the spirits' in the difficult area of Africa in which they were working. They had wondered why their words seemed to be ineffective. It also transpired that other people had been there a year or so previously and they had 'bound the spirits' as well. I asked them, 'How many times does it have to be said, before the spirits are bound?' Obviously, when we look at it like this it does appear to be nonsense. I went on to ask the missionaries whether the churches in the area that they were involved with were free from the cultural strongholds that they were seeking to bind. They replied, 'No. Many of the problems that are there in the world are also in the church.' I said to them, therefore, 'How can you by a formula bind the spirits when those spirits are operating through cultural strongholds which are as yet undealt-with in the church? Surely, the way to deal with those evil powers is first to set people free from them in the church. As people are set free from the evil spirits governing their culture, then "binding and loosing" has taken place. The effect is that the enemy is bound and the people are set free.'

Another friend of mine was saved on the 'hippie trail' in Iran. He had been involved in the New Age movement before he committed his life to Christ, so when he came back to England, and to his home in the Peak District, he gathered some friends and went to all the high places which he knew had been centres of demonic activity and sought to 'bind' the works of the enemy in those places. However, he found he was having to get into more and more detail about the works of Satan as he pursued this path. Have we covered this? Have we prayed about that? Other people had done the same thing in the same area. Why had their 'binding' not worked? What he decided to do eventually was to plant a church there with cells in different villages and small towns. I believe that by seeing churches established that preach the gospel, he will more effectively restrict the work of the enemy there and see many saved.

Spiritual mapping

Spiritual mapping is the drawing up of the spiritual profile of a city or area based on careful research. A mixture of historical and sociological research is used, combined with 'prophetic revelation', in order to obtain an understanding of the deception that the enemy has brought over the lives of unbelievers in a particular area. Some would argue that it is necessary to reveal the nature of the demonic hierarchy and the names of demons that rule in a given place. To this end, it is considered that people with gifts of prophecy and discernment of spirits are considered necessary to expose what the enemy has been doing. If we thus discover 'the devices of Satan', we can more effectively pray against them. Some, again, would argue that it is helpful to get the proper names or functional names of these demonic powers. Knowing their names helps us to gain power over the demons and specify the exact nature of the oppression.

Is this helpful? I have considerable difficulty with the notion that we need to know the names of demons in order to have authority over them. I think this comes too close to pagan concepts of spiritual authority. I also believe that, as with my friend in the Peak District, we can become over-occupied with pursuing stories about what occult activity may have taken place in the past. We also have to be careful to distinguish between genuine prophetic revelation and merely human speculation. Nevertheless, there may be distinctive factors in each place that keep people from responding to the gospel. To research this could bring positive benefit. Our ministry is to pray, to preach the gospel: but also to recognise particular characteristics of spiritual oppression in particular areas and to cast out demons. If we find a stronghold in people's thinking, a particular cultural attitude which prevents people understanding the gospel, particular prevailing sins in the community, then that alerts us as to how we should pray, what we should teach on, what demons we may expect to encounter and so on.

As I said in Chapter 1, when I take stronghold seminars in different places, my concern is to set people free from the evil forces in their culture that have distorted their thinking and bound them up. To know what these issues are can be helpful in setting people free.

Identificational repentance

The idea here is that the sinful behaviour of a community or a nation in the past has provided openings for high-ranking principalities and powers to establish spiritual strongholds. Obviously, non-Christians will not express corporate humility and repentance themselves and so Christians must do it for them. There are many examples nowadays therefore, of people repenting before others for the sins of their nation or city. We find people apologising for sins that one nation may have committed against another when they are preaching or taking a conference in that other nation. It is even said sometimes that we cannot expect to see revival until we have fully repented of particular issues in the past.

Now it is true that our western individualism can sometimes blind us to the corporate and structural nature of some evils and the corporate guilt that this entails. Daniel and Nehemiah

did identify themselves with the sins of their people and confessed them to God.[40] However, the sins they confessed were
those of the people of God of whom they were a part. They did
not confess the sins of Assyria, or Babylon, or Persia where
they were living on behalf of the Assyrians, Babylonians or
Persians who would not do so. Paul makes no bones about
clearly identifying and condemning the sins of the Roman
Empire in Romans chapter 1. We do *not* find him confessing
them.

I believe that we do need to take more seriously the wrong
attitudes that have characterised the church as the people of
God and put these right through acknowledging them and
through relevant teaching from the Word of God. We have to
admit that our churches have often become affected by the
ungodly culture around. As we will see in a later chapter, we are
often unconscious of this. Where it has characterised us, it is
right to acknowledge it. It can help us build bridges with other
believers. Recently I had a meeting with the leaders of a Punjabi
speaking church in the town of Bedford where I live. We were
exploring the way in which our churches could work better
together in the future. We recognised that it was not right to
have churches divided on racial lines. However, at the beginning
of this meeting, I acknowledged to my Punjabi friends that one
of the major reasons why there were white churches, Asian
churches and West Indian churches in our communities was
that in the 1950s the English church had been unwelcoming to
many of the new immigrants whom God was blessing us with
in our nation at that time. One of the Punjabi pastors found
that very helpful and said that he was sure that his people would
as well. It is right to act in humility where we as the people of
God have acted wrongly, even though I was not around as a
responsible adult in the 1950s.

However, we still have to be careful. We must not just recite
trite formulae concerning the past. This sort of repentance

must reflect an attitude in prayer and humility before one another rather than a formula to 'bring revival'. For example, how often do we have to say we are sorry before the past is dealt with? I remember after preaching at a major conference, I received a letter to the effect that my message had been a bit triumphalistic and what about repenting for the sins of the Protestant reformers at the time of the Reformation? I am ready to acknowledge that there were wrong things done by the leaders of the Reformation. It was not right, then, to send to the stake those they considered heretics. When we teach church history on our training courses, we look at the issues raised by such practices. However, how many times do I have to refer to this when I am preaching on the future glory of the church? Does the fact that another twenty-first century Christian believer may also have acknowledged the wrongs of the past in this respect deal with it, so that I do not need to mention it? We can get into very complicated, and in the end futile, arguments if we push too far this line of identificational repentance even with the past actions of the people of God.

I am not claiming that my acknowledgement to my Christian Punjabi friends 'broke something in the heavenlies', nor do I believe I was doing so on behalf of all white English Christians. I do believe I was trying to work out with humility the truth of 'one new man in Christ'.[41]

It is certainly very questionable whether we are authorised to represent our non-Christian community by confessing their sins and then expecting them to be 'remitted'. Again, we can get into all sorts of practical difficulties; how do we know what the sins of our community are, either in the past or the present? There is ample scope here for so-called 'words of knowledge' or 'prophetic insight' which we may be completely unable to test in a biblical manner. And in any case, proxy confession will not save anybody. Individual repentance is required as people come to believe in Christ. If that happens on a large scale, it will have positive effects for the kingdom in transforming our communities.

Nevertheless, we do need, always, to maintain an attitude of humility, whether regarding past sins of the people of God, or of the nation we belong to, when we are involved in situations that could otherwise create offence or misunderstanding. For example, if I were to be ministering in a nation where British colonial power had caused suffering to the local inhabitants, I would bear this in mind when teaching and in my relationships with the people. I would be constantly aware of the need not to be patronising, but would acknowledge the wrong that had been done to the people involved. We have to be careful that we do not miss the sense of corporate responsibility because of our individualistic worldview.

Cleansing the land

Much has been said by a number of people recently about our responsibilities for 'the land' in the sense of the physical location of the towns in which our churches are situated. People are engaging in spiritual warfare to 'cleanse the land'. They will go to 'high places' of supposed former demonic activity and deal with the spirits there. They will take great interest in 'ley lines' – lines of supposed occult power dating from a pre-Christian era in the history of our nation.

I believe this represents a misunderstanding of old covenant theology, which does not apply to us today. Joshua may have been led to cleanse the Promised Land of idolatry but we are not promised a physical land today. Our inheritance is Jerusalem above.[42] We gladly rejoice in the fact that the nations have been promised to Christ as His inheritance.[43] However, the New Testament makes it perfectly clear how that inheritance is to be claimed. It is by us going into all the world, and not by 'cleansing the land', not by 'nullifying the effects of the ley lines', but by preaching the gospel and making disciples of every nation. Christ's inheritance is a redeemed people from every tribe and tongue and nation.[44] The literal drawing of lines on maps that some advocate as a means of plotting 'demonic corridors of power' seems, in itself, more akin to divination than to proper spiritual discernment.

I was once asked to give advice to an Anglican Church where there had been considerable difficulties. It was felt that spiritual warfare issues were involved. As I discussed the matter with some of the leaders in the church, it was suggested to me that the problem might well be that the church had been built on a ley line. My reply was that there were issues that the current members of the church needed to put right and repent about. There were divisions and wrong attitudes within the church. One church member was even initiating legal action in an ecclesiastical court against the vicar for altering the central heating system without following the proper consultation procedures! There was an outcry in the church because the vicar had permitted the front two pews to be moved to make room for a worship band. With those sorts of issues within the life of the church, we had far greater things to worry about than the situation of the church building on a ley line. The enemy could gain far greater access through wrong attitudes amongst church members.

But doesn't it work?

One reason why many feel diffident about questioning some of these teachings on spiritual warfare is that they do seem to work in certain parts of the world and we long to see the same effective evangelistic breakthrough in our own nation. We must not be afraid to come back to what is a fundamental principle of the Christian faith. What governs our belief is what God reveals in Scripture and we dare not adopt any other belief until we can be shown its validity from Scripture. It is true of course that we must always be open to God revealing more from His Word, and I hope I am open on this issue.

Chuck Lowe suggests in his book that there are many other reasons why God is now blessing nations such as Argentina with such wonderful evangelistic fruit.[45] Yet in resisting what we believe to be an unbiblical approach to spiritual warfare, we must seek to emulate the fervent prayer of many who advocate this approach. In the end, why God works in a particular place ahead of working in another is hidden in His own sovereign wisdom. Our responsibility is to pray, do the work of the kingdom and trust God for His mighty breakthrough.

We also need to be very careful about the use of stories that may be second or third hand. Many of the examples of these principles of spiritual warfare allegedly working are from stories that it is very difficult to verify. You will notice that in this book most of the stories are from my own experiences, or have been directly recounted to me by the people involved. Chuck Lowe refers to a story that he was in a position to verify because it concerned the town where his wife was born and brought up. Sadly, in that case, many of the facts went against the stories recounted by those advocating strategic level spiritual warfare.[46]

Having said all this, I recognise that those advocating various practices of spiritual warfare have a genuine passion for God to move in power. Their concern is to frustrate the efforts of the enemy to blind people's minds, and to see thousands swept into the kingdom. I very much share their passion and recognise my own need for greater prayer to this end.

My concerns are twofold:

- That in our genuine desire for breakthrough, we are not diverted into spiritual warfare techniques that are unhelpful and unbiblical.

- That in our reaction to extremes of spiritual warfare, we do not back off the subject altogether. I believe that many people have been uneasy about some of these areas of spiritual warfare and have therefore withdrawn subtly, and perhaps unconsciously, from the battle. If we avoid these issues by withdrawing altogether, we become less bold in dealing with demonic strongholds in people's lives, less bold in casting demons out from people – and all because we fear being off beam and extreme in our approach to spiritual warfare.

God honours faith and it is possible to be 'correct' in doctrine but not bold in faith. I want to try to be both. I believe that we are taught in Scripture how to combine the two. We are called to pray; God moved on the day of Pentecost as His people obeyed Him and waited in the city as He had commanded. They were fervent in united prayer. We are called to preach the gospel. It is the gospel that is God's power unto salvation.[47] We are to do the works of the kingdom, reaching out to the community in practical acts of compassion, kindness and service. We are to pray for the sick to be healed and those demonised to be set free. As we do that, God himself will move and deal with the forces of darkness that hold people in bondage.

Effective Strategy Number 4: Concentrate on prayer and on doing the works of the kingdom, whilst recognising the characteristics of enemy activity in a particular nation, culture or place.

NOTES

[1] *Confronting the Powers*, C Peter Wagner; [2] Wagner, page 21–22; [3] *Territorial Spirits and World Evangelisation?*, Chuck Lowe; [4] *Spiritual Warfare,* Clinton Arnold (Marshall Pickering, HarperCollins Religious, 77 Fulham Palace Rd, Hammersmith, London, W6 8JB. Used with permission.); [5] Ephesians 3:10 (RSV); [6] Ephesians 6:12;

[7]Daniel 10:12–14; [8]Daniel 10:13; [9]Daniel 10:20; [10]Mark 5:1–13; [11]Mark 5:9–10; [12]Acts 12:23; [13]Acts 19:11; [14]Acts 19:15; [15]Acts 19:10,20; [16]2 Timothy 3:17; [17]*Confronting the Queen of Heaven,* C Peter Wagner, page 12–13; [18]Arnold, page 195; [19]1 Corinthians 10:20; [20]Wagner, page 148; [21]Matthew 12:24; [22]Ephesians 6:12; [23]Jude v 8; [24]Jude v 9; [25]Isaiah 24:21; [26]Luke 10:17; [27]Luke 10:19; [28]Luke 10:18; [29]*New Testament Commentary – Luke,* William Hendrickson, page 581 (The Banner of Truth Trust, The Grey House, 3 Murrayfield Rd, Edinburgh, EH12 6EL. Used with permission.); [30]Luke 8:24; [31]Matthew 16:19; [32]*New Testament Commentary – Matthew*, William Hendrickson, page 651; [33]Matthew 18:17; [34]Matthew 18:18; [35]Matthew 12:29 (RSV); [36]Matthew 28:18; [37]Matthew 28:19; [38]Matthew 12:29; [39]Luke 10:18–19; [40]Daniel 9:1–19, Nehemiah 1:4–11; [41]Ephesians 2:15; [42]Galatians 4:26; [43]Psalm 2:8; [44]Revelation 5:9; [45]Lowe, page 121–127; [46]Lowe, page 116–118; [47]Romans 1:16.

Chapter 5

UNDERSTANDING STRONGHOLDS

It may be helpful to read 2 Corinthians 10:1–6 in conjunction with this chapter.

What are strongholds?

Much Christian spiritual warfare seems to be like fighting with one hand tied behind your back. For the church to take the kingdom into enemy territory more effectively, we must first see strongholds demolished that the enemy has in us.

Paul talks to the church at Corinth about the issue of strongholds. He says, 'The weapons we fight with are not the weapons of the world. On the contrary, they have divine power to demolish strongholds.'[1] The context here is that some false teachers had been undermining Paul's ministry amongst the Corinthian Christians. He refers to these false teachers elsewhere as 'super-apostles' who were making 'super-spiritual' claims and enticing the people at Corinth away from the truth. These false teachers would laugh at Paul, saying that although he was a wonderful letter writer and his written words were powerful, when he came to visit Corinth he was not very impressive in his public teaching style.

Paul dismisses this almost irrelevant distortion of his ministry. He believes that he has very powerful weapons at his dispo-
sal. They are not, however, of the world. Paul dismisses the
weapons of outward show and clever words. As he has stated
earlier in this letter, he will have nothing to do with manipulation or deception or distorting the Word of God.[2]

The weapons he is interested in have 'divine power to demolish strongholds'. What are strongholds? The context makes it
clear – they are wrong thinking. They are wrong arguments and
pretensions.[3] Strongholds consist of thoughts that have not
been taken captive to Christ, that have not been submitted to
His lordship. The fact that he uses these military terms, 'strongholds' and 'weapons' also suggests that there is something very
powerful about this whole system of wrong thinking that he is
seeking to demolish. The reference to 'setting itself up'[4] suggests the work of the devil who originally, as we have seen, rose
up against God and sought to challenge God's rule and sovereignty. Strongholds are wrong thinking patterns that challenge
God and His sovereignty today. The devil seeks to establish an
alternative, autonomous way of thinking. Behind all these
thought patterns, philosophies and practices is an enemy who
is experienced; an enemy who maintains a vast array of spiritual forces that are self-sufficient and God-rejecting.

This was the nature of the devil's temptation to Adam and
Eve in the Garden of Eden. He challenged them by daring to
question the words of God Himself[5] (has God said?) and substitute an alternative way of thinking, 'You will be like God'.[6]
Thus was erected the first stronghold of wrong thinking
amongst human beings, inspired by the evil one himself.

The whole of the world's system is set up against God under
the influence of the prince of this world. Strongholds have been
erected. The world's system of trade, commerce, false religion
and independence of God is symbolised in the book of
Revelation by the city, Babylon. The evil powers lodging in that

city are described as follows, 'Fallen! Fallen is Babylon the great! She has become a home for demons and a haunt for every evil spirit, a haunt for every unclean and detestable bird. . . . In her heart she boasts, "I sit as Queen; I am not a widow"'.[7] The world's system is haunted, therefore, by demonic power.

So what are strongholds? I describe them as 'wrong thought patterns and ideas, which Satan and his demons influence, and behind which they hide, that can govern or dominate individuals, communities, nations, and even churches'. Strongholds need to be demolished, otherwise they continue that domination.

How do strongholds affect individual Christians?

So how does this work out for individual Christians? I think it is helpful to look at other ways in which the word 'stronghold' is used in Scripture.

Ancient fortified cities in Old Testament times were built with a wall around the outside. This would not be very practical today, with aeroplanes, bombs and guns, but then it was a powerful defence. Such walls were strong enough to keep out all but the most determined invader, but the inhabitants would also build a secondary defence in the centre of the city in the shape of a tower. This was called a 'stronghold', and could be defended by just a few soldiers, so that if an attack came, the people of the city could crowd in for protection, confident that the tower could be easily defended. However, this wasn't always successful, and even the stronghold's defences could be breached.

Sometimes the word is used in a context of blessing for us in Scripture, for example, 'The Lord is my rock, my fortress and my deliverer; my God is my rock in whom I take refuge. He is my shield and the horn of my salvation, *my stronghold*'.[8]

However, the word is also used in the negative sense, of something that needs to be pulled down. So the book of Proverbs says, 'A wise man attacks the city of the mighty and *pulls down the stronghold in which they trust'* (italics mine).[9] The idea behind this is that sometimes only the outer wall of a city would be taken but a wise general attacking that city would also pull down the stronghold, so that his enemies had no defences to hide behind.

I believe that many people come to Christ, give their lives to Him, and in that sense the outer wall of their life is taken. However, the stronghold is not taken and that stronghold represents a way of thinking from before the time they were saved. It will have been influenced by their culture, their past sins, their upbringing, experiences and events that have happened to them. In other words, they are Christians, but in their deepest thinking, they are still influenced by strongholds of the enemy.

Exactly how this works can be seen from the story that I told of the Indian couple who could not have children. The wife was brought up to believe in a powerful superstition that if a teenage girl killed a cobra instead of calling a man to do it, she would not be able to have children. She had been a Christian for quite a while, but had never been set free from this superstition. This stronghold in her thinking had never been attacked and destroyed, and had resulted in there remaining a demonically powerful block on her ability to have children, even though there was nothing physically wrong with her. The stronghold was a part of her old life that had not been demolished, even though the 'outer walls' of her life had been torn down sufficiently to allow Jesus to enter. As soon as the curse over her life was broken, the stronghold was demolished, her thought processes were changed and her physical body was affected so that she could bear children.

In my 'strongholds' conferences, when I tell this story, everybody is able to see the point. I make sure now that I start my conferences with this story because it means people are with me right from the outset of my talks. They can see how strongholds from our culture can affect our thinking even though we are Christians. It is often helpful to see an issue in another culture so that we can understand the principle, because we are often blind to the strongholds in our own culture. You see, there aren't many cobras in England, and this superstition is not fundamental to our society. But there are similar satanic strongholds here and everywhere. They can be found in the thought processes of most individuals and communities; they exist through our cultural pre-suppositions and even at a national level in the political systems, governments, and rulers of nations. But more of this later . . .

Even the very occasion of my praying with this couple in India concerning the cobra had an effect upon others around. When I was praying with the couple concerned, I was not praying on my own because I believe in ministering in a team. I had with me Sydney and Cheryl who are leaders in one of our churches in India. I was unaware, until they told me afterwards, that they were also unable to have children. Cheryl had forgotten all about it, but my prayer for the first lady had reminded her of a superstition that she had been told as well. It was not quite the same. She had been told that the menstrual rag after a girl in puberty's first period must be burnt because otherwise a snake might go over it and then the girl would be unable to have children when she grew up. Cheryl remembered that that story had caused her some fear at the time, but she had subsequently forgotten about it. I prayed again for this stronghold of superstition to be demolished. Soon after that Cheryl conceived and it was wonderful at our Stoneleigh Bible Week, a year or so afterwards, to meet the miracle child who was the result of strongholds being demolished.

These are encouraging stories, but I am using them by way of illustration because, like Cheryl, we are unaware of many strongholds in our thinking. It requires both revelation and teaching from the Word of God on this subject to open our eyes to the strongholds in our own lives that will need demolishing.

So a stronghold is in my mind, and reflects the way that I *used* to think. That is the way of the world and I will need teaching to renew my mind.

Strongholds can also be in our emotions. For example, self-pity is not just in the mind; it is in the emotions as well. It can be the result of emotional pain in the past. I will need teaching, to renew my mind and help me to learn to take responsibility for my wrong reaction to hurt, but I will need the healing power of Christ flooding into my emotions, too.

Strongholds can also have a spiritual, demonic, dimension. Now I will not only need teaching to renew my mind, I will also need deliverance from any evil spirit that has attached itself and that reinforces the stronghold in my life.

Most Christians will never need deliverance from an evil spirit, but we will all need our thought lives changed to renew our minds.

A different sort of weapon

Let us now return to what Paul was writing in 2 Corinthians 10. Note that he says that we are living in this world.[10] The 'super-apostles' were living on a 'super-spiritual' plane that totally denied the reality of everyday living. The sorts of people that Paul is talking about here are 'super-spiritual'. They start every sentence with 'God told me . . .' and do not seem to live in the ordinary world at all.

Paul does not talk about some super-spiritual experience that separates us from the real world. He tells us that we are not living out in the stratosphere when we face spiritual powers. Instead, he cuts right across this attitude and starts by saying that we *live* in the real world. This is just as true today. We face these powers in our everyday lives, meeting with spiritual forces in the supermarket, facing strongholds at work and overcoming attacks from the evil one at home in our family relationships.

This is where we work out the realities of spiritual warfare.

Paul says that we are not to use worldly weapons to overcome the enemy, worldly weapons that are designed to impress. He talks about weapons of divine power, handled with humility, and contrasts this teaching with that of the 'super-apostles'. They love the big platforms, they love to make a name for themselves, but spiritual warfare is not about how loud you can shout; instead Paul talks about appealing to the Christians in Corinth by the meekness and gentleness of Christ.

This might not be our normal understanding of spiritual warfare, but Paul is commending divine power, handled with humility in the form of the meekness and gentleness of Christ. We are not to use manipulation, or to show how clever we are. We are not to get involved in personality cults, or insist on pomp and ceremony or try to shout the devil out. It is not about winning arguments, he seems to suggest. It is possible to win an argument but still see no change in the other person. Paul calls us weak people who rejoice in our weakness but have powerful spiritual weapons.

John Paul Jackson puts it as follows, 'When we engage in spiritual warfare, we can become endangered by our own knowledge and by the enemy, if we do not learn to take our stand in the cross and die to pride that can arise from our knowledge. Operating in knowledge, like operating in the flesh, may be perilous when we face a powerful foe'.[11] Jackson in this context is talking about the heresy of Gnosticism, which is the supposed acquisition of a special, superior knowledge unavailable to ordinary believers. There is a danger that seeking to have too much knowledge about the operations of the devil beyond those revealed in Scripture can subtly lead us into that danger.

Effective Strategy Number 5: Understand that strongholds are wrong thinking and learn to use godly power to pull them down.

NOTES

[1]2 Corinthians 10:4; [2]2 Corinthians 4:2; [3]2 Corinthians 10:5; [4]2 Corinthians 10:5; [5]Genesis 3:1; [6]Genesis 3:5; [7]Revelation 18:7; [8]Psalm 18:2; [9]Proverbs 21:22; [10]2 Corinthians 10:3; [11]*Needless Casualties of War*, John Paul Jackson, page 55 (Streams Publications, a division of Streams Ministries International, P.O. Box 101808, Ft. Worth, TX 76 185. Used with permission.).

Chapter 6

UNDERSTANDING OUR FREEDOM

There is sometimes an impression given that after we become Christians we just sail through life, that everything becomes easy and nothing gets in the way. In reality, nothing could be farther from the truth.

Words that are used in the Scriptures speak of battles and wars, labouring, striving and fighting against spiritual attacks. These words do not paint a picture of an easy life, especially when many of the battles that we face involve dealing with old ways of thinking and reacting, what is called in the Scriptures 'putting to death' whatever belongs to our former way of life.[1]

On top of this, there is a spiritual struggle that we have to face against the devil. Some of us might choose to imagine a battlefield with two armies facing one another; we might choose to visualise Satan's huge army on one side, with all his demons and evil spirits, while on the other side are massed the even greater and more powerful armies of God.

What we need to remember when we use pictures like this, however, is that God has already won the war, even though it is true that Satan might appear to win the occasional battle. Remember that the devil is *not* equal to God.

It is amazing, but sad, how many Christians are still affected by things controlling their lives even after twenty or thirty years. These things should have been dealt with soon after they were saved; yet they are still not resolved. In our church, we now run a course for new Christians called *Breaking Free*. We first encouraged the whole church to go through it. The purpose is to ensure that issues from people's past lives (strongholds) are dealt with. The idea is that people now go through this *Breaking Free* course soon after they have come to Christ. The first session in this course is always about who they are in Christ, what His victory has secured for them. It is important that we know this before we approach any footholds the enemy may have had in us.

Perhaps we should go back to the beginning to refresh our minds about exactly what happened at our conversion to Christ, before going any further in this book. So you should consider this chapter as a spiritual MOT, just like the medical check-up that you have at the doctor's, to make sure that you are walking as free as God intended you to be in Christ.

Completely new people

From the start, as soon as we become followers of Jesus Christ, we find that we are new people. It is not just that certain things have changed, like maybe we now go to church on Sundays, or we read the Bible and pray regularly. Plenty of people do those things without necessarily making a personal commitment to follow Jesus.

Salvation is not presented in that way in the Bible. Instead, what we are told is that we become entirely new people; this is what it means to be born again. A change has occurred inside us and we are no longer the same people that we were. Once we were born in the natural way to live a 'normal' kind of life, with a 'normal' destiny, what the Bible calls flesh giving birth to flesh.[2] Now we have been born again to live a different kind of life with a different destiny. Many people are surprised to find out what God has done in them after they have made a commitment to Christ.

A good example of this was a man who was converted at our church. He got saved on Sunday, then went to work as normal on Monday. When he got home that evening, he said that he was amazed at the way people in his place of work were swearing and blaspheming all the time; he just could not believe it and it really upset him. In fact, the people where he worked had not changed. They were behaving just as they had always behaved. They were not swearing more just because he had become a Christian. They had not changed . . . but he had. He had become a new person inside and all the swearing that went on every day was now upsetting him; whereas he had not even noticed it before.

It might not happen that way for everybody, not straight-away, but this is the sort of difference that being born again makes to people. The *reason* why we behave differently is the same for everyone. It is because we now basically want to please God in what we do, to do what God wants us to do. The important thing now is that we are aware of the difference. God has written His laws in our hearts[3] and we can begin to tell when we get it wrong or want to go our own way.

Under new authority

If that was all there was to it, that really would be something. However, it does not end there. Having been born again, been made new creatures, means that we do not have to conform to our old way of life. The old creature that we were in Adam no longer lives under the same authority. We have died to that life; that is why the next step is to be baptised, to symbolise the death of our old life and our rebirth as new people.

Paul wrote to the Roman church about this. He explained

that all those who are baptised into Christ Jesus are baptised into death and because of this, they have now died to sin.[4] He said that they are buried through baptism and raised to live a new life. Paul then draws the logical conclusion that if they are dead to sin, the natural consequence is that they should not live in it anymore. The way it is presented in the Bible is that everybody is born naturally into the same order of manhood as Adam. However, when someone believes in Jesus, they transfer from one order of creation to another. They are now born into the same order of manhood as Christ . . . they are now 'in Christ'. Consequently, since Christ died, they have died. Since He has been raised from the dead, everybody that is in Christ has been raised with him.[5]

Totally accepted

This also means that we are totally accepted in Christ. If we are in Christ, God accepts us in just the same way as He accepts Jesus as His Son.[6]

I was in a church in Africa on one occasion, surrounded by several hundred Basuto people who had only recently become Christians. These people had suffered terrible discrimination under the apartheid regime in the part of South Africa where they lived.

During the year before I met them, they had seen many new things. To start with, they had travelled to Cape Town to go to a Christian conference. This was an exciting adventure, because many of them had never travelled away from their home district. They had other many experiences, most of them far beyond their expectations, yet when they were asked what was the most important thing to happen to them during that year, the answer that they gave might surprise some people. The most important thing that had happened to them was hearing a preacher called David Adams, who had visited their church from Cape Town, tell them that God accepted them and all that this acceptance meant. Almost all of them agreed that this was the most significant thing that had happened to them during that year. They were a people who had not known acceptance. They had been discriminated against, rejected and ill-treated. God's acceptance was an amazing revelation.

There are many other things that also click into place when we become new creatures. Our future immediately becomes secure; we are blessed with every spiritual blessing; but what is perhaps more important for many people is that we no longer live under condemnation.[7] God does not condemn Jesus, so if we are in Him, God does not condemn us either. It just cannot happen; so if God does not condemn us, how can anyone else?

Let us summarise it to remind ourselves . . .

1. We are born again.[8]
2. We are a new creation.[9]
3. We are accepted.[10]
4. We are secure.[11]
5. We are blessed with every spiritual blessing.[12]
6. We are not condemned.[13]

That all sounds pretty good, doesn't it! Now, how about replacing the words 'We are' with 'I am', just to make it feel even better?

Weapons against the accuser

Understanding these truths is ever so important in the context of spiritual warfare. Why? Because one of the descriptions of the devil is 'the accuser'.[14] The devil seeks to accuse us before God and accuse us in our own minds and hearts. 'Do you call yourself a Christian with such serious problems in your life?' 'Look at the foul thoughts that come into your mind; if other people knew, they would be horrified.' 'You ought not to have missed that opportunity.' 'Can God really forgive someone with a background and life history like yours?' 'You're a failure, you always have been, you always will be.'

If we do not know how to deal with these accusations, we will be ineffective in the fight and in our witness to Christ. Sometimes, even when we are about to be 'lost in wonder, love and praise' in our worship, some accusation of past failure will come into our minds and cause us to hold back as unworthy.

Satan keeps trying to accuse. The prophet, Zechariah, had a vision of the high priest of Israel standing before God in filthy clothes.[15] Satan was standing beside him to accuse him. The Lord said, 'The Lord rebuke you, Satan!' God confirmed that He had taken away the man's sin; new, beautiful clothes were put on him. He was to be regarded as someone rescued from the fire. That's what God does for us. He has extended grace, undeserved love, to us who only merited judgement. He has rescued us and clothed us in all the righteousness of Christ. We are no longer under the law with all its condemnation.[16] An understanding of the grace of God is essential to spiritual warfare otherwise it is us striving against this powerful enemy in our own puny strength.

Disciples

Right, so what comes next?

Well, according to the Scriptures, we are to become disciples of Jesus. For some, this is the difficult part. The word 'discipline' can frighten them. Let us look at what it means to be a disciple. It is simple, really: a disciple is a follower or learner. Jesus said that this is what disciples do; they learn to become like their teacher.[17] This means that there are certain responsibilities that we have to consider.

The difficulty here is that discipleship is all about change and by coming to Christ, we are now committed to that process of change. For most of us, change is not easy. We now have a responsibility to live out all the changes that God has already made in us, and we have to make a decision to do that. Every day, in every situation, there is a choice to be made: shall I go back to live or react like the old creature that I was, or shall I live as the new creature that I am? It also means that I am willing to be corrected by others who input my life.

How about something else that Jesus said about being disciples? He said that anyone who wants to be His disciple must take up their cross and follow Him. Now, anyone living in the days when Jesus lived knew exactly what He meant by that. If you lived in those times and you saw someone carrying their cross, you would know where they were going. You did not have to ask. They were going to be crucified. They were going to die. So, if we take up our cross, then we are to die. What did Jesus mean by that? Certainly there must be the willingness literally to lay down our lives for Jesus. It also means, if we read what Paul said, that we are to die to our old self, our old way of thinking.

What does this mean in our everyday lives? What are the practical issues? Well, for a start, when we become Christians, it does not mean that we immediately become perfect. There will be some things that need to change straight away as part of our repentance when we become a believer. For example, if we are living dishonestly or immorally it must stop. We will gradually become aware of other issues we need to address as we are 'discipled' by a more mature Christian. This is all part of the responsibility that we now face as disciples. We have to live out the life that God has given to us.

Paul is clear. He says that we are to put to death the things that belong to our earthly nature.[18] These are the attitudes, desires and responses of our old lives. These might be things that we want or even enjoy, but they are things that are not good for us, and can actually do us harm. The trouble is that as soon as we give them up, we look round and there they are again. Paul says in response to this that we are to count ourselves dead to them and alive to God.

Perhaps you were always a 'poor old me' sort of person; full of self-pity, believing everything always went wrong for you. However, now that you are in Christ, all that has gone and you are not like that any more. All that old stuff has gone . . . or has it? No sooner do you say that then up it pops again, and you are going through the same old routines. So you have to make a decision here. You can either enjoy it . . . or put it to death. How do you do that?

Paul says that we are to clothe ourselves with the things of God, like: compassion, kindness, gentleness and patience.[19] For most of us, these sorts of things are not naturally part of our lifestyle. The best way of throwing off the old is by embracing the new. The best way to dispel darkness is not to try to sweep it out, but to open the curtains and let the daylight in.

Renewed minds

The way that we do this, Paul tells us, is to renew our minds. They are a bit like a computer, really. A computer is programmed to do things in a certain way. If we want to do things in a different way, or to do different things, we need to re-program it, or install different software. For those like me, who know very little about computers, a computer has 'software' that tells it how to work. Software is just a set of instructions, a program that tells a computer how to do what you want it to do. The trouble is that software sometimes gets corrupted, (a bug), and then the computer might not do anything at all, or it might go off and do something totally different to what it is expected to do. When this happens, it can sometimes affect everything that uses the software.

This is a bit like us when we were in Adam. We were open to all sorts of demonic power. Satan, the god of this world, rules through this demonic power. This means that when we were in Adam, these things were affecting our lives, even ruling the way that we lived. That is why we need to have new 'software' installed.

Now we are in Christ, we have come under someone else's authority and we have a new set of software installed that is clearing out all the 'bugs', all the corrupted instructions that were written into our program. However, for many of us, those bugs, those demonic influences that affected us have become so strong that we need to be set free practically. Luke tells us that many of those who had believed came and openly confessed, and a number of people involved in sorcery brought their scrolls and burnt them.[20] In other words, some time after they believed, they suddenly realised that all those old demonic things should not be in their lives anymore, so they dealt with them. Because of our position in Christ we have power through the Holy Spirit to deal with the things of the past.

As well as understanding our *acceptance* in Christ to enable us to overcome the accuser, it is also vital for us to know our *authority* in Christ over all the powers of darkness.

New authority

To understand our authority over the enemy, we need to look at Paul's letter to the Ephesians. Ephesus was a city devoted to the occult. The temple of Diana (one of the seven wonders of the ancient world) was there. The cult of Diana was centred in Ephesus. It was in that city that Paul had his most dramatic confrontation with the powers of darkness.[21] It was there that Christian converts burnt occult manuscripts equivalent to 50,000 days' wages![22] If any new church might be justified in dwelling on the overwhelming strength of the powers of darkness, it was the church at Ephesus. Yet it is to that church that Paul writes most powerfully of the victory of Christ and of our victory in Christ.

As we have already seen, the Bible speaks of a spiritual realm, which is just as real as the physical world that we can handle and see. One of the expressions the Bible uses to speak of this spiritual reality is 'heavenly places', or 'heavenly realms'. This is a characteristic expression of Paul's letter to the Ephesians. The book of Ephesians also refers to the evil forces of darkness, using terms such as 'rule and authority', 'power and dominion', 'rulers and authorities', 'principalities and powers'.

What does the book of Ephesians say about these things? First, it makes clear that Christ has triumphed over all these evil powers. He has conquered them. It talks about Christ being not only raised from the dead but seated at God's right hand in the heavenly realms. There He is far above all rule and authority, power and dominion.[23] And, not only has He conquered, but the power in which He conquered is available to His church. Paul is praying that we may be fully aware of the 'incomparably great power of God for us who believe'.[24] It is that power which has caused Christ to be above all these principalities and powers, and that same power is available for us as we live as overcomers of the power of the Evil One.

Furthermore, if Christ is above all these evil powers, where are we? Answer; we are in Christ, blessed with every spiritual blessing in the heavenly realms in Him.[25]

The Ephesian letter then goes on to talk about what we were before we were saved. Previously we used to be under the authority of the 'ruler of the kingdom of the air' – that is the devil.[26] Thus we were dead in our sins; but we have been saved from that. Not only have we been saved, but God has seated us in a new place. Where? In Christ in the heavenly realms. In other words, as soon as we are born again we are placed into Christ, which means we have His authority over all the powers of darkness. We are secure and safe in Him. We need not fear.

More than that, the church is to be a demonstration to these evil forces of the wisdom of God. In other words, as the church demonstrates what it is to be one in Christ, from all nations, with all barriers broken down; it is a demonstration to these evil principalities and powers of how wise God is.[27]

It is from this understanding of our position of victory, that Paul urges us, later in the epistle, to stand firm as we wrestle against these same evil forces of darkness.[28]

As believers, we must be secure in this before even approaching the subject of spiritual warfare. Many people get bugged by a sense of failure or a sense of weakness, or even foreboding because of all that the enemy can do against us. We must be set free from this to realise our authority in Christ. We are involved in the spiritual world now. And in that world, we are more than conquerors through Christ.[29] We overcome because we are overcomers. The church as a whole will demonstrate God's victory and wisdom to all these evil powers. This is the basis upon which we can approach the whole subject of spiritual warfare.

Effective Strategy Number 6: Understand your authority in Christ

NOTES

[1]Colossians 3:5–7; [2]John 3:6; [3]Hebrews 8:10; [4]Romans 6:2–3; [5]Romans 6:4; [6]Romans 8:14–16, Galatians 4:4–7; [7]Romans 8:1; [8]1 Peter 1:3; [9]Corinthians 5:17; [10]Romans 15:7; [11]Romans 8:38–39; [12]Ephesians 1:3; [13]Romans 8:1; [14]Revelation 12:10; [15]Zechariah 3:3; [16]Romans 7:6, 8:1–2; [17]John 13:14–17; [18]Colossians 3:5; [19]Colossians 3:12; [20]Acts 19:18–19; [21]Acts 19:11–12; [22]Acts 19:19; [23]Ephesians 1:21; [24]Ephesians 1:19; [25]Ephesians 1:3; [26]Ephesians 2:2; [27]Ephesians 3:10; [28]Ephesians 6:12–13; [29]Romans 8:37.

Chapter 7

CHRISTIANS AND DEMONS

I am going to raise some difficult issues here, but it is important that foundations are established before we build any further. If you have been reading this book from the beginning, you will have realised that I do believe demons exist. However, how these demons can affect Christians is a controversial issue, so it is important to clarify what we are talking about here.

As we have seen in Chapter 2, the Bible reveals to us that there are two worlds that affect our lives, the spiritual world and the physical world. We all know the physical world. That is the one that we can touch, taste or feel, the one that we relate to through our senses. However, there is also a spiritual world that is just as real and often described in the New Testament as 'heavenly places'. Demons, which are part of the evil spiritual world, are evil, malevolent spiritual beings with personality. They are under the direction of Satan and can inhabit people and places.

Please try to understand me when I say that nowhere in the Scriptures is the phrase 'demon-possessed' used. You may argue that it is used in your translation of the Bible, but it is important to remember that the Bibles we use are translations of the original text and, moreover, that words change their meaning over time. The King James Bible uses the phrase 'possessed with devils', and these words can strike fear into people's minds because of our modern understanding of the word 'possess'. We take it to mean total control; 'possession' suggests something that is owned, taken over and deprived of any independence. Thus 'demon-possessed' suggests total ownership and control by demons or by Satan. In the seventeenth century, when the King James translators were at work, 'possessed with' carried a much less extreme meaning, (it could simply have meant 'imbued', 'inspired by', 'permeated with' or 'inhabited by') and it is not helpful for us to retain this word in a context where it is now so prone to misunderstanding.

The original word that is most frequently used in Greek manuscripts is *daimonizomai*,[1] which is translated literally as 'demonised'. The word 'demonised' can be defined as a situation where an evil spirit has got a hold on someone's personality or on their physical body to a greater or lesser extent.

So we have in Scripture the situation where Legion was confined to a graveyard and had to be chained up to prevent him from cutting himself.[2] This was a case of severe demonisation. By contrast, there was a man who sat in the synagogue regularly without any problems, until Jesus walked in the door; then a demon manifested itself. This was a milder case of demonisation.

In my experience, people can have a demon that affects certain aspects of their life. For example, someone might have a deep-seated problem of rejection that a demon has got hold of – a spirit of rejection. This does not mean that every aspect of their life is affected. It simply means that they are likely to experience deep, almost uncontrollable, feelings of rejection whether or not this is called for in the situation.

Other expressions that are sometimes used in the Scriptures include:

- 'Having' a spirit. Examples of this include 'having a dumb spirit'[3] or 'having a spirit of infirmity'.[4]

- Someone can be described as 'with a spirit' as in the case of a person with an unclean spirit.[5]
- Someone can be 'troubled by a spirit' or 'afflicted by a spirit'.[6]
- In the case of Ananias and Sapphira, they were described as being 'filled' by Satan in the same way that a Christian is filled by the Holy Spirit.[7]

The important thing to remember is that the phrase 'demon possessed', in its modern meaning, is not used anywhere in the Scriptures, so I would counsel that we do not use it at all. This means if I am asked a question 'Can a Christian be *possessed*?' my answer will be 'No', because that is not how the Scriptures describe it. However, I do believe that Christians can be *affected* by demons, that they can be *demonised*.

Why do I believe that a Christian can be demonised? Whilst there may not be a straight theological statement to that effect, there is, in my view, plenty of clear biblical evidence.

Scripture describes the phenomena. Demons are either cast out or come out in a way that is clearly noticeable, eg 'With shrieks, evil spirits came out of many'.[8] It is never stated in Scripture that a demon can simply disappear without any sign that it has done so. We presumably all agree that people can have demons before they come to Christ, so if someone with a demon becomes a Christian, what happens to the demon? Let us look at a parallel situation. We are told to preach the gospel, heal the sick and cast out demons. If we preach the gospel but do not heal the sick, are they automatically healed? Does it just happen? Most of the time it does not, and if it does, there is clear evidence of it – the person is healed! Similarly, if we preach the gospel but do not cast out demons, do they just disappear of their own accord? There does not seem to be any clear scriptural evidence that they do. If they do leave, there are clear signs of it, as we have just seen.

As I will cover in more detail in Chapter 16, Scripture does not seem to encourage bringing deliverance to unbelievers without them coming to faith. If a person from whom a demon goes out is not filled with the presence of God, then the demon could come back and bring seven worse with it. Jesus clearly encourages setting people free from demons, but not in the context of leaving them empty.

Furthermore, many of the warnings in Scripture of demonic activity are addressed to believers and Christians are also said to be vulnerable to attack and defeat. So:

- Satan can devour.[9]
- Satan can deceive the believer.[10]
- Satan can bewitch Christians.[11]
- They can go back into slavery to 'weak and miserable principles'.[12] This phrase translates the Greek word *Stoicheia*, which almost certainly describes spiritual forces.
- They can become the mouthpiece for Satan, as they were once the mouthpiece for the Holy Spirit.[13]
- They can be taken captive by Satan to do his will and thus oppose anointed leadership within the church.[14] Surely being 'taken captive' to do the devil's will must imply some degree of demonisation.
- They can evidently enter into relationships which defile them and the references to 'Belial', 'idols' and 'unclean things', in this context, suggests the potential of demonic influence.[15]
- They are warned by Paul not to walk according to the fruit of the flesh. In this list Paul includes witchcraft.[16] The parallelism of this section with the fruit of the Spirit may imply that just as the Holy Spirit is the source of positive character traits, unholy spirits can work behind the sins of the flesh listed. This is indisputable in the case of witchcraft, but may also lie behind such sins as hatred and drunkenness.
- Christians are warned not to walk in unforgiveness which may eventually lead to them being handed over to demonic

tormentors.[17] Bitterness, unforgiveness and anger can so easily lead to strongholds of resentment, thoughts of murder, hatred, depression and even suicide. These are surely like being tormented in a dungeon.

- If we hold on to anger, we can give Satan a foothold or landing strip, which implies an entrance of demonic influence into a believer's life.[18]
- As we have already seen in Chapter 3, James teaches that polluted streams of demonic wisdom can flow into a believer's life through vulnerability created as a result of sins of the flesh.[19]
- It is recorded that Jesus healed a woman with pronounced curvature of the spine by casting out a spirit of infirmity.[20] We get the impression that he was angry because this particular woman was afflicted. To understand why, we need to interpret what Jesus said to her. He called her a daughter of Abraham. He seemed to be implying something very specific here. Abraham was known as a man of faith and I believe Jesus was saying that this was a woman of faith, part of the people of God, who was in bondage because of a demon.

The cumulative effect of all these biblical warnings and statements surely suggest that demons can infiltrate the life of the believer. They can attack them, bring them into bondage, induce sickness, trouble their minds and oppress their spirits. This is what we mean by demonisation. Furthermore, Greg Haslam has suggested, in an unpublished paper, that there is additional confirmation in the story of the Syrophenician (Canaanite, NIV) woman. She was a Gentile woman who sought a specific type of healing, namely deliverance, for her daughter. She was told that it was not right to take 'the children's bread'[21] and give it to the dogs. It would seem that Jesus meant that deliverance was 'the children's bread'. If deliverance is staple food for God's children according to Jesus, this further endorses the view that it is generally more effective in the lives of believers than those who are not. It is intended to set free those who come to Christ from what previously had held them in bondage. In addition, we are warned consistently, as believers, not to succumb to the devil's infiltration as we continue in our Christian walk.

I recall praying for a pastor in a prayer meeting at a church in another European country when he suddenly fell to the floor. When he got up again and I asked him how he felt, he said that it was not very pleasant at all. He actually described it as being very weird. So we arranged to meet the next day to pray into the situation further.

We met and talked around a few issues. He told me that he was one of a large family and he was, apparently, the least successful. This had left him with a desperate fear of other people's opinion. I began to pray for him and a demon started manifesting itself. I cast out a 'spirit of the fear of man' and he was set free. His first words were 'We don't believe in that!' Needless to say, he does now, and he has become very effective for God in delivering people from demons all around his nation and elsewhere.

What about those filled with the Spirit?

Leading on from the question about Christians being demonised is another that says 'What about Christians who are filled with the Spirit?' The inference here is that if someone is 'filled' with the Holy Spirit, nothing else can get in.

Again, I suggest this involves a lack of understanding of what is meant by being 'filled with the Spirit'. If I take a glass and fill it to the brim with water, nothing else can get in. If I then empty the glass by drinking it, for example, then anything can now be put into it. This is how many would picture in their minds being 'filled with the Spirit'.

I would suggest a better illustration is the idea of a sailing boat being blown along by the wind. Here, the idea of the sail being filled by the wind is a more dynamic picture than the glass being filled with water. The sail does not contain the wind; it is acted upon by the wind. I believe it is sometimes possible even for people who have been filled with the Holy Spirit to also have part of their lives affected by a demon.

There are scriptural examples of people who had previously been filled by the Holy Spirit becoming demonised. The Holy Spirit came on King Saul and he prophesied.[22] Yet, we find a little while later that an evil spirit, that only David could subdue with music, was tormenting Saul.

Helping new believers

It is, in my view, essential that our churches lay proper foundations for a life of discipleship for new believers. So we need to ensure that deliverance from demons forms part of the package that we offer when we preach the gospel, or at least early on in making disciples. The writers of the New Testament seem to suggest that people were set free as they responded to the gospel, or during the early challenge of living the Christian life. However, in practice, many people may have been Christians for a long time without issues of demonic influence from their past life being challenged. In this event, demonic strongholds may come to light at a later stage and we have to deal with them at that time. I deal with how we set people free in Chapter 16.

How can demons affect Christians?

I believe that demons are at work, as far as Christians are concerned, in three ways:

- To tempt us, though it is not right to say that all, or even most, temptation is demon induced.[23] I try to ensure that I do not watch certain female pop singers on the television. I believe there can be seducing spirits at work, which it is not helpful to watch.

- To oppose and attack us.[24] We can all experience demonic counter attack, as we have seen elsewhere in this book.
- Demonisation. This is where an evil spirit is able to get a grip, to a greater or lesser extent, on people's personalities or physical bodies, producing bondages and patterns of temptation and weakness that are not changed by repentance.

In the first two categories, we simply need to submit to God and resist the devil. However, where there is demonisation, the demons need to be cast out.

It is easy to see that we need to be very careful what language we use when dealing with these sorts of issues. For example, using an expression such as 'having a spirit of lust' might be inappropriate; it may simply be that the person referred to is giving in to desires of the flesh, not that he/she is being affected by a demon of lust. In a similar way, people might speak of a meeting as having a 'spirit of heaviness', when in fact it is more likely that people had a late night on Saturday, got up late on Sunday and had an argument on the way to church; so by the time they got there, the last thing they felt like was praising God. This is not to say that someone cannot have a spirit of lust or there cannot be a situation where a church is under attack and the meetings are heavy. What I am trying to say is that we should be sure we are using the right words for the situation.

Demons, places and objects

I have also found that places where occult activity has gone on may be affected, for a time, by evil spirits. For example, I have been asked to pray in houses where the occupants have complained about strange things going on. After we prayed, people noticed a difference almost immediately, evidence apparently that demons had inhabited the place and had now gone. I have also known situations where objects that have been used in occult ceremonies have demonic attachments and need to be destroyed. Please do not go to extremes, however. It does not mean that all 'ethnic' art is suspect because there may be witchcraft in a particular community; I am only talking about objects specifically used in witchcraft, curses or as superstitious charms.

Although I do believe that Christians can be affected by demons, it is important to maintain that this does not mean that all Christians need deliverance ministry, or even a majority, of them. As I make clear many times in this book, we are fighting against the flesh and the world, as well as against demonic forces. Most of our problems arise because we give in to the flesh or the principles of the world, rather than any direct demonic activity.

When considering this issue, I think we need to be reminded of John Wimber's words. He used to say on many occasions that he was less concerned with what a demon could do to a Christian than what a Christian could do to a demon!

Effective Strategy Number 7: Do not back off from setting Christians free from demonic power because of lack of clarity on this issue. I will explain how to set people free later in the book.

NOTES

[1]Matthew 4:24, 8:16, 28, 33, 9:32, 12:22, 15:22, Mark 1:32, 5:15, 16, 18, John 10:21; [2]Mark 5:2–5; [3]Mark 9:17; [4]Luke 13:11; [5]Luke 4:33; [6]Acts 5:16; [7]Acts 5:3; [8]Acts 8:7; [9]1 Peter 5:8–9; [10]2 Corinthians 11:3, 13–15; [11]Galatians 3:1; [12]Galatians 4:8–9; [13]compare Matthew 16:23 with Matthew 16:17; [14]2 Timothy 2:25–26; [15]2 Corinthians 6:14–18; [16]Galatians 5:19–21; [17]Matthew 18:32–33; [18]Ephesians 4:26–27; [19]James 3:15; [20]Luke 13:11–12; [21]Matthew 15:26; [22]1 Samuel 10:6, 10–11; [23]Acts 5:3, 1 Chronicles 21:1; [24]Acts 13:6–10, 16:18.

Chapter 8

STRONGHOLDS IN CULTURE

In Chapter 5, we showed how the way we think is affected by our culture. In our course on strongholds, for new Christians, we look at how their culture and upbringing may have caused strongholds to be erected in their thinking. In this context, we need to look at the subject of our 'worldview' because this affects the way we understand a given situation.

What do I mean by 'worldview'? This whole subject could fill a book, but I will try to summarise the issues involved. Some excellent material has been written on this subject and I would particularly encourage you to read David Burnett's book *Clash of Worlds*[1] if you want to study this important subject further. Worldview is about our personal philosophy; the way we look at life and our presuppositions, usually unconscious, about right and wrong, appropriate or inappropriate.

Our worldview depends upon the way we were educated, the way we were brought up, the friends that we mixed with and the place where we live. Most of the time, we are not aware that we have a worldview, let alone its influence on our thought processes. Many aspects of our worldview are not really very important. For example, if you lived in Britain during the earlier part of the twentieth century, and you did not hold your knife and fork properly while eating, you would have been rapped across the knuckles. This would not happen very much nowadays, but to previous generations, it was part of the way they looked at life. It was important to them. On its own, it may seem quite unreasonable, but taken in the context of the period when that attitude was common, the principle was generally accepted. People upheld certain standards, called 'good manners' and this was part of the training that helped to maintain them.

There is nothing wrong with this viewpoint . . . but there is nothing right with it either. It is simply a worldview, the way many British people of the time expressed who they were. People in other countries ate with their fingers or used chopsticks, but the English ate 'properly' (as they saw it) with a knife and fork.

A definition of worldview is 'a set of pre-suppositions or assumptions which we hold (consciously or sub-consciously) about the basic make-up of our world'.[2]

I once heard a story of a man who travelled to Siam (Thailand), and met the king. Because this happened two or three hundred years ago, the king did not have much experience of the 'outside world' and enjoyed listening to the stories that the man told, mysterious stories about windmills and canals and strange boats. The king was amazed; he had never heard of such things. Then one day the man told the king how the canals froze over during the cold winters in Holland, and how the ice got so thick that an elephant could walk on the water. This was too much for the king; until that point, he had believed everything that the man told him, but the idea of an elephant being able to walk on water offended his worldview. The king said that this was impossible, and that the man was obviously a liar. From that time on, the king refused to trust anything that the man said.

Somewhere in the Pacific Ocean, there is an island called

Yap. I once stopped over on this island while on business in that area. David Burnett tells how the people of that island refused to accept that babies arrived as a result of sexual intercourse; they believed it was a spirit entering a woman. An anthropologist eventually managed to demonstrate the principle using the results of breeding imported European boars with native sows. The people's response was one of amazement that the anthropologist should imagine that human beings reproduced in the same way as pigs!

On another island in the Pacific, I stopped over for a weekend on banking business and decided to go to a church that I had noticed. The only problem was that I couldn't find out what time the meeting started on Sunday. Eventually I asked someone, 'What time does the service start?' and received a puzzled look in response to my question. 'Obviously he doesn't understand English', I thought, so I checked. Yes, he understood English perfectly; so I asked again and got the same response. Again I asked the question; this time I got an answer. 'Why, the service starts when the people get there!' Of course it did. How stupid of me! That was my problem. It wasn't a language problem, it was just that our worldviews on the issue of time had come face to face and we could not readily understand each other. I regarded time as a measure; he regarded it as an event.

Taking this a step further, we can sometimes even look at the Bible through the spectacles of our own worldview. For example, there was a preacher in one part of Africa who was telling the story of David's affair with Bathsheba. 'Isn't it amazing', he said, 'Such deep repentance for such a minor sin?' How could the preacher call adultery a minor sin? Of course it isn't a minor sin. However, in the culture where he was preaching, adultery was a more or less socially acceptable way of life. To these people, looking at the story with their own worldview, David's affair was not all that serious.

We are probably unaware, unless it is pointed out to us, that we too can approach Bible text through our worldview. Preaching in many other cultures has helped me to examine this possibility. What is needed is for us to renew our minds so that we can understand the biblical worldview.

For example, what about the story in the gospels about the man who needed a loaf of bread for a visitor?[3] He went to his friend's house after midnight and knocked until his friend came to the door to find out what the problem was. We cannot understand that in Britain today. It is just not something we would do. We might go to a 24hr supermarket, but more than likely we would not bother, or we might leave it until the next day. So when we hear many Western preachers speaking on this passage, we look at it from the perspective that to knock on a neighbour's door at midnight is unreasonable and requires great boldness and persistence. However, in the Middle Eastern culture of that time (and today!), hospitality was more important to them than almost anything else. So, if you ran out of bread when someone came to visit, you could not go to a supermarket, but you could go to a friend's house at any time of day or night and know that they would help you out, because a failure to show hospitality would bring shame to the whole village. Kenneth E Bailey in his book *Poet and Peasant and Through Peasant Eyes*[4] suggests that Jesus is telling a humorous story to the effect that if a guest has arrived and the host is borrowing bread to show him hospitality, you cannot imagine someone giving silly excuses about locked doors and children in bed. If this interpretation is right, it would suggest that the story is there an affirmation of the confidence we may have as we approach our Heavenly Father in prayer. So perhaps we too can sometimes read Scripture through the perspective of our worldview that will contain strongholds of wrong thinking.

Strongholds in 'fallen' culture

Because of sin, every culture is 'fallen' and in all cultures there are strongholds of wrong thinking, which sometimes may be demonic.

As I indicated in Chapter 1, when I go to teach on strongholds in any particular nation, it is important that I understand something of the culture of the people there in order to help them practically to be set free from the strongholds of wrong thinking in their culture. There will always need to be an adjustment of thinking; sometimes it will also require deliverance because of the demonic power that may have attached itself to that wrong thinking through the occult, idol worship, witchcraft, or other sins in the individual concerned or their family.

To start with I will often use an illustration from another culture. This is because it is very easy to see the strongholds in other cultures, but not so easy to see the ones in our own. Seeing strongholds in another culture helps us to see the principles of cultural strongholds, which we can then teach people to apply to their own culture.

Churches can easily absorb the culture around them to the extent that there is hardly any difference between them and the non-believers around them. The church was always intended to be counter-culture. This does not mean counter-culture by dressing in styles that are forty years out of date, or playing music that is years out of date, or introducing Western religious music to drum-playing Africans. Indeed, churches that appear 'old-fashioned' can actually adopt many ways of thinking from their culture without noticing.

I often have to deal with the issue of cultural superiority: the assumption that the way we were brought up is the right way. Many people in Britain have traditionally thought this way. We think that the Italians are much more excitable, Scandinavians are much less excitable, but the British are in the middle and that is just the way that it should be!

This was made very clear to me on one occasion in a strange way; I really had not met this situation before. I was looking to see set free somebody whose father was very judgmental. I found I actually had to confront a demon of the 'Colonial Englishman who always thinks that he is right'. I do not know if this was its name but it responded and left! I later found this story helpful when ministering on strongholds to white South Africans!

To illustrate this, I will take you through a number of the strongholds I deal with when teaching this material in Britain. Much of it applies to other Western nations, as we will see.

The stronghold of Western worldview

This particular stronghold has developed through the educational system and affects the way that we are trained to think. We accept as true only those things that we can see and understand, and if we cannot understand it then we assume that either it is not true or it belongs to the 'less real' spiritual world.

What happens is that intellectual analysis is exalted above faith. The intellectual's attitude is patronising and we frequently hear people talking about Christians having a 'blind' faith, followed by the nauseating 'patting on the head' that goes with the remark: 'Well if it is a comfort for you, that's okay'. It is the sort of intellectual superiority that sees Christianity as being for old ladies and little children at Sunday School, but not for sophisticated, educated adults. Many have to face this patronising attitude of 'You don't really believe that, do you?' at work, at college, at school. It can be undermining of our faith and we need to fight boldly against this principality of our culture in just the same way as those in

India saved from worshipping Hindu idols have to renounce and stand against the strongholds of their culture. The spiritual world is either denied by most people, or seen as less than real. The only things they accept as real are those that can be explained by the laws of science. The biblical worldview, by contrast, is that the physical world and the spiritual world are equally real, both created by God.

Christianity must of course be seen as a reasonable faith, that is, a faith that can be reasoned intellectually and argued doctrinally. However, Paul said that both his message and his teaching were not with wise and persuasive words.[5] Instead, he tells us, they were supported by a demonstration of the power of the Holy Spirit. His purpose in this, he says, is so that our faith is not based on man's wisdom but on God's power.

Our Western worldview, with its exaltation of knowledge and intellectual understanding above faith, can undermine our effectiveness in doing the works of the kingdom, because it tempts us to equate 'knowledge' with 'effectiveness'. For example, we may think that if we go to enough seminars on healing, we are effective in healing people. If we go to enough seminars on prophecy, we may consider ourselves 'prophetic', even if we never bring effective prophecy in a meeting.

It is this stronghold of the Western worldview that makes it such a struggle to pray for the sick with real, believing faith. In some parts of the world, it would be regarded as strange if Christians did *not* pray for the sick and expect to see many healed. But in the West, I believe prayer for healing is a battleground where we wrestle against the principalities and powers behind the Western worldview every time we seek to pray for the sick. So endemic is this stronghold that even when we see people healed, we find ourselves wondering whether there is another more 'rational' explanation for the healing.

The stronghold of atheism

The logical conclusion of a rationalist worldview which excludes the supernatural is atheism. As a teenager in the 1960's, I remember *Time* magazine running the front-page headline 'God is Dead', and it seemed that the philosophy of atheistic humanism had triumphed in Western thinking. A society that could build atomic weapons and put men into space seemed to have 'come of age' and have no further use for the supernatural. (Humanism is the name for the worldview that ignores or denies the existence of God and regards human beings as autonomous, essentially good and able to solve their needs and fulfil their potential by rational means and human effort.)

In fact, atheism was not a new philosophy, but one formulated in the nineteenth century by the German philosopher Nietzsche. Ravi Zacharias points out in his book *A Shattered Visage* that Nietzsche 'prophesied' that because God had 'died' in the nineteenth century, the twentieth century would be the bloodiest in history and a universal madness would break out.[6] This 'universal madness' may be what Malcolm Muggeridge had in mind when he wrote 'If God is dead, somebody is going to have to take his place. It will be megalomania or erotomania, the drive for power or the drive for pleasure, the clenched fist or the phallus, Hitler or Hugh Hefner'[7] (of *Playboy* magazine).

We can easily find ourselves on the defensive when unbelievers remind us of the wars and atrocities perpetrated in the name of religion, and we have to admit that the Christian church has too often failed to heed Jesus' words that His kingdom does not belong to this world, otherwise His servants would fight.[8] However, we can answer this by pointing to the far worse record of the atheistic rulers of the twentieth century: Hitler, Stalin and Mao alone have caused unprecedented human suffering and death through wars and appalling abuses of human rights by their oppressive regimes.

Again, we have to admit to some 'Christian' abuse of human rights, such as the notorious Spanish Inquisition and the martyrdom of Reformation activists on both sides at the hands of fellow Christians of the opposing faction. But on the whole, Christians have an excellent historical record of providing social care (education, hospitals, ministry to the poor, etc) and have been effective in promoting justice and morality in society.

Let us not cower before the massive, mocking stronghold of atheism in our culture, but go on the offensive and take the battle to the enemy's camp. Our faith stands up to intellectual and moral scrutiny: humankind is far from 'coming of age' intellectually or morally; the evil in our world is in the hearts of fallen, sinful individuals. In the cross of Jesus Christ, we have the answer to that evil.

The stronghold of hedonism: the pursuit of pleasure

In our culture personal pleasure has become, for many, their greatest goal. Our judgement on issues is, *how it affects me*. 'Let us eat and drink for tomorrow we die'.[9] We do not have to spend time demonstrating how this has become a dominant stronghold in our culture. We only have to look at the advertisements on our television screens. However, as Christians, we can become affected by our culture and this stronghold can have outworkings in church life. I want to suggest a number of ways in which this can happen.

- The therapeutic movement. This movement has taken the middle class Western world by storm. Now, please do not misunderstand me. I regularly teach a counselling course. I believe in biblical counselling and its necessity and effectiveness to help people who have been damaged through the problems of life or their own past sin. However, in the Christian church, just as in the world, counselling can become 'me' centred. The objective so often is to make me 'whole'. Actually, this is a false promise. I will not be 'whole' until glory, because the kingdom of God has not yet come in all its fullness. Being set free from the bondage of past hurts, or the effect on my emotions of past sins, is not to make me feel better, it is rather to enable me to be free to serve in the body of Christ and to spread the gospel in the world. The objective of Christian counselling is more effective Christian service and a life lived to the glory of God, not that I should 'feel' better.

- I believe that some of the excesses of what is called the 'prosperity gospel' are, in fact, pandering to a spiritualisation or 'Christianisation' of this particular cultural stronghold. The goal of faith is to please God and live in sacrificial service for His purposes. This does not mean that poverty is to be sought as a goal to be attained, though it is sometimes something to be endured for a season. The issue is rather that whether we have much or have little, we are content[10] and we live to the glory of God.

- A consumerist attitude to church. Consumerism is one of the by-products of this particular stronghold. It flourishes in Western capitalism. Our whole economic system is based on consumers making choices. This may work well for economics but it is not how we should approach our responsibilities in church life. We can often have a consumerist attitude to church. If one church isn't suiting me, then I can transfer and go to another church which meets 'my needs' better. This is a parallel to consumer choice in the world where, if I do not like one store I can easily go to another. It means that church structures and programmes are geared to what are described as 'felt needs'. The result of this is that I can say that a particular church no longer meets 'my need'. *It was never intended to!* It was intended to be a body of people to whom you could be committed in order to advance the kingdom of God together. This stronghold is reflected in the expression 'the sort of church I like . . .' What about the sort of church that God likes and has described in His Word? It can also result in a lack of commitment, particularly over the long term. Sadly, in church life today, it is often easier to ask people to commit to a short-term rather than a long-term involvement.

The stronghold of individualism

This is a stronghold of 'me first'. It is therefore linked to the stronghold of hedonism but has other characteristics as well. I think of *my*self, *my* career, *my* success; or at best that of my immediate family, rather than thinking of my community as a whole. I prefer not to think of belonging to a community, or how others will be affected by my actions or decisions.

This is even stronger in the USA than in Britain. In America, the rugged individualist who carves out his own success is almost a cult figure. In Britain the attitude was epitomised by Mrs Thatcher's statement 'There is no such thing as society. There are only individual men and women and there are families'.[11] It means, that if I can make a success of my own life, then I do not need to take any responsibility for the rest of the community; for the poor, for the weak. After all, 'They had the same opportunities as me', we say 'and they blew those opportunities'. 'It is their fault'. 'How does this affect me?' we ask, when the government introduces a new policy or a new tax. 'How does it affect me?' can equally be our reaction when a change needs to be made in church life so that the church can more effectively reach the needy people in our town. 'How does it affect me?' can insidiously creep into our minds when our cell group needs to 'divide' (oops! 'multiply', I mean) because it is becoming too large to be effective in gathering new people. We can say of our money 'Well I earned it; I can do what I like with it'. True, you are free to do what you like. However, we often do not notice the verse that speaks about one of the motives for going to work being that we 'may have something to share with those in need'.[12]

In many parts of the world, people think less individualistically and more corporately; as Westerners, we can fail to understand this.

There is an African saying, 'It takes a village to raise a child'. Africans can find it difficult to understand how we expect to heal people by taking them out of their community and putting them into a hospital on their own. Surely, they say, healing takes place within the community. I am not saying that hospitals are wrong; I am only trying to make a point about the principle of community as a way of life. So an African village leader might consider that it is right to come to Christ, but will want to affect the rest of the village so that they want to come as well.

Even the English language can confuse our thinking on this point and can cause us again to read Scripture through our own worldview. The key here is contained in that little word 'you'. In English, it is either singular or plural. So if I say 'you' in English, I can mean either you as an individual, or you as 80,000 people of mixed gender in a football stadium. In many other languages, there are separate words for the singular and plural forms of 'you'.

The trouble here occurs when we read the Bible. We easily assume that when the word 'you' appears, it means 'me personally'. A good example of this is in Ephesians 5, where Paul says that 'you' should not get drunk because it leads to debauchery. Instead, he says, 'you' should be filled with the Spirit.[13] Many of us see that 'you' as referring to me as an individual – that I need to be filled with the Spirit. However, the context, as well as the use of 'you' plural in the original Greek, shows us something different, for Paul continues by telling us to speak to one another in psalms, hymns and spiritual songs, then tells us to submit to one another. This is only possible in the context of a community. What Paul is saying to us here is that *as a community*, we should be filled with the Spirit. This is a very important issue for our Christian life and our corporate church life.

God exists in perfect community as Father, Son and Holy Spirit. We were created to be a community because we were created in God's image, created to present a corporate image to the world as the body of Christ. Even many of the good things of evangelicalism can lead us unwittingly to remaining in bondage to this stronghold of individualism. We speak of our 'personal salvation', our 'personal walk with God', our 'personal ministry'. These are all essential, but let us not forget the equally important truth of corporately being the body of Christ with a kingdom concern for justice and righteousness in society around us. Otherwise, it is always 'I am going to do this'. We say that '*my* ministry does not fulfil *me*', or that '*I* am not fulfilled', or '*I* am doing this particular ministry in the church, but it doesn't fulfil *me*'. Who says that we should be fulfilled? Personal fulfilment can be an idol.

Ministry is about serving others; meeting others' needs as part of a community. Submitting one to another is a part of our life as a community and in doing that, the community is blessed. Because we do not think like that, servanthood is devalued; we are prevented from considering others to be more important than ourselves as we are commanded to do.[14] This stronghold causes personal preference, race or even colour to be exalted; God wants His body to reflect a culture that has no racial barriers. Lack of understanding of the corporate also hinders our witness to more corporate cultures, in particular the world of Islam.

The culture of the Bible does not reflect individuality either. When Jesus spoke to the woman at the well, the first thing she did was to run to the people of her village to tell them about this man who knew all about her life. Immediately she needed to relate to her community, to include them in her experience.

It is not that *I* cease to matter as an individual. It is that part of my *mattering* is that I am *part of a body*.

When people read the Bible, they sometimes fail to see the point in the lists of names that it contains, for example, Numbers 26 and Nehemiah 7. What these lists do is to maintain people's sense of identity and history as a community. The whole concept of identity is important in Scripture, but what these lists tell us is that we can only really have an identity if we are part of something. For example, I am David, of the family of Roy, of the clan of Devenish, of the tribe of English people. In Christ, I am even more part of a new family expressing its life through a local church to which I am fully committed. Within local churches, healthy outward looking cell groups are to reflect this biblical priority for community and engage in spiritual warfare against the stronghold of individualism.

Stronghold of Mammon

Mammon is another stronghold that is of huge dimensions in our culture. Many people understand the concept of materialism, the giving of undue value and importance to material possessions, and believe it to be wrong; yet Jesus speaks not of materialism as a concept, but of Mammon as a false god.[15] The NIV translates Mammon as 'money', but the KJV reproduces the spirit of the original more accurately by retaining the word 'mammon', which we may thus interpret as the personal name of a false god, rather than a general term for 'money' or 'riches'. Mammon is a principality that can be represented as a god or idol in the same way as Baal, Ashtoreth or Moloch in the Old Testament; it is an evil spiritual force, established as a demonic cultic ruler.

It may seem strange and outdated to speak of 'gods' and 'idols' as demonic forces that still exist, but we have New Testament authority for this view; Paul told the Corinthians that demons lay behind the pagan gods[16] and while they may not operate through such directly 'religious' forms of idolatry today, their presence and power is demonstrated by the effects that we see in our culture.

Mammon is one of the most powerful of these forces and affects the western world in particular, where it has millions of worshippers, though it has gained millions more elsewhere over the last few decades. Its attributes are covetousness and greed, which is specifically described in the Bible as idolatry.[17] We expect Hindus to burn their idols when they come to Christ, but how many Western Christians renounce their worship of the idol Mammon?

An idol is a substitute for the true God. If we worship an idol, we will look to it for the sense of security, purpose and identity, which we should rightly find in God. This may be seen particularly clearly in the case of Mammon; *our security* becomes rooted in what we earn, *our purpose* becomes to earn more, and we see *our identity* in terms of the size of our salary and what it buys for us. Insurance companies pander to Mammon by offering us a 'secure future' in the form of secure income. We serve Mammon in our jobs and the accompanying quest for promotion, by seeking there a false sense of *purpose* (to earn more in order to provide ourselves with more *security*) and an inadequate sense of *identity* that is built on what we earn and own.

Indeed, one of the many ways in which Mammon is successful is the way we assess people by its standards: 'They live in a big house', 'He drives an expensive car', 'She is a company director in her own business'. Even pastors may be heard talking respectfully of the rich visitor they have received, or the amount someone gives to the church. If these things become the standard by which we judge people, then Mammon is in our midst. James made it clear that we must never discriminate between rich and poor in the church, or judge people's worth by their material possessions or social position.[18]

It is the *love of money* (i.e. the worship of Mammon) that is a root of all kinds of evil;[19] a passage of Scripture that is often misquoted. The love of money brings with it a temptation to cheat and lie, to fight, scheme and manipulate and to fail to give enough time to our families. This is subtle because there is a tempting deception for men to believe that it is all done on the grounds of providing for their wives and families. The love of money can also breed terrible bitterness in families, for example, over the division of inheritances.

One of Mammon's chief weapons is anxiety. Jesus himself warns us of this in the same passage in which He says that we cannot serve God and Mammon.[20] He tells us not to worry about our lives, or the future, or our material needs – what we eat or wear. Our heavenly Father knows what we need, and we should trust Him rather than give in to anxiety, which is a powerful cause of emotional stress and even physical illness. When we find ourselves becoming anxious, we need to recognise it as a tool of Mammon and start declaring: 'This is one of Mammon's tools, and I am not going to let it come between me and God!'

To fight the stronghold of Mammon is the equivalent of burning our idols, just as Jesus, in effect, asked the rich young ruler to do.[21] I am not saying that everyone should give away all they have to the poor; this was a specific command to this one man, because Jesus discerned that love of money was his problem.

How, then, are we to fight the stronghold of Mammon?

First, we do so by generous giving, which may seem crazy to those around us. The Bible records certain churches that gave beyond their ability.[22] In the Old Testament, the people of Israel on one occasion gave too much for the leaders to cope with.[23] What a blessing that would be for church treasurers today! The biblical practice of tithing is a first step towards this. When we tithe, we are stating: 'I am determined not to be governed by materialism, so I will make it a priority to give a tenth of my income to the Lord.'

Connected closely with this, we fight the stronghold of Mammon by individual or corporate acts of faith. Sometimes, it is helpful for a church to have a building project they can scarcely afford, not just in order to have a useful building at the end of the day, but to have an opportunity to stretch their faith and overcome the principality of Mammon by generous giving.

We also fight Mammon though dying to possessiveness towards our material belongings, and cultivating a genuine willingness to share our possessions with others, as the early church did in Jerusalem.[24]

Finally, we fight Mammon by having an eternal rather than an earthly perspective. Giving money away is actually the best investment. As we give, we lay up treasure in heaven.[25] Jesus told a rather strange parable about an unjust manager.[26] The man was commended, not for his dishonesty, but for his wisdom in being generous with his master's property, in order to benefit from the gratitude of those to whom he gave it. Jesus is saying that handling money wisely involves being generous with it, recognising that it belongs not to us, but to God. If we give generously, we will be welcomed in the 'world to come' by those who have benefited from our generosity. Imagine being greeted in heaven by a currently unreached people group, who express their gratitude to you because your generous giving enabled the Bible to be translated into their language so that they came to faith! Jim Elliot's famous quotation is applicable here: 'He is no fool who gives what he cannot keep, to gain what he cannot lose.'[27]

The stronghold of Postmodernism

In the generation born after 1965, sociologists would say there has been an embracing of a new way of thinking. This is often called 'postmodernism' and the sociological term for the generation which has been impacted by this change is 'Generation X' (after the title of the book by Douglas Coupland[28]). This new way of thinking is derived from the philosophy of 'existentialism' – and in particular, the version of existentialism developed in the 1940s and 1950s by writers such as Jean-Paul Sartre and Albert Camus.

The centre of this philosophy is 'being' and 'enjoying being'. It is truly 'eat, drink and be merry, for tomorrow we die'. Furthermore, we are what we choose to be. Choice is thus the centre of existence. Moreover, it says that any choice I make is completely arbitrary; it need have no rational purpose whatsoever, other than what I choose to give it. The universe is absurd, according to these philosophers, so meaninglessness is something we have to come to terms with. Whatever we choose is right for us.

This results in a supermarket approach to belief. You are offered 83 different varieties of potato crisps, and it is up to you which you choose. It really does not matter which you choose because they all taste about the same anyway; and the choice is getting bigger all the time. According to this philosophy, it also does not matter if your choices do not quite hang together. You can be equally passionate about saving the lives of whales and promoting the killing of unborn babies through legalised abortion. This may be illogical but it does not matter.

This philosophy spreads over into the areas of spiritual belief as well. So people will say 'Oh well, if that's what you believe, I'm glad for you; but I choose to think a different way'. So they mix and match Buddhism and Hinduism and blend it with a seasoning of 'acceptable' Christian doctrine and call it their belief. For them, it is just as valid as your belief. There is no sense of having to believe something because it's true; truth is related to choice. Whatever you choose to believe is true for you and it does not matter if someone has a completely different view. This can lead to the idea of 'tolerance' being the final authority rather than the Word of God. Indeed this whole philosophy is tolerant of everything except a belief in absolute truth, which it interprets as intolerance!

Now there is much that is positive about the so-called Generation X. There is a greater sense of community and an openness to the supernatural. These characteristics need to be seen as doorways through which we can reach Generation X.

We need to be careful that this 'mix and match' philosophy does not invade the church and bring an attitude of choosing which Bible teachings are acceptable and which are not. As Christians, we must 'bow the knee' to revealed truth in God's Word, whether or not it is palatable to the modern age or our personal preferences.

Another outworking of this change of philosophy is a growing tide of cynicism, which is affecting British culture. British humour is growing more and more cynical. It has a tendency to undermine what is good as well as exposing what is hypocritical. Our mass media tend to over-idolise people of celebrity status and then cynically pull them down again off the pedestal on which they themselves first placed them.

Cynicism is very undermining of faith. Cynical humour can develop within the Christian church and weaken our faith in the operation of a powerful, wonder-working God today. It is true, sadly, that sometimes false claims are made concerning the miraculous and we need to be very careful to avoid this hostage to fortune. However, let us also be careful that even in the church, we do not allow a justifiable exposing of hypocrisy and ridiculing of the 'super-spiritual' to leave us with a vacuum of unbelief. Otherwise, just as in one town in Israel,

Jesus may not do many works of power amongst us because of our unbelief.[29]

Non-Western strongholds

Up to this point, this chapter has focused on the cultural strongholds of British (or Western) thinking. If I am teaching in another culture, I do not focus on these issues but on strongholds that are appropriate to the relevant culture.

• *Superstition*

These are beliefs which arise from family or cultural traditions and are binding upon people's lives. They are exploited by evil spirits and can act as a curse if the superstitious taboos are transgressed.

Many superstitions are to do with combating sickness or ill fortune, and are often connected with the 'rites of passage' – significant times of change in people's lives, such as conception, birth, entering adulthood, puberty, marriage and death. Some friends of mine are working in the Middle East. When the wife became pregnant, the women around her told her a range of the things she must and must not do while carrying the baby. And when it was born, they were horrified that certain ritualistic procedures were not followed. However, this became a wonderful opportunity for her to testify to the power of Christ who protected and prospered mother and baby without any recourse to superstitious charms and practices.

Other superstitions look to the spirit world to bring bad 'fortune'. In many cultures, the 'evil eye' is a powerful superstition; somebody may be perceived to look at you or your child with the 'evil eye', which will bring a curse or bad fortune. All sorts of charms may be employed to ward off the effects of this supposed evil look.

Another group of superstitions relates to animals and their

behaviour, such as the idea that when a dog barks unaccountably, it means an evil spirit is passing by. Many cultures have superstitions relating to black cats.

• *Syncretism*

In some countries, I will teach on syncretism. Syncretism is the attempt to reconcile or combine diverse or opposite beliefs and practices. For example, it can happen where Roman Catholicism has brought Christianity to a country and there have been baptisms without personal faith. Then old pagan gods can still be worshipped but the names of Catholic saints be substituted for them.

• *Witchcraft*

There is the issue of Shamanism where an occult practitioner works in co-operation with the spirit world with the alleged aim of achieving healing and prosperity within the community. This often ends up 'controlling' the community as well. This is 'so-called' white magic. I will also teach about witchcraft and its effects that many still fear, even though they have been converted to Christ. In one place I visited, witchcraft ceremonies had been enacted against people's properties. Every meeting I was in, people came forward for prayer on this issue. I remember one lady at an evangelistic meeting at which I was speaking. It was her first visit to the church. She had witnessed some spices being placed strategically around her property. Her neighbour had told her that this meant that somebody had been practising witchcraft against the property. It turned out to be a distant member of the family who was coveting the property and was determined to get this lady and her family out. The result had been that during the previous year, her father had died, her mother had died, and her brother had died. She was now the only one left and was understandably in great fear. We need to tackle these issues and I explain how we do so in

later chapters with respect to deliverance. Teaching about our
security and authority in Christ is very important too in this
context.

• *Patriarchy and matriarchy*

Sometimes there are cultures with an outward patriarchy but
hidden matriarchy. This is very subtle because we then have to
deal with the strongholds on 'both sides'. For example, we have
to teach men to serve their wives as Christ served the church. A
friend of mine was teaching this in a particular place and heard
afterwards that one of the leaders had responded with indignation. 'How dare he suggest that I should make my wife a cup of
tea?' The 'macho' distortion of godly masculinity needs to be
confronted in some places in this connection.

However, at the same time, in some cultures that are out-
wardly male dominated, it can still be said, 'A man is not free
until his mother dies'. Mothers urge their sons to get married
so that they can have daughters-in-law to act as servants. So not
only is the man not free, but the daughter-in-law's life is a 'hell'
of servitude until her mother-in-law dies, and the daughter-in-
law re-establishes the tradition! I deal with more of these issues
in the chapters on the stronghold of control and the Jezebel
spirit.

Other cultural strongholds

In many places, the strongholds of racism and tribalism need
to be confronted. The idea of 'tribe' as a group that conveys a
sense of 'belonging' is actually a helpful safeguard in an age of
the breakdown of community. We can therefore see its re-emer-
gence in many cultures because of political and social isolation
and uncertainty. However, tribal*ism* is an evil force, a form of
'dissension' and 'factions', that Paul described as works of the
flesh.[30] His reference to it in this connection shows that it can

invade the church. Many supposed religious conflicts are in fact tribal.

Linked with this issue of discrimination is the evil of the caste system in India. The caste system is a form of institution-alised 'rejecting' and 'rejection'. I remember hearing the testi-mony of a lady in India from a high caste background testifying to the release she experienced when she was willing to use the same cup as her servant and not have a separate cup for her.

Of course, this has similarities in Britain. I have often set people free in prayer from the effects of the class system, either 'a chip on the shoulder' or a feeling that 'leadership is not for people like us' – or both. John Wesley battled successfully against this stronghold when he not only saw many conversions amongst the working classes, but he also made leaders of thou-sands of them.

In some places, we need to oppose the particular form of tri-balism that we call 'racism'. Again, it is totally contrary to our Christian inheritance. In Christ there is neither Jew nor Gentile, barbarian nor Scythian.[31] The term 'barbarian' was a deroga-tory one used of people of a different language and, by illogi-cal implication, of an inferior 'barbaric' culture. 'Scythians' were a people group traditionally mocked at that time.

Where there has been intense conflict, we need to minister to the effect of militarism on the one hand and intense pain and rejection on the other. I remember ministering to a man who had served for many years in the South African army in the apartheid era. He needed to be set free from huge strongholds of anger, racism and militarism.

Strongholds can sometimes be amongst a people because of their history. A whole nation can have a 'chip on the shoulder' because of its ill-treatment by another nation. However, in the church we must set people free from these attitudes.

Where there has been dictatorship, there can be tremendous passivity and lack of taking responsibility amongst people in the church. This can result in a dearth of Christian leaders willing to take initiatives. It can also mean that even in the church, domineering leaders can take over. We need to teach on these issues, see people set free and seek to train men to move out of the stronghold of passivity and take responsibility. Sometimes because of a nation's history, men can be wrongly honoured. When I was in the Ukraine recently, I was told that after the Second World War, in many cases, perhaps only one or two men returned to a whole village. The woman who got that man was greatly envied and the man was spoilt! This resulted again, in men not being able to take responsibility in the new era in that country.

I have ministered many times in Denmark. In their culture they have what is called 'Jante' law. This came into Danish culture through somebody whose intention was to keep people humble: we must not boast, we must not think too much of ourselves. However, it came to mean that nobody should take a higher position than another; no one may do better than another. This can drain the initiative and energy of leadership. If somebody seems to make progress beyond you, then it is legitimate to pull them back. Who are they to tell you what to do? It is sometimes pointed out that crabs can be left in the bottom of a bucket without a lid on. If one crab starts to climb up, the other crabs will pull it down. This is a stronghold that manifests itself in different ways in a number of cultures!

Pulling down the cultural strongholds

How does all this relate to our strategies for spiritual warfare and demolishing wrong strongholds?

It is important to see, as we said in an earlier chapter, that it is not enough to use a formula to 'bind' these strongholds. Sadly, there can be much 'binding' or 'rebuking in prayer' when the need is rather to rebuke their influence in the church by exposing them, teaching against them and setting people free from their effects. By recognising the cultural strongholds in this chapter, we have sought to demonstrate that by teaching people so that their minds are renewed, and helping them to walk free of the demonic dimensions of their culture, we can see churches truly set free and then made effective in evangelism. If deliverance for individuals is needed as well, then we must not hold back.

These are vital issues of spiritual warfare. We must see our churches set free from the power of the strongholds in their culture. Only then can churches be truly counter-cultural and radical as God intended.

Effective Strategy Number 8: Recognise the strongholds of wrong thinking in a particular culture and see people set free through teaching and applying the Word of God, and seeing them released from any evil spirits associated with the cultural wrong thinking.

NOTES

[1]*Clash of Worlds*, David Burnett; [2]*The Universe Next Door*, James Sire, page 17 (IVP, 38 De Montfort St, Leicester, LEI 7GP. Used with permission.); [3]Luke 11:5–8; [4]*Poet and Peasant and Through Peasant Eyes*, Kenneth E Bailey; [5]1 Corinthians 2:4–5; [6]*A Shattered Visage*, Ravi Zacharias, page 23; [7]Zacharias, page 25; [8]John 18:36; [9]Isaiah 22:13, 1 Corinthians 15:32; [10]1 Timothy 6:6–8, Hebrews 13:5; [11]*Woman's Own*, 31 October 1987; [12]Ephesians 4:28; [13]Ephesians 5:18–21; [14]Philippians 2:3–4; [15]Matthew 6:24 (KJV); [16]1 Corinthians 10:19–20; [17]Colossians 3:5; [18]James 2:1–4; [19]1 Timothy 6:10; [20]Matthew 6:25; [21]Matthew 19:21; [22]2 Corinthians 8:3; [23]Exodus 36:4–7; [24]Acts 4:32–35; [25]Matthew 6:20–21; [26]Luke 16:8–9; [27]*Shadow of the Almighty*, Elisabeth Elliot, page 15 (Hodder & Stoughton, 338 Euston Road, London, NW1 3BH. Used with permission.); [28]*Generation X*, Douglas Coupland; [29]Matthew 13:58; [30]Galatians 5:19–20; [31]Colossians 3:11.

Chapter 9

STRONGHOLDS IN GOVERNMENT

Once there was a great king. He ruled much of the world. He was a great soldier. He should have been one who could sleep peacefully at night. However, night after night he had terrible nightmares. In the morning he could not really remember what these were; they were so real, so terrifying. In desperation he sought help from his spiritual advisors as to what the dream could mean.

A man called Daniel then went to the king (whose name was Nebuchadnezzar) and offered to interpret these terrifying dreams through God's revelation. The king had dreamt of a huge image with gold on top but a terrifyingly weak mixture of iron and clay at its feet. This huge image represented the great empires of the world. What the king saw was a stone, not cut by human hands, which struck the image. The image was smashed and scattered in the wind. The stone eventually grew and became a mountain that filled the whole earth.

The image that Nebuchadnezzar had seen in his nightmares represented the kingdoms of this world. They were cruel, terrifying and seemingly all-powerful, and yet founded on an unexpectedly weak mixture of iron and clay. The tiny stone represents the kingdom of God, which was inaugurated supernat-

urally when Jesus came into the world. The picture demonstrates that all empires fall, all human rulers, however despotic,
come to nothing. The kingdom of God grows until it fills the
whole earth.

This picture and similar pictures in the book of Daniel show
on the one hand the terrifying power of human government.
They also show that we can trust God because His kingdom
will grow in the midst of these empires and will flourish until
it fills the whole earth. Jesus spoke about this when He
described the kingdom as being like a mustard seed planted,
which became a huge tree.[1] He said that the gospel of the
kingdom must be preached in every nation and then the end
will come.[2]

I would like to say more in this context about the kingdom of
God. However, my purpose is to write about the biblical view
of human government.

Later, Daniel himself had a terrifying vision. He saw fierce
grotesque animals. One was like a bear with ribs in its mouth,
another like a lion that could fly, another like a leopard with
four heads and then an indescribably evil looking beast with
iron teeth which trampled everything underfoot.[3] As he was
thinking about this dream, the picture suddenly changed. He
saw the throne of God, the Ancient of Days seated upon it, and
a river of fire flowing from it. Daniel was being told that there
would be dreadful times in world history from demonically
inspired governments. These governments would oppress
God's people. They would terrify the inhabitants of the earth.
The assurance was, however, that the throne of God was there
and that His kingdom would be worked out.

These are pictures of the operation of human government in
history. They are worked out at all times all over the world.
Human history has followed this pattern. The century that has
just ended has, in particular, experienced some terrifying realities of demonic power inspiring human governments.

There have been two world wars. There have been millions killed, as we have seen, in the holocaust of Nazi Germany, in the oppressions of Stalin and Mao ZeDong. There has been exploitation of many people groups all over the world by colonial powers. We have seen the 'beast' of apartheid in Africa, we have seen the 'beast' of cruel communist dictatorship, the 'beast' of fascism. Governments have released terrifying persecutions against the church of Jesus Christ. What about the atrocities of genocide and ethnic cleansing in Kosovo, in Bosnia, in Rwanda, in Angola and in Sierra Leone?

All this is the outworking of the demonic forces, which have usurped authority in this world through the fall of man. The book of Revelation takes up the theme of human government and institutions being the haunt of evil powers. The spirit of anti-Christ is at work.[4]

The Bible teaches two parallel concepts of human government. On the one hand it teaches that the 'powers that be' are ordained of God.[5] We are to submit ourselves to them. We are to pay our taxes. We are to obey the law. This is one picture of human government, but there is another which is familiar to Christians who have experienced terrible persecution; familiar to all those who have suffered through genocide. This is the picture of the dreadful 'beasts' representing demonic power. As Christians, we must hold these two ideas of human government in tension. The Bible does this. We must recognise that although we are to obey the government, unless their commands offend the Word of God, we must also recognise the evil powers at work through them.

What does this mean for us in practice?

• We must not stress one aspect at the expense of the other. For example, in South Africa in the apartheid era, many white Christians said that they must obey the laws of apartheid because the government is ordained of God.

They did not recognise the evil bestial nature of the government.

- We must recognise that in encounters with government, there is exposure to evil forces at work there. This means that we must pray for those Christians who sense the call of God to be involved in politics. Covering them in prayer is an aspect of spiritual warfare. We must also pray for Christian organisations that are involved in lobbying governments for justice to be maintained.

- We must obey the command of Scripture to pray for those in authority.[6] This is often omitted in our churches today.

- Those who engage in politics as Christians must recognise that they will encounter insults and attempts to ridicule them because of their faith, and be prepared to persevere in spite of it. On the other hand, although in Western democracies, they have to get involved in party politics, they must remember that their first loyalty is to God and not to their party. They must discern when their party is following principles that come from the demonic forces at work within the political arena, and be prepared to go against the flow when necessary.

- We must not be surprised that in the political arena, governments can fall prey to pressure groups promoting evil practices.

- We must not fall into the trap of seeing Third World dictatorship as wholly bad and failing to recognise the evil influence of Western exploitation, both throughout history and today.

- We must remember that all human governments are accountable to God, whether or not they recognise it. Nebuchadnezzar's second vision led him to understand this principle of accountability.[7] We must pray for governments to recognise this principle.

Effective Strategy Number 9: Pray for rulers and governments, and particularly for Christians involved in them, whilst fully recognising the capacity for terrible evil within the institutions of human government.

NOTES

[1]Matthew 13:31–32; [2]Matthew 24:14; [3]Daniel 7:7; [4]1 John 4:3; [5]Romans 13:1 (KJV); [6]1 Timothy 2:1–2; [7]Daniel 4:34–37.

Chapter 10

THE CHALLENGE FOR MISSION

Here for Mission!

God has a cosmic destiny on His heart, which the enemy opposes. Furthermore, God has revealed that destiny to us in Scripture – not in fine detail, but in broad brushstrokes. God's ultimate purpose, planned before time, accomplished through the death and resurrection of Christ, is to bring everything under Christ's authority in the final day.[1] His desire is to see glory given to God in the church and in Christ Jesus for ever and ever but starting now through worshippers of every generation.[2] He will eventually have people from every tribe, language and nation praising him.[3] In this context the word 'nation' means every ethnic group.

We can summarise this to the effect that it is God's purpose to receive worship from a glorious church composed of people from every ethnic group. When this is achieved, Jesus will return and the whole of creation will be brought into the good of it in submission to Christ, finding its ultimate expression in a new heaven and a new earth.

God, in His grace, has decided to work through us to bring these purposes about. We are here for mission. Jesus has commissioned us to go and make disciples of all nations.[4] Every people group is to be reached with the gospel. We are believing for glorious, self-propagating churches in every people group in the final days. We are believing for the church all over the world, even in areas that seem most resistant now to the gospel, to be a city set on a hill.[5] 'The mountain of the Lord's temple will be established as chief among the mountains; it will be raised above the hills, and all nations will stream to it'.[6]

The issue of spiritual warfare is directly related to mission. It arises because the church of Jesus Christ is invading the darkness, advancing the kingdom. That is why the enemy fights against us; he is seeking to protect his strongholds against the advance of the gospel. Spiritual warfare must not be seen as a separate issue of church life, the sphere of a few specialists who understand about these things. I am concerned lest we allow a few of what I consider unbiblical emphases in spiritual warfare to deflect us from our mission. As we have seen, it was as the seventy-two disciples went out on their mission, preaching the gospel, healing the sick and casting out demons, that Jesus saw Satan falling like lightning from heaven.[7] The primary challenge for mission, therefore, is for us to be actively involved in doing these primary works of the kingdom (what some would call low level spiritual warfare!) and seeing God at work in the spiritual realm.

As we saw in the last chapter, we are confronting massive strongholds of Satan. Our objective is to see Christians released from the power of these strongholds so that the church can be built free of demonic influence. It is not that we do not believe in the strong evil powers at work in this darkness; we recognise the enormity of the task. Our commission is to rescue people from these enemy strongholds and in that way build New Testament churches in enemy territory.

The challenge of culture

Over recent years, missiologists have been very wide-awake to issues of culture. There is an understanding of the need to be culturally aware, to respect other cultures. It is recognised that we should not try to impose Western cultural values and styles upon others. The gospel needs to be free of any cultural shackles.

Gospel truths are unchanging, but as genuine servants of the gospel, we can adapt to each culture in order to reach that culture. 'Though I am free and belong to no man, I make myself a slave to everyone, to win as many as possible. To the Jews I became like a Jew, to those under the law, I became like one under the law . . . , so as to win those under the law. To those not having the law I became like one not having the law . . . , so as to win those not having the law. To the weak I became weak, to win the weak. I have become all things to all men so that by all possible means I might save some. I do this for the sake of the gospel, so that I may share in its blessings'.[8] This clear, unambiguous statement of Paul's is a good plumbline for our approach to culture as those willing to serve. I recall the point being made at a mission conference, that Paul released the gospel from its Jewish clothes; that Martin Luther released the gospel from its Latin clothes. What is happening today is the release of the gospel from its distinctive Western clothes.

I believe there are three elements to each culture and it is essential that we understand the difference between these, if we are to be effective in our mission to reach them.

1. Every culture has things that make that culture open to the gospel

A missionary went to Irian Jaya in Indonesia, to preach the gospel to a particular tribe there. The missionary learnt the language of the people, and became acquainted with their culture. He read the gospel story to them in their own language and as they listened, he was amazed how they became more and more excited by the story. This was going to be so easy. Then, as he reached the end of the story, he realised that something was wrong. They appeared to have misunderstood. It was not Jesus they wanted to give their lives to, but Judas! You see, in that culture, betrayal was one of their highest values, and this was the most incredible story of betrayal they had ever heard, so they understood Judas to be the hero, not Jesus.

In a culture with such strongholds, how would he ever get them to understand the gospel story? How could he present it as anything other than a story of betrayal? Then he realised that since betrayal was so common, it caused many wars between villages. When people wanted to end such a conflict, they would take a young child and present it to the other village as an offering of peace. The child was called a 'peace child'. Here was the opportunity! Here was the factor that made that culture open to the gospel. He told them all about the peace child called Jesus, whom God had sent into the world![9]

The apostle Paul did something very similar when he went to Athens. All he could see were idols; so many, that he was almost overwhelmed. Then, as he walked around the city, he noticed an altar that had inscribed on it 'To an unknown god'.[10] So he praised the Athenians for being so religious and continued, 'Now what you worship as something unknown, I am going to proclaim to you.'[11] He had found his entry point – the factor in their culture that made them open to the gospel – and told them of the unknown God who sent His Son into the world to die and be raised to life again

Every culture contains elements that make it open to the gospel, and we need to be wise in finding and exploiting these elements so that we proclaim the unchanging truths of the gospel in a way that reaches the hearts and understanding of our audience.

2. *Every culture has neutral things that can be used to the glory of God.*

Neutral things include the way that people sing and dance – art and expression. I have preached several times in Africa. I particularly remember a recent visit to Lesotho. When they started to sing (as in much of Africa), the worship leader gave them a starting note, then after a brief few moments, the rest of the congregation joined her, all in perfect harmony. Their dancing is wonderful too, but makes me, as a Western European, feel I have no innate sense of rhythm at all. Of course, worship in an African church should be expressed through an African style of dancing.

I remember another visit to Africa, this time to Uganda. We were at an African church there. The leaders of the church were from Singapore and they were doing an excellent job. However, the early part of the worship was led by somebody from Singapore who was speaking English in an American Southern States drawl. Yet when she spoke to us after the service, she did not speak with that accent at all. It was just that there must have been an almost unconscious perception that 'That is how you speak when you lead worship'. That first part of the meeting did not flow very well, but the people entered with enthusiasm into the second half, which was led by Africans playing their African drums.

Last year I was in Crimea in the south of the Ukraine. After one of my messages, I sensed that things were a bit heavy and felt that it would be good to sing a triumphant song and encourage the people to dance. I did not know at the time, but the pastor of that church had only two weeks before come to the conviction that it was all right to dance in worship in church. He would previously have not allowed it. The people therefore were unaccustomed to dancing in worship. I asked the band to sing a lively Russian language song and then encouraged people to go out into the aisles and to the front of the hired cinema building where they met and dance. They all responded wonderfully, but they had never learnt the 'charismatic two-step'! They were only accustomed to their own cultural form of Cossack dancing. I found myself being thrown around all over the place! Once again, I realised I had little innate sense of rhythm.

All these cultural expressions, used to the glory of God, demonstrate His multi-coloured wisdom.[12]

3. *Every culture has strongholds that must be demolished.*

We have seen this in the previous chapter. We have seen that churches can adapt to their culture in wrong ways. We have seen that people need to be set free from whatever the strongholds of the enemy are in that particular culture.

Consequences for spiritual warfare

This understanding of culture has a number of consequences for the issue of spiritual warfare. One danger is that we can fail to discern the strongholds because we are so concerned about being culturally relevant. I remember praying for some people from a part of the world where, in one particular people group, because of a matriarchal culture, it is required that a man once he gets married must go and live in his in-laws' house to maintain matriarchal control. Now this is a part of the world where there has been much Christian influence over the years and, indeed, some revival in the past. I was praying for a young man about the effects of this culture upon him. I asked him whether the church historically had done anything about these issues. He said that no, the church had not done so because they considered them to be 'cultural'. The problem is that though cultural, they are unbiblical and having a detrimental effect on the raising up of godly leadership.

Another danger is that we can teach the 'major' truths of Christianity and because they are accepted, ignore the strongholds. There is an excellent book entitled *Filipino Spirit World*,[13] which studies this phenomenon in the Philippines. What this study showed was that first the Roman Catholics went into the Philippines and taught some of these major truths. They taught the doctrine of the One true God, they taught about the Trinity, about heaven and hell, about the cross of Christ and the Virgin Mary. Many of the people of the Philippines came to acknowledge these doctrines but their practical lives were still lived out according to their traditional beliefs in spirits and so on.

When Protestant missionaries arrived, they 'corrected' the teaching on some of the high truths of Christianity that I have referred to earlier. They added the truth of justification by faith. However, they did not deal with the strongholds either, which were actually governing the way people lived in practice. Hence the stronghold of the Filipino spirit world was not taken so far as these Christians were concerned, though they had apparently adopted either Catholic or Protestant forms of Christianity.

When I recently met with Daniel Balais, the pastor of Christ the Living Stone Fellowship, Metro Manila, and a leader in intercession in the Philippines, I was encouraged to hear that they were still using as a basis for their prayer and teaching the concepts raised in the book, *Filipino Spirit World*. It is really encouraging when we see the issue of strongholds being taken seriously in this way.

Often the strongholds in a culture are not what they appear on the surface. For example, in many Islamic countries, people are in practice bound up by superstition and what is called 'Folk Islam'. Bringing freedom from evil spirits could be a way in for the gospel rather than concentrating on theological differences between Islam and Christianity.

We must be careful not only to distinguish between positive and negative aspects of the culture to which we are taking the gospel, but also to distinguish between the gospel we are called to preach and the cultural trappings that we have brought with us. We may well have cultural strongholds in our own lives that we are not set free from. This calls for great humility and a willingness to listen to those to whom we are ministering.

Battle for the first fruits

Another aspect of spiritual warfare in terms of our mission is the issue of what I would call 'the battle for the first fruits'. It is the biblical pattern that the entrance into new areas will often be costly in warfare terms. As the gospel expanded in the book of Acts, we see tremendous persecution. There were mysterious sicknesses such as, it seemed, Paul succumbed to in Galatia.[14] When in Corinth, Paul seemed almost to fall into a depression until God encouraged him in a vision.[15]

Paul was obviously aware of the very great danger of new converts falling back. As we have already seen, he wrote to the church in Thessalonica talking about his deep concern that 'The tempter might have tempted you and our efforts might have been useless'.[16] You might say, 'That sounds like negative confession, Paul.' No, it is the reality that many find when they are seeking to break through to new areas in mission. Moreover in the same context, Paul refers to the fact that he had tried to get back to see them time and time again, but he says, 'Satan stopped us'. Again, this is familiar for those engaged in pioneer mission work. They have just seen some new converts established. Then suddenly, they have to leave the country; it is difficult to obtain a visa to get back in again. We are in a battle for the first fruits.

It may be coincidence but it does seem as though people sensing the call of God to go to new areas are often dismayed by mysterious sicknesses that they face. They find things going wrong in their extended family, which could easily keep them from their call. Sometimes when new converts seem to be going on well, suddenly some pressure comes upon them either from their culture of from their families and they give up. What is going on? Again, it is a battle for the first fruits. It is vitally important that those engaged in these battles are supported in prayer. The outstanding book *Mountain Rain,*[17] concerning the life of Frazer of Lisuland, is a wonderful example to us in this respect. Frazer had to battle it out for many years, scarcely seeing any results, finding that those that seemed to make a profession of faith fell back. He would write home regularly about the battle. People were supporting him in prayer, calling upon God to deal with the strongholds in that culture. In the end there was breakthrough and a time of wonderful revival as many found Christ.

It is very important that our caution about certain methods of spiritual warfare does not blind us to the need to engage in fervent, continuous prayer for breakthrough in new areas of mission. We must ensure that we cover in prayer those who have gone from us. We need have no doubt that they are coming face to face with the reality of the powers of darkness.

It is also a battle to see churches built in these new areas. We must not shrink from this task. We must see mission, not simply as gaining converts, but as building churches able to reproduce themselves in their own areas and cultures. It will be a battle to raise up indigenous leadership. It might be easier to move on and do something else. We must not give in; our task is to follow the principles laid down by Jesus and His apostles to see the church built in such a way that the gates of hell will not prevail. We go into more detail about this in a later chapter.

Breaking down the wall of hostility

There is another factor that we must consider here. God's heart is not just about reaching every nation. His desire is to heal the nations through the church and the preaching of the gospel, and to break down barriers between people. At the cross, the wall of hostility between Jew and Gentile was smashed; to create one new man in Christ.[18] Paul goes on to speak about this in more detail in Ephesians, chapter 3. He says that there was given to him the revelation of a mystery that was not known about in Old Testament times. What was this? It cannot be the fact that all nations will be blessed, because the Old Testament prophets were aware of this and wrote about it. It was rather that people from every nation would be brought to be one in Christ. All barriers would be smashed. There is a key verse here for the issue of spiritual warfare. Paul reveals to us God's purpose that now, through the church, the manifold wisdom of God should be made known to the rulers and authorities in the heavenly realms.[19] If it is God's purpose to see the nations brought together in Christ and it is God's purpose thereby to demonstrate how wise He is to all these evil principalities, then obviously there is going to be opposition from the enemy as we seek to build united, multi-ethnic churches.

This is very important in the context of spiritual warfare. In the UK, for example, there are many churches specifically for different ethnic groups such as Asian, Indian, Chinese and West Indian churches, to name but a few. While there is a positive aspect, a place for recognising the different style each has to offer, the negative aspect of this is all the walls that have been created between them. God really wants to break down those walls and destroy the barriers so that He has just one multi-faceted church.

We recently brought together Christians from different ethnic groups to do some outreach. We have held evangelistic meetings where three languages, Tamil, Punjabi and English were used; we even had three worship bands singing in each of those languages.

Men have made attempts to unite the nations. Conquering Empires have sought to subjugate the various people groups so that superficially they seem to be one. We see examples of this in the former Soviet Union and the former Yugoslavia. However, what happens when those empires fall is that the enmity between the various people groups is shown to be a strong as ever. The United Nations – the force of humanism – has been unable to reconcile people from different nations. However, it is God's heart to do so and His intention to do it through His church. Satan will oppose it; it is an issue.

'The church as a multi-racial, multi-cultural community, is like a beautiful tapestry. Its members come from a wide range of colourful backgrounds. No other human community resembles it. Its diversity and harmony are unique. It is God's new society. And the many-coloured wisdom of the church is the reflection of the many coloured wisdom of God.' – John Stott.[20]

This has quite a challenge for mission. As we move into a new unreached area, we may at first have to work with just one people group or even one community within that people group. For example, in many third world major cities, there are gatherings of people from rural areas who stick together and have considerable mistrust of others. The evangelistic method as commended by Jesus is that as we enter a community we find a 'man of peace' there.[21] We seek to find somebody who will receive us and be a gateway into that community. As we see people saved, it will often be an appropriate strategy to leave them in their communities to reach others of their community. If they were taken out they would be separated from those that otherwise they could reach with the gospel. It takes a while to establish trust.

However, we are not going the full way in terms of God's purposes if we do not see the mistrust that there is between different communities or different races broken down in Christ. It may take a long time, but our objective must be to see people from different backgrounds embracing one another in Christ, finding some opportunity to demonstrate their oneness in Christ.

Homogeneous units?

Some 'church growth specialists' have advocated the point of view that it is better in church growth terms to work through 'homogeneous units'. In other words, we seek to build church with people who are like us. The problem here is that the result would be different churches amongst different racial groups, even if they were in the same geographic area. We would see middle class churches, working class churches, youth churches, twenties churches. This may be easier in terms of church growth but it does not fulfil the purpose of God to demonstrate through His church that all barriers are broken down. God wants to demonstrate that His church can truly be a family embracing all ages, all backgrounds, rich and poor, old and young, different races. I believe this is an issue of spiritual warfare that we need to fight for. It is certainly a challenge for our mission.

The challenge of legalism

I believe that outward rules of behaviour can be imposed on Christians, with the result that they see their acceptance by God as being conditional on observing rules. This legalism can be superimposed over strongholds without demolishing them first; the Law has no power on its own to demolish strongholds. It is like an impotent husband.[22] It has no power to impart life. Yet it can produce a veneer of respectability and conformity whilst not dealing with the underlying strongholds and therefore rendering the church ineffective in its evangelism against the strongholds in that particular culture. I write more about this subject in Chapter 17.

Learning from other cultures

I also believe that we need each other so that we can humbly learn from each other and see the strongholds in our various cultures demolished. For example, when I travel to India and many other parts of the world, I come to realise the strength of community and hospitality. That enables me to discern better the lack of hospitality in our own culture. It is the stronghold commonly known as 'the Englishman's home is his castle'. In the New Testament we are commanded to show hospitality. This does not only mean having our best friends round for a meal occasionally; it means kindness to strangers. In New Testament churches, hospitality was considered so important that it was a qualification for eldership.[23] I do not believe I will be able to be set free to be fully who God intends me to be without my brothers and sisters from other cultures. I believe it for me as an individual, I also believe it for our churches.

It may not be possible all at once, but in our mission, we will want to see eventually Kurds and Turks embracing one another in Christ. Similarly, Serbs and Kosovan Albanians recognising that the gospel of grace has reached both communities. Russians and Chechens being able to stand together, one in Christ, against the true enemy of our souls; God's multi-coloured wisdom blazed through the church.

Effective Strategy Number 10: Ensure that when we are involved in mission, we are seeing people clearly set free from strongholds to make them, in turn, effective in their own mission.

NOTES

[1]Ephesians 1:9–10; [2]Ephesians 3:21; [3]Revelation 5:9–10; [4]Matthew 28:19; [5]Matthew 5:14; [6]Isaiah 2:2; [7]Luke 10:18; [8]1 Corinthians 9:19–23; [9]*Peace Child*, Don Richardson; [10]Acts 17:23; [11]Acts 17:22–23; [12]Ephesians 3:10; [13]*Filipino Spirit World*, Rodney L Henry;[14]Galatians 4:13; [15]Acts 18:9–10; [16]1 Thessalonians 3:5; [17]*Mountain Rain*, Eileen Crossman; [18]Ephesians 2:16; [19]Ephesians 3:10; [20]*The Message of Ephesians,* John Stott, page 123 (IVP. Used with permission.); [21]Luke 10:5; [22]Galatians 3:21; [23]1 Timothy 3:2.

Chapter 11

STRONGHOLDS CAUSED THROUGH PAST SIN

In this chapter I want to look at things that might have created a stronghold through past sins. I referred earlier to the course we run in our church to help people get free of strongholds in their lives. We find that many of these strongholds relate to wrong thinking as a result of past sins in their own lives or in their families, which become real bondages.

It is important to remember in this context that there is no condemnation for those who are in Christ.[1] Some of the issues that I need to deal with in this chapter are serious ones, but no matter what we have done or suffered, we are accepted in Christ and that acceptance does not change. I have listened to people confessing many serious things, but it does not change God's acceptance of them. However, God will not let it rest there; He wants to deal with issues in our lives to enable us to walk free from all of them. So there is no need to feel guilty if anything in this chapter applies to you now. You simply need to respond to the leading of the Holy Spirit, get it dealt with through repentance and walk free of any bondage.

Occult Activity

The occult is sadly on the increase again in this country; many people who are saved through our witness may well have had occult involvement. Occult activity is forbidden in the Scripture, in both the Old and New Testaments, because it is direct involvement with a forbidden evil spiritual world.[2]

We have access to the supernatural power of the Holy Spirit through Jesus Christ. However, occult involvement attempts to use supernatural power that is the direct result of contact with evil spirits. If someone has been involved with any of the things listed below, quite often deliverance will be necessary as these strongholds are demolished.

Fortune telling: Ouija boards, tarot cards and any other kind of fortune telling such as tea leaves, palmistry or a crystal ball.

Spiritualism: Horoscopes, spiritualism, so-called Christian spiritualism, séances and mediums, automatic writing, spiritualist healing and clairvoyance.

Magic: Black and white magic, table lifting, levitation, casting spells and hexes.

Mystical: Transcendental meditation, astral projection, mind-reading, mental telepathy, thought transference and mind-expanding drugs.

Religious: Satanism, idol-worship.

Sometimes people will have been involved in three or four of these things. When we are praying, we may find that some past occult activity has resulted in a demon affecting them. Other activities may not. (Hints at how to help and discern this as we are praying are given later in Chapter 16.) The reason for this, I believe, is that although that Satan's kingdom might appear to be well organised, it is probably chaotic or haphazard.

Superstition

This is related very closely to occult issues and can take many forms depending on the culture. In some cultures it is stronger than in others. Superstition is a very legalistic thing – you must do this, you mustn't do that. I have dealt with this issue in some detail in Chapter 8.

Superstitions are handed down from generation to generation without question. They act like a curse if the superstition is transgressed. I remember in Africa praying for a woman about a stronghold related to fear, and nothing was happening at all. Then the person praying with me about this asked the woman whether she had a piece of red string tied around her waist. We both asked her to get rid of it, she broke it and threw it on the ground, and we were able to see a spirit of fear clearly leave her. The string was a symbol of the superstition that held her in its grip.

False religions

False religions all need dealing with according to the type of belief involved. For example, where idols or literature are involved, these need to be destroyed and the person involved needs to burn them. This can be a powerful release, but it is often necessary to identify the names of the gods or idols involved and go through deliverance ministry, commanding the relevant evil spirits by the names of the false gods to leave the person. The purpose of this is to help identify and specifically renounce the sin.

New Age

New Age beliefs are becoming increasingly widespread in the West. There is a strong link with Hinduism and other eastern religions.

Legalism

Another area of great concern is that of religious legalism, often built around Christian principles, but where a set of man-made rules is added over the top of the basic Christian belief. Legalism is described as 'doctrines of demons' in the Bible.[3] Sometimes people who have been in bondage to very legalistic or excessively ritualistic forms of Christianity or the cults need to be specifically set free from them.

Freemasonry

Freemasonry is a secret society and when anything is a secret we need to beware! The word occult, as I have mentioned elsewhere, means hidden, and again, as with witchcraft, there is much in masonry that is to do with exercising control over others, using curses, oaths and the idolatrous names of so-called gods.

There is a high level of insecurity in masonry, coupled with love of money and power, because it gives people in particular areas or business groups a degree of power over others. People are frequently led into masonry because of the attractions of money and power, sometimes because of simple deception. However, there is a risk of curses being passed from generation to generation, particularly relating to poverty or continuous ill health. (It is important to remember that although this does happen we should not expect it in every case and become morbidly interested in the power of freemasonry in previous generations).

One young man I prayed for had tried for a long time to obtain a well-paid job in accordance with his qualifications and had been unable to do so. We broke Masonic curses in the family and within a few weeks he had a good job with a reasonable salary.

Past generations

We referred earlier to sins, which may have been carried out in earlier generations. Some of these may relate to the occult. Others may be obvious, such as fear coming down from generation to generation. However, we should not go searching for this or act only on the basis of 'words of knowledge' without some confirmation. We can become very inward looking if we are constantly worried about what previous generations in our family line may have been involved in.

If there is a problem, God will reveal the source of it as and when He chooses, and it can be dealt with when that happens. Issues coming through the family line tend to occur if there is a high degree of control in a family. Such a situation could be a good indicator of occult involvement, and might suggest an area of investigation. We deal with the issue of control in Chapter 12.

Solutions

Resolution of any area of these activities requires repentance first. This is where I confess my sin, express my sorrow at having transgressed God's requirements for my life, and then turn away from the sin, and refuse to have any further involvement with it.

If the sin was committed not by me but by previous generations of my family, then obviously I cannot express personal repentance because it was not my sin. In this situation, I must renounce the sin by naming it and refusing to have anything to do with it.

Sexual Strongholds

I believe the church is often weakened in its battle and its witness by the presence of undealt-with sexual strongholds in the lives of church members. Whenever I have begun to teach on this subject, all sorts of sexual problems creep out of the woodwork such as men, including leaders, who need to be released from pornography. John White talks about this in his book *Eros Redeemed*. He says, 'Many conservative churches either remain silent on the topic of sex or else condemn sexual sins publicly but practice them secretly. Charismatic and non-charismatic churches seem equally vulnerable.'[4] The end result is that the world becomes very cynical about the gospel that we preach.

I am determined that the church should get rid of this sort of clutter and garbage so that we can begin to see the people in the world set free, because the world is so dominated by sexual sin. If we are trying to fight the powerful principalities in the world when we have weaknesses in these areas in the church, then again it is like trying to fight with one hand tied behind our backs. We are undermined if we do not have a godly approach to sexuality.

Sexual sin is not necessarily the greatest sin; that is, arguably, pride. However, it is described in the Scriptures as having a particularly weakening effect on Christians. Paul says that sexual sin is a sin against our own bodies. I am not fully sure what he means by that, but he tells us to flee from sexual immorality because all other sins that are committed are outside a man's body, but sexual sin is against his own body.[5] He questions whether we fully realise that our bodies are the temples of the Holy Spirit and reminds us that because we were bought at a price, we should honour God with our bodies.[6]

In the Old Testament, Balaam, who was a false prophet, tried to defeat God's people through witchcraft or by cursing them. God turned it around and Balaam's curses became a blessing. Balaam then tried a different track; he introduced the people to sexual immorality. He then defeated God's people easily, and they came under the control of the false gods in whose name he was trying to curse the people.[7]

Similarly, in both David's and Solomon's lives, sexual sin undermined their authority to rule. By way of contrast, Joseph was able to overcome when Potiphar's wife attempted to seduce him, and he became a godly ruler. We are intended to be people who bring in God's kingdom rule in this world, but sexual sin undermines our capability to rule.

We are living in a society that is saturated with sexual symbols, where sex is used as a tool for control and where people are being undermined by the evil principalities that have a powerful hold over their lives through sex. It is not that our society has slipped a bit, although that is perfectly true: it is that our society has again given itself over to the worship of false idols and the battle for sexual purity is not just an issue that needs dealing with in our personal lives; it is also a major issue of spiritual warfare.

Reading through the Old Testament gives us a picture of the interaction between Israel and the people around them. Often we read of God's anger against the people of God because they become involved in the cultic religions of local cultures, and the Scriptures give a picture of what some of the religions involve. There are three specific idols that are most frequently mentioned: Baal, Ashtoreth and Moloch. Two of these in particular, Baal and Ashtoreth, were fertility gods whose worship involved sexual activity through cultic prostitution, both male and female, for the purpose of improving the fertility of the land, to provide crops for their families.

Sex for worship is not very far from the worship of sex. These practices of Old Testament times distorted the original purpose of sex as a unique gift that was originally given by God.

Those ancient gods are manifesting themselves again in the sexually unrestrained culture that exists today. Baal and Ashtoreth are again being worshipped through the constant stream of sexual exploitation that exists in our society. These evil principalities are again seeking to control people's lives through the saturation levels of innuendo, advertising, films and television. This is why it is so important to deal with sexual strongholds in people's lives in the church and as part of our discipling process when people are converted.

Soul Ties

One result of past sexual sin is often the creation of a tie to the person with whom the sin was committed. We often call these 'soul ties'. I admit this is not a biblical term, but it is a biblical concept.[8] The spiritual effect of this joining is something that often needs to be broken. It applies to wrong sexual relationships through adultery, pre-marital sex, homosexuality and even emotional dependency.

The Corinthians were known in their day for their sexual depravity; indeed, the common swear-word of the day was to 'Corinthianise'. They had a saying to the effect that you take food for the body and the body was for food. Part of the implication of this belief was that sex had no more than a physical effect and that illicit sex was the equivalent of several good meals.

Paul refused to accept this and pointed out that sexuality is not just a physical thing; it involves emotions and spirits.[9] When people have had a number of sexual partners, they need to be set free from all sorts of spiritual bonds that bind them to their previous partners. These bonds must be broken otherwise they will form a foothold for the enemy. I remember one situation where I was speaking on this and a man came to see me afterwards. He explained that his relationship with his wife was not very good and that he needed help. We talked around this sort of issue and he confessed to an illicit sexual relationship from before his marriage to an older and manipulative woman. I prayed for him, broke the soul ties from that relationship and when I next saw them a week later, his wife told me that their relationship had improved dramatically.

There are all kinds of emotional and mental difficulties that can result from the spiritual joining created by these sorts of situations, and when we are preparing couples for marriage, we try to work through these issues, especially if one partner has not been a Christian very long or has a history of promiscuity, to ensure that each one enters into marriage free of all previous soul ties.

Pornography

One thing that really does amaze me is the level of interest in pornography in the church. It doesn't seem to matter how long people have been Christians; the problem still exists. This is serious and I have seen many men set free during seminars on this particular subject. Because pornography is a hidden thing, practised in secret, this very secrecy gives it power. It also becomes like a drug. Users of this sort of material find they crave it more and more, frequently moving on to increasingly extreme forms of pornography and it becomes an addiction. Bondage like this needs drastic action. Jesus said that if your right eye offends you, you should cut it out,[10] and while we are not suggesting that this should be taken literally, it indicates the level of severity that is necessary in dealing with it.

Release from the effects of pornography therefore takes

drastic action, through openness, releasing prayer and frequent and very confrontational accountability.

One man, a leader in a church in another country, was in agony. He confessed to me that he had a problem with pornography. I prayed for him, and instructed him to ensure that there was someone to whom he could maintain a high level of accountability. This level of relationship was not normal in his environment. I pressed him to make sure that there was someone that he could be accountable to, and eventually he acknowledged that there was someone in a nearby town that he felt able to trust in that situation. So I told him to write to me after my holiday that year to tell me he had established contact with this man, and if I didn't hear from him, I would write to remind him of his undertaking. I didn't hear after my holiday, so I wrote to him as I had promised and he responded quickly. With help from his friend, he was finally able to make progress.

Auto-sexuality

Auto-sexuality is not a phrase in everyday use, but is essentially sex with oneself solely for self-gratification. It can involve obscene or masochistic acts designed to give orgasmic pleasure and there have been a number of high profile cases in the media in recent years where people have even died through this form of self-indulgence. I have known cases where self-worship has become a serious problem. This whole issue will always require a high degree of accountability to resolve and overcome, as well as prayer ministry.

Sex was not intended to be self-indulgent or worshipped, but was intended to be a loving and giving creative act between two people in a marriage relationship – two people of the opposite sex. Masturbation makes a god (an idol) of my bodily sensations. I am not talking about an odd isolated act, but where it has become obsessive. My sexuality is for the benefit of my marriage partner as an act of giving. I am to be concerned about the degree to which I am giving myself for the pleasure of my spouse – not for the idol of self-satisfaction.

Homosexuality and lesbianism

I know this is controversial today but the Bible makes it clear that homosexual acts are sinful.[11] The gay scene is an example of the way enemy strongholds operate in a sub-culture rather than simply territorially. Male homosexuality can be, in my limited experience, the result of one or more of the following things:

- An inability to establish a good relationship with an important male in early life, usually a father or father figure. (Elizabeth Moberly in her book *Homosexuality, a New Christian Ethic*, deals very thoroughly with this subject).[12]
- A domineering mother. This is a frequent problem.
- Sexual abuse as a young boy, usually by another boy or man. Often there is a mixture of hating the act and yet still having temptations.
- Rejection in heterosexual relationships.

Homosexuality invariably needs more than just ministry sessions; a reorientation of thought life and relationships by building good open and accountable relationships in the body of Christ.

Female homosexuality, or lesbianism, can likewise have a number of causes.

- Infantile deprivation: a lack of care and affection from a mother at an early age.
- A possessive and domineering mother with a devouring love that is easily sexualised.

- Estranged femininity: usually caused by a father who wanted a son and treats his daughter as a boy.
- A fear or hatred of one's father or other men.

These issues are too complex to go into more detail in a book on spiritual warfare, but we need to recognise the strongholds created in people's thinking and actions. The identification of 'causes' of wrong practices does not, of course, excuse them. Repentance is essential. However, understanding the 'roots' of an issue in someone's life can be of help in assisting them to walk free.

Distortion of role models

A whole generation is in danger of becoming confused about its sexual identity as a result of militant feminism, the constant bombardment of sexual corruption and the advocacy of homosexual relationships. For example, media role models of men show them as 'macho', or 'wimps', or 'men behaving badly' – none of which are appropriate for a man created in God's image.

Male and female were created to be different but complementary and this needs to be taught in churches so that we can present a biblical model in contrast to our culture.

There is a massive attack by the enemy on biblical standards of masculinity and femininity that the church needs to respond to through its teaching regardless of the response of others. We must not be afraid to teach on it even though it goes against the trend of the times. I would commend particularly in this connection the essay on *A Vision of Biblical Complementarity*, in the book edited by John Piper and Wayne Grudem entitled *Recovering Biblical Manhood and Womanhood*.[13]

I have taught on the subject of sexual strongholds in many different cultures and find that although the manifestations may be different, the underlying issues are the same. Many other issues could be discussed under this subject heading. In a later chapter we deal with the pain of abuse but, of course, where people are sexually abused, there are also abusers. This in itself is a huge stronghold, which we often do not like to talk about or deal with in our churches. It is important that our churches have clear values and known procedures both to protect children and to minister to those who have been abused.

I recall teaching all this material to men in India and in a men-only context, we could be very open and frank about the situation – indeed my translator had to be very specific in order to make it clear what I was saying! The result was many men coming forward to confess that before they had become Christians they had been involved in wrong sexual activity and that this still had a grip, to a lesser or greater extent, in their lives. Many were set free from demonic power and the domination of sexual strongholds.

Abortion

One of the major feminist issues has been that of abortion – the freedom to rule your own body and to choose whether you want to carry the baby that has developed inside it.

However, as with sexual sins, this is an issue for spiritual warfare, because the key force behind abortion is demonic. Of the three main cultic gods that Israel got involved with, two (Baal and Ashtoreth) have already been mentioned in relation to sexual sin. The third was Moloch, who was a very powerful evil force.[14] Moloch was worshipped through child sacrifice. In one situation,[15] Israel had defeated the King of Moab in a battle, so the king sacrificed his own child to Moloch and released immensely powerful spiritual forces that defeated Israel and caused them to flee.

This principality is again being worshipped through the two

evils of abortion and child abuse. It is not just that abuse and abortion are morally wrong, but that those involved are giving themselves over to demonic forces which are becoming very strong in our culture. If someone has had an abortion, or has counselled someone else to have an abortion, there needs to be repentance, healing of the emotions and the committal of the child to God. I think that such committal will help the parents to express their emotions about it properly and help them to walk free of any emotional hang-ups that might otherwise occur.

Rebellion

This attitude is usually demonstrated by the person stating that no one is going to tell them what to do. It has a tremendously negative effect on discipleship, and we are told in the Scriptures to make disciples, not just converts.

What is a disciple? Someone who has been taught how to obey; in particular, to obey the Scriptures. 'Discipleship' might appear to be a cover-up word for simply telling someone what to do, but in fact it has more to do with explaining what the boundaries are, as defined in the Bible. Rebellion can be a real barrier to effective function as a Christian and moving into leadership.

Rebellion is often a reaction to abuse of authority in the past, and the people in rebellion may have actually been sinned against, rather than sinning themselves. This needs dealing with sympathetically but firmly, and healing of the emotions may be involved. Sometimes the problem is caused by an angry reaction to a lack of 'fences'; that is, not being given any boundaries as a child. Whatever the reason, the stronghold of rebellious thinking and action must be overcome.

Rebellion can become such a way of life in someone that it becomes a character 'strength' that they would find difficult to live without. I remember praying for a woman like this who really could not face the idea of losing the rebellious spirit, because she thought that she would be weaker as a result. The rebellion had become so much a part of her life that it had become perceived as her strength.

Addictive behaviour

Alcoholism is a subtle addiction that frequently occurs before you notice it. It is easy to recognise an alcoholic who is lying in the gutter unable to stand. It might not be so easy when it is someone with a responsible job who cannot get through the day without a half-bottle of whisky to help them to cope, or a housewife getting through a bottle of sherry every day to combat loneliness and frustration.

Alcohol is not wrong in itself. It does not say anywhere in the Scripture that we must not drink. Jesus turned water into wine. However, it does command that we do not get drunk. There can be an almost childish attitude these days of thinking it clever to drink until you are unable to stand. This is portrayed in the media as 'men behaving badly', but it is not the godly image of masculinity and we have to be careful we are not misled and trapped.

When teaching new converts to walk free from these strongholds, we would obviously ensure that any other addictive behaviour, such as drugs etc, come to the surface so that they can be dealt with.

Effective Strategy Number 11: Identify strongholds in people's minds and emotions that are a result of past sin, so that they can be delivered and walk free.

NOTES

[1]Romans 8:1; [2]Exodus 22:18, Deuteronomy 18:10–11, 1 Samuel 15:23, Acts 19:18–19, Galatians 5:20, Revelation 21:8; [3]1 Timothy 4:1–5;

[4]*Eros Redeemed*, John White, page 14 (Eagle, 6–7 Leapale Rd, Guildford, Surrey, GU1 4JX. Used with permission.); [5]1Corinthians 6:18; [6]1 Corinthians 6:20; [7]Numbers 24:1, 25:1–3; Revelation 2:14; [8]1 Corinthians 6:16, 2 Corinthians 6:14; [9]1 Corinthians 6:12–17; [10]Matthew 5:29; [11]Romans 1:24–27; [12]*Homosexuality, a New Christian Ethic*, Elizabeth Moberly; [13]*Recovering Biblical Manhood and Womanhood*, Piper & Grudem; [14]Jeremiah 32:35; [15]2 Kings 3:27.

Chapter 12

THE STRONGHOLD OF CONTROL

In 1994, at a time when God's Spirit was moving in a powerful way, a woman we had great respect for came to see Scilla and I. She was a godly woman, eager to move on into the presence of God, but she had begun to develop uncontrollable anger at what was happening with the fresh move of the Spirit and the situation was beginning to upset her deeply. We asked her about possible causes of her anger, and she said that although she desperately wanted to be in the move of God, it made her angry. When we asked why, she said that it was because the move of God was something that could not be controlled. This gave me a clue. I asked her if her mother was very controlling and she said yes, then went on to give examples. Then I asked her if her grandmother had been very controlling too. Again, she said yes. What was really worrying her was that her children were approaching their teens and she was liable to try to control them wrongly, at a time when she knew that she should be beginning to release them.

We were able to recognise from all this that there was a powerful controlling spirit affecting her life which had come down through the female family line. When we prayed for her release, she was set free of a demonic controlling force and was soon able to enjoy the move of the Spirit. This was wonderful, but she later also related an interesting side effect.

She was out shopping for clothes one day when she saw something that she liked and immediately decided that she would buy it. As she did so, she quickly realised that this was the first time she had bought something that she liked, and *not* put it back on the hanger because her mother wouldn't have liked it.

The story demonstrates the effect of control that goes back through several generations of a family. Why can 'control' sometimes be a demonic force? The essence of witchcraft is control. When somebody is using witchcraft against another person, they are trying to control their destiny, sometimes for something bad to happen to them in revenge, sometimes to prevent them from taking a particular course of action.

Now little things like what clothes you wear do not really matter but they can reveal a deeper problem. I shared this whole story when teaching on strongholds in Mexico and when I came to the clothes illustration, a woman there suddenly realised that this was a problem in her own life which revealed something deeper and from which she was set free.

The weapons of this ungodly control are manipulation and domination and they can be very powerful. When people start to use this form of control, their desire is to have an effect in people's lives that they are unable to have in any other way. People who use manipulation might not be aware of this. It is particularly sad to see this happening in an otherwise godly person.

When I teach on the issue of spiritual authority, I always teach the principle that ungodly authority is always binding, and that godly authority always releases people into their calling and gifting, and to fulfil their destiny under God.

Manifestations of control

You can see this principle at work in different cultures through-out the world. The spirit of control often works through the long drawn-out machinations of bureaucracy, a frustrating problem in many countries (though sometimes, we British taught them how!). Bureaucracy can be a form of injustice; the rich and well educated can work through it, either by bribery or 'knowing the system', whereas the disadvantaged just have to wait for justice and are often powerless.

The same sort of thing happens in offices: bureaucratic control by small-minded individuals who want to control all the little details of people's lives; forms that have to be filled in even when they are not specific to your circumstances. These are not the silly examples they seem to be but manifestations of small-minded and oppressive control.

The stronghold of control works through cultural situations such as the caste system in India or, historically, the class system in England. It works through dictatorship where people are rendered passive and lacking in initiative.

Religious control

It can even work in the church, through domineering rather than equipping leadership. Peter instructed the church elders not to 'lord it over those entrusted to you'.[1] In some churches traditionalism can be a controlling force, as can extended families who have dominated a local church, often for generations. Similarly the insidious enemy of legalism can be functioning through this stronghold often under the guise of 'maintaining godly standards'.

I mentioned in Chapter 1 that I was brought up in the Exclusive Plymouth Brethren, as was my wife Scilla, and it took some time for us to gradually break free of the problems we brought out with us. Scilla's immediate family are still within the movement and, under its controlling influence, have cut her off for thirty years now.

The Exclusive Brethren are very particular about clothes and hairstyles; women have to wear their hair in a certain way. Scilla was fairly free, but there were a number of areas where she was not fully entering into the things of the Spirit. One day, she decided to have her hair permed. This was not within the Exclusive Brethren's dress code, and when she emerged from the hairdresser's with permed hair, she suddenly realised that she was free. For Scilla, having her hair permed was a powerful symbol of her freedom from what had been an emotionally controlling influence in her life. Of course, that does not mean that having your hair permed is a formula for getting released from control! It was simply a symbolic expression of freedom that made Scilla freer to serve God and be open to the Holy Spirit.

Family control

Another area where control is often used is that of the family, just as in the story which opened this chapter. In a control situation like this, parental or family domination is often extreme. In the evangelical church we rightly speak in support of family and authority within the family, but we must distinguish between authority which is godly and control which can be demonic. Our desire must be to see the family function in the manner prescribed in the Scriptures.

A few years ago, a young man I know was just about to get married when he was taken ill by a crippling disease. The disease was similar to symptoms of ME, so that he was unable even to read a book. This was very unusual, and there was nothing obvious in his life that might have caused it. One day I was praying about this situation, asking God what it might be and how we might be able to resolve it when an answer came immediately that he was under women's control. I have learned to obey such promptings so I decided to ask the young man about it. His fiancée was there when I asked him, and she was immediately in floods of tears. As I prayed for him there were demonic reactions manifested. I knew him well and I really hadn't expected this response. However, we prayed for him to be released and he was immediately healed. It turned out that he had reacted wrongly to his mother and her role in his life. He had also been involved in another wrong relationship with a woman in the past. This was what was making him ill, because he was about to get married and move out of 'control' into a new godly relationship.

The extended family continues to operate in many countries, and brings much blessing and security. However, the downside is that if biblical principles are not followed, ungodly control can be even stronger in such situations. In Genesis, God said that a man should leave his father and mother and become united with his wife. This is a very important principle. However, throughout Genesis and beyond it often did not happen. Men were not leaving their father and mother to be devoted to their wives. There are many cultures today where this biblical 'releasing' principle is not respected

In one language group in West Africa, a friend of mine was translating the Scriptures. When he got to Genesis 2:24 about a man leaving father and mother, the local translation helper said that he could not translate this because there were no words in their language that he could use! What he meant was that it was an impossible concept culturally. It is interesting that later the translation helper was the first person in that culture to do just that. He became the first man to move out of his parents' home and live separately with his wife in a hut he built on the edge of the family land.

Control through family tradition

An almost superstitious form of control can appear in family situations, particularly where family traditions are concerned. When two people get married, responses such as 'Well, in our family we always do it this way,' are a warning sign of a clash between two family traditions. Sadly, the argument is too often settled by giving into the dominant family line, rather than the couple telling both families that their marriage constitutes a new family who choose to do it the way they believe is God's will for them.

Family get-togethers such as Christmas are another common problem area. 'We always go to my mother's on Christmas Day.' If that is a free choice that you are happy with, that is fine. If it is the result of family domination and an almost superstitious taboo against breaking the tradition, then it is not fine. This is a stronghold that needs to be broken before it breaks the marriage.

Family control through occult activity

Family control sometimes operates though some form of occult activity, whose power is harnessed for purposes of control, and transmitted from generation to generation. Some cultures are particularly open to this wrong principle operating. For example, in cultures where ancestor worship is practised, family control and fear are likely to be prevalent and to have dangerous consequences. The very worship of ancestors gives an idolatrous view of the family and its past history, which can have a strong hold over people and prevent them from Christian effectiveness, undermining their boldness in witnessing – particularly witnessing to their own family. There can be great fear not only because new converts may feel all the pressure of going against family tradition, but also because there have been witchcraft spirits in the family which are being directly challenged.

Godly principles of family life

A common result of control is a victim mentality. Those who have been abused or dominated often tend to be passive and pessimistic, unable to take initiatives, and expecting things (usually unpleasant things!) to happen to them, which they regard themselves as helpless to oppose or prevent.

God is able to set us free from this sort of mentality. We can reign as 'those who receive God's abundant provision of grace and of the gift of righteousness'.[2] Recovering the ability to take the initiative is wonderfully liberating in such circumstances!

To walk free of wrong control, but still respect and honour God's institution of the family, we need an understanding of godly principles of family life.

• *Family is ordained by God*

This means that God established it. It derives from Him. He is the pattern of Fatherhood.[3] We recognise that family can be expressed in somewhat different ways in different cultures, but biblical principles must always apply. We must fight for it as an institution, because the evil forces of humanism are seeking to undermine it by defining almost any relationship as 'family'. Facing that is spiritual warfare too.

• *Marriage, like every other institution, is affected by the Fall*

As a result of the Fall, marriage became an institution of conflict and idolatry. When the Fall occurred, Adam immediately blamed his wife for the problem and conflict, and blame shifting resulted. Cain's killing of Abel was again family conflict as a result of the Fall.

As well as conflict, there can be idolatry in the family. This might seem a strange word to use in this context, but what it means is that family starts to claim a loyalty that should only be given to God. Our first loyalty in worship is to God and not to family. In families where a wrong loyalty is claimed, this loyalty becomes an idolatry issue, because it undermines first loyalty to God. Obviously, children under adult age should obey their parents,[4] but this, too, can be undermined through the humanistic spirit of our age.

• *Male–female relationships came under the curse, leading to authority conflict*

God said to Eve that her 'desire would be for her husband', and that he would 'rule over her'.[5] This desire and rule were not promised as something good and godly, but were part of the curse that followed the Fall. The word 'desire' is the same word as in Genesis 4:7, where God warns Cain, 'Sin *desires* to have you', or perhaps, 'Sin is out to get you'. This desire is an ungodly craving to impose one's will on someone else by exerting a manipulative influence over them. The idea of 'rule' in this Scripture is a harsh rule, not the godly leadership that was intended in creation. As a broad generalisation therefore, there is a tendency for a husband to seek to get his own way by abusing his position of authority in a domineering manner, while the wife seeks to get her way by manipulation. Both domination and manipulation are wrong and represent authority conflict. A godly marriage must seek to work out God's standards as expressed in Scriptures such as Ephesians 5:22–33, rather than work out the effects of the curse in authority conflict.

• *The original concept of family is releasing*

One of the first things said about family is that a 'man shall leave'. A man who left his father and mother to be united with his wife was moving out from underneath his parents' authority to establish his own family under his own authority.

Parents need to recognise that they do not own their children. We bring our children up in order to release them. As we train our children for adulthood, we need to prepare them to be released into taking authority for running their own lives. Many families have a problem in practice with this principle; it is something that they are not prepared to do. If I am asked to take a wedding, I ask both sets of parents during the wedding service to release their children into the new relationship of marriage. At risk of upsetting some readers, I have to say that quite often it is the mother of the bridegroom who will have the problem, not the father of the bride!

• *Family loyalties must take second place to our relationship with Christ*

If family is to be something that will be established properly and not built on an idolatrous foundation it is vital that our relationship with Christ takes priority over any family loyalty. When Jesus spoke about hating our mothers and fathers,[6] this was what He meant. He was saying that we cannot be His disciples unless we put Him first. As soon as we come face to face with Christ and become His disciples, this must take precedence over *every* other relationship.

Family relationships are then worked out in submission to Christ and based on biblical teaching. So, husbands are to love their wives as Christ loved the church, and thus become an example of true servanthood. Wives are to submit to their husbands as to the Lord. Children are to honour their parents and fathers should try not to offend their children.[7] My eldest son, Tony, read me that verse publicly at my fiftieth birthday party!

• *The church is to become a new family that expresses God's heart for relationships*

Mark gives us a very clear example of the way Jesus demonstrated His freedom from parental domination as a single man.

In the story,[8] Jesus was teaching in a house in His home town. A crowd had gathered and it had grown so large that He was unable to eat. His mother and brothers went to the house and tried to take charge of the situation. In a culture where the family has real authority, they wanted to take back control over Him. So Mary arrived with the rest of her family and they sent someone in to bring Him out, saying that He was out of His mind.

This was a situation where Jesus had to confront family control, and the situation was tense. However, He cut right through the family claims to authority over Him and said in front of everyone present 'Who is my mother?' He moved out of His family's authority, in front of a large number of people who were living in that culture. What Jesus said could well have been considered offensive to His family. We often forget that Jesus is described as a 'rock of offence'.[9] He often caused offence where religious or cultural practices cut across the will of God for people's lives. That is effectively what Jesus is saying here. His obedience is to a different authority, and He pointed to the people around Him and said that they were His family now; those who do the will of God, those who are genuinely God's people. The church is to express God's heart for relationships.

It was not that Jesus did not honour His mother. This can be seen from another situation, at the foot of the cross. Then, He was caring for His mother, ensuring that she would have someone to take His place as the eldest son. He asked John to replace Him and to care for His mother.[10] That was a very different situation, where He fulfilled God's command by making sure that His mother would be looked after. Blessing results from honouring our parents.[11] However, He was committed to the will of God first, and He would never be *controlled* by His mother. This is the example for both single and married adults to follow.[12]

Effective Strategy Number 12: Recognise that godly authority brings release and therefore challenge anything that would bring people under ungodly control and manipulation, whether in society, culture, family or religion.

NOTES

[1] Peter 5:3; [2] Romans 5:17; [3] Ephesians 3:14; [4] Ephesians 6:1; [5] Genesis 3:16; [6] Luke 14:26; [7] Ephesians 6:4; [8] Mark 3:20–21, 31–34; [9] Romans 9:33 (KJV); [10] John 19:26–27; [11] Ephesians 6:2–3; [12] a book that develops this subject quite helpfully is *Families at the Crossroads* by Rodney Clapp.

Chapter 13

THE STRONGHOLD OF JEZEBEL

Please read 1 Kings 16, 18, 19 and 21, 2 Kings 9 and Revelation 2:18ff in conjunction with this chapter.

In recent years a lot of interest has been shown in issues relating to what has been called the 'spirit of Jezebel', and although other writers have covered it, I have been asked many times for my own tapes and seminar notes that explain my understanding of the issues involved. This is why I decided to cover this issue separately in this book.

The first thing to understand is that the spirit of Jezebel is a powerful force for evil. It can be devious and subtle. One of the main groups at risk are pastors who have this problem in their churches, so I wanted to deal with the issue with them in mind. Jezebel is a powerful stronghold that can affect people, churches, communities and even nations.

Jezebel exploits the tension between the sexes, which has come as a result of the Fall. However, I am not making a 'sexist' point. Though the spirit of Jezebel may be expressed through some women, it may also be equally expressed through some men who function manipulatively. They may even be leaders who dominate churches. A friend of mine once said, whilst preaching, 'Give the women a break. Don't keep on going on about a spirit of Jezebel!' However, when I am addressing the issue of Jezebel in this chapter, I am talking about an evil spirit, which worked in the same way as Jezebel in the Old Testament and can work through manipulative people of *both* sexes. It is more obvious in certain cultures, but that does not mean that it is absent in others, so cultural issues are another aspect that I want to deal with here.

Francis Frangipane underlines the seriousness of this problem in his book *The Three Battlegrounds*. He says 'When we speak of Jezebel we are identifying the source in our society of obsessive sensuality, unbridled witchcraft and hatred for male authority.'[1] They are strong words, so let us examine the issue.

'That woman Jezebel'

The gravity of this particular stronghold can be seen in the book of Revelation. Here amongst the letters to the seven churches, is one to the Church at Thyatira, a city in Asia Minor – modern day Turkey. 'Nevertheless, I have this against you; you tolerate that woman Jezebel, who calls herself a prophetess. By her teaching she misleads my servants into sexual immorality and the eating of foods sacrificed to idols.'[2]

When Jezebel is referred to in Revelation, I doubt whether it is literally a woman called Jezebel. There may well have been a particular woman causing trouble there but the title 'Jezebel' means, I believe, that the writer is talking here about a spiritual principle that can work in some people. This same demonic spirit still has considerable effect today world-wide.

We are told that the problem in this church was that she misled many people by leading them into sexual immorality and by her work as a false prophetess.

This subject is quite complex, so to make it easier to

understand, I have broken this chapter down into separate sections. Let us start by looking at the scriptural background to demonstrate that the spirit of Jezebel is a real demonic influence. By looking at scriptural examples, we can find out what Jezebel was like as a person so that we can begin to see how this demonic influence can affect people today

• *Jezebel in the Old Testament*

We have already looked briefly at Jezebel in the book of Revelation, so now we will look at the original Jezebel from whom the name derives. Although many kings get a mention in the Old Testament, it is noticeable that very few of their queens are mentioned at all. Jezebel's life is detailed relatively clearly and this makes her an unusual case. From her story, we can determine her character, behaviour and personality and through this identify the sort of person she was. This will help us to recognise the signs of the influence of the spirit associated with her name.

Ahab, son of Omri, was a king in Israel and the Scriptures speak of him as having done more evil in the eyes of the Lord than any before him. Much of this was a result of his wife Jezebel's influence. Jezebel came from a family that worshipped Baal, and she was responsible for leading Israel away from worship of God to the worship of this idol. Baal is the seat of a stronghold of sexual sin, as well as idolatry, and sexual sin is one of the most powerful tools that Jezebel uses.

Ahab and his queen lived at the time of Elijah. We are told that Elijah overcame more than four hundred false prophets of Baal on Mount Carmel, yet immediately this was over, he was unable to face Jezebel's anger and ran as fast as his legs would carry him. Such was Jezebel's power that he was not just scared, he was completely demoralised. It was this tremendous feeling of discouragement that was the real issue, not just his fear. He was a strong man, full of faith, but somehow Jezebel was able to cause him to lose that faith at a time when he should have been moving on to even greater things.

Nevertheless, Jezebel got her just deserts and died a horrible death. Her eunuch priests threw her over the city walls where she was trampled on by horses, then eaten by dogs. All that remained were her bones.[3] This illustrates the need to deal drastically with manifestations of the Jezebel spirit.

• *The character of a Jezebel*

The name Jezebel means literally 'without cohabitation' and is used to describe the character of a person who is rebellious, and cannot accept authority. Jezebel refuses to dwell with anyone unless she can dominate and control the relationship. A person demonstrating the key behavioural patterns influenced by this particular demonic force is said to have a Jezebel spirit. (The name of Balaam, the false prophet, is used in a similar way to denote those working in the same way as Balaam did.[4])

The character of the Jezebel spirit is *always* concerned with power seeking. Whether through control, manipulation or overt sensuality, the eventual aim is always power. Some current forms of militant feminism, which despise men and masculinity, offer a clear example of the extremes that this power struggle can attain to. As I said before, it is not a straightforward male-female issue. However, a Jezebel spirit always exploits the tension between the sexes that came about as a result of the Fall.

Another characteristic of Jezebel is fierce anger when crossed, opposed, or where it fails to gain or keep control. This anger is more powerful than any normal form and seems to exert the demoralising influence that frightened Elijah so much. Jezebel's anger left him totally discouraged and undermined even after seeing God at work in tremendous miracles.

One of the strange characteristics of this problem is that there is often a 'passive' Ahab equivalent in a close relationship, whether in a family, in a church or in business and the effect is always the same. A Jezebel character almost always tries to make the men around look less masculine, and undermines any authority or initiative they may wish to exhibit.

Just how sensitive an issue this is was revealed to me in a situation where I was praying with a man whom I did not know, but who I found out later had been a leader in a church. I mentioned the word 'emasculate' when praying and got an immediate reaction. 'That's just what it was like', he shouted. At that moment his shoulders and neck froze as if held in a powerful yoke. Incidentally, this was a situation where he had suffered under a manipulative *male* leader.

This form of manipulation can often be sexual in form, although that depends on the individuals involved. However, a seductive glance is often enough to exercise control.

Sometimes in cultural or family situations there is the readiness of a Jezebel spirit to use witchcraft and occult power to fulfil its purposes.

An often-overlooked aspect of this character is a possessive desire for ownership of property. The story of Naboth's vineyard is an example where Jezebel was quite willing to murder the rightful owner so that her husband could take control of the property. Ahab's only purpose in wanting it was because it was next door to his land. He actually tried to deal fairly with Naboth and offered to either buy the vineyard or trade it for another piece of land. However, the vineyard had been in Naboth's family for generations so he was unwilling to part with it. Jezebel had Naboth falsely accused, then stoned to death. It is of note that Jezebel uses deception here in this incident. Deception is another characteristic of the Jezebelic spirit; to a disinterested observer her accusations would have seemed reasonable.

I was once praying with a lady in South India who had responded to my teaching on this subject. She had inherited a property in North India from her aunt who had always controlled her life. Her aunt had said before she died that this lady must never sell the property but keep it in remembrance of the aunt. The property had actually been of no use to her and she really wanted to sell it but did not dare. As we prayed, she was set free and able to deal with that property as best suited her.

I have seen situations where church property, or property around the church building, has become an issue of control or dispute. I have seen this in countries as diverse as India, Mexico and USA and believe that a Jezebelic spirit is at the root of it.

• *Influences of a Jezebel spirit in church leadership*

We know from the Church in Thyatira that Jezebel can be a major influence in church life. When this stronghold finds its way into leadership, the results can be devastating. Francis Frangipane, for example, said, 'We are going to confront a stronghold of immense proportions, it is a way of thinking that exists unchecked in most churches.'[5] I have to admit to hoping that he is wrong, but as I have travelled round the world, I have begun to accept that it is widespread. In many of the places I have travelled to, it has been a serious problem.

Pastors who fall under the direct influence of this spirit become manipulative and authoritarian. They refuse to be accountable to any other authority except their own, although they will use any form of deception to hide that fact. Sometimes the leader might be in a controlling situation, dominating weak members of the leadership group or congregation. Alternatively, it could be that a group or person within the church is constantly seeking to undermine the leadership. Such a person or group does not always need to be on the platform, in fact sometimes they prefer not to be too visible, as long as the leader(s) can see them or feel their effect. Some people manipulate with their eyes, their size, their body language or alternatively, through anger or sensuality. Whichever method is used, it can undermine leaders' authority and cause them to compromise or waver from giving the clear, prophetic leadership the church needs.

A friend of mine who is a pastor in India became very ill when there was a dispute about his church property with someone in his family. He was taken into hospital where they were concerned as to whether he would even live, though it was not known what was wrong. In the end a group of other leaders prayed over him and specifically rebuked the spirit of Jezebel. He made a full recovery. We must not underestimate the power of this spiritual force to cause physical sickness even when it is confronted. I have often seen this pattern. Sometimes leaders have fallen ill immediately when they have confronted the spirit of Jezebel either in the church or in another leader. Obviously, we must not be fearful because, as that and many other stories illustrate, Jezebel can be overcome through prayer and faith.

• *Influences of a Jezebel spirit in the lives of individuals*

One area where the Jezebel spirit has been particularly active outside the church is in family life, especially where there has been a history of witchcraft going back for generations.

This is an extreme form of the 'control' issue dealt with in the previous chapter. I have seen clear demonic manifestations and wonderful release when people have come forward in clear repentance from having acted under the authority of this evil spirit. They were probably unaware of it until I taught on the subject. I have had people thank me years later for the release they have experienced.

The matriarchal influences of a Jezebel spirit occur in many cultures and challenging these brings its own problems. Many of the attacks that I suffered through the early days of my ministry occurred as I preached against the spirit of Jezebel. The situation has eased since I have been receiving strong prayer support.

When I first started to teach on control and manipulation, even naming the spirit of Jezebel was quite difficult, and I had to overcome considerable resistance in my own mind as I was speaking. On one particular occasion, every time I tried to use the name, I could not get the words out, and tried to say it in a different way. I realised that my anointing was ebbing away. Finally, I spoke the name 'Jezebel' out, and saw many people set free. I have to say that it was in a culture where this particular influence is very powerful.

In Goa, on one of the first occasions I preached on this subject, I was the target of the most grotesque demonic visitation I had ever experienced. It woke me up in the middle of the night, coming through the door of my bedroom. I have to admit that I did not do very well. It would have been nice to have been like Smith Wigglesworth, and say 'Oh! It's only you, I'll go back to sleep again', but I did not have his faith, so I called out in some fear until I had calmed down enough to pray.

It is important to recognise this potential for counter-attack, although it is not a reason to be afraid. The God we serve is more than capable of handling Jezebel; but He wants us to learn how to do it as well.

I mentioned in Chapter 1 how my son, Neil, was attacked when I was teaching on this subject in India. Incidentally, there were many men set free from matriarchal domination on the day when Neil was attacked.

• Cultural aspects of the Jezebel spirit

In almost every culture there are examples of this stronghold exercising control and manipulation. Jezebel is often represented as part of a culture's mythology. In the Hindu culture, the goddess Kali has the same attributes. She is usually represented as being angry with and dominating a male. In some countries with a Roman Catholic influence, so-called manifestations of the Virgin can be tainted by this stronghold and become something that is given too much authority. They then have an effect on the people's culture as the Virgin of Guadeloupe does in Mexico. In our own culture, the more extreme forms of feminism can be operating under the same spirit.

In the *Sunday Times* a few years ago, there was an article called 'The decline and fall of the nuclear family'. This reported the vote of viewers of a particular television programme who chose the 'ideal family' from a selection of finalists:

> Choosing from a selection of finalists, viewers voted that the new model family was the milk-maidy, pretty divorcee Michelle Jones, her bright eyed but not overpoweringly cute daughter Mia, and her boyfriend who stays at weekends and gets called Daddy Paul. He was once her colleague, now he's her lover.
>
> The child's father lives 260 miles away and sees his little girl a few times a year. In such meetings the two daddies get tense. It's a little confusing, but they get by.
>
> This trio didn't inch their way in, they were voted for by an over-whelming majority. . . . The BBC viewers chose, not only who they thought was the most attractive family, but also the ones they most identified with.

It goes on to say,

> Today's model family is more isolated and more integrated. The mother lives alone with her child, one child is now the norm, and at the weekend she integrates with her boyfriend and her boyfriend's family. On alternate weekends her child goes off with its father. Women are more independent, men are more emasculated. The child gets a different sort of attention. The mother is more domi-nant and matriarchal, there is none of the "wait till I tell your father".
>
> Children respond to artificial niceness with great suspicion, but they know how to manipulate the paradoxes of what is called 'quality time'. The child goes to the zoo, to Thorpe Park and goes

laser gunning with its dad. . . . This is creating a new breed of manipulators. Manipulators are self-motivators; they also get confused. They have a weekday bedroom and a weekend bedroom, they are everywhere and nowhere. They eat on their own.[6]

This is how we are re-creating our society and will develop more opportunities for the spirit of Jezebel to further undermine godly relationships.

• Dealing with Jezebel in leaders in the church

Where a leader has been operating in a 'Jezebelic' way, a common barrier to resolving the problem will be a refusal to face confrontation, especially in the area of his personal accountability. This will make it quite difficult to bring any form of authority into the situation. Leaders who operate in this way become expert 'wrigglers' as far as their personal accountability is concerned.

If the leader recognises and is willing to admit to the problem, then it can be dealt with through confrontation and re-training. If the problem has resulted in immorality, (and that is often the case), the stronghold is rarely identified until this has already happened, in which case the normal discipline for a leader involved in immorality should be applied.

It is perhaps worth explaining the link between Jezebel and the leader's immorality in more detail. Firstly, the Jezebelic spirit seeks to entice a leader into immorality. Secondly, having fallen into immorality, the leader resorts to employing manipulative methods to maintain his position because he is not 'walking in the light' and leading in a godly way.

However, if there has been manipulative leadership in the church, the body of the church will also need re-training to help them to overcome the destructive effects of the Jezebel spirit.

This involves teaching on the following areas:

- The effects of the Jezebel spirit
- An explanation of true spiritual authority
- The spiritual authority of servant leadership
- Man's responsibility
- True prophetic ministry
- The release of ministry

The last of these is important because when this type of leadership occurs, other men in the church are undermined and emasculated, and people stop contributing or taking on responsibility.

Because a stronghold is built within our thought processes and influences, this sort of teaching should occur in every situation where there has been leadership influenced by the Jezebel spirit. Since re-training could take a long time, it should begin as soon as possible after the leader has repented or been removed. If that does not happen, I think the stronghold will still be exerting its influence spiritually in the church.

• *Dealing with Jezebel in the church – non-leaders*

Where the person influenced 'Jezebelically' is resisting spiritual authority it becomes necessary to look at other issues. The problem is that this stronghold often operates very subtly. It is difficult to get hold of specific examples of its operation which can be confronted, although we might be sure of its existence – a 'gut' feeling, if you like.

As in all things, there are varying degrees; there might be a small amount of control, but not necessarily as a full Jezebel. We do not want to go overboard, as some do, and attribute every problem in church life to a Jezebelic spirit. If it does occur, those with true spiritual authority need to ensure they do not give it any space to operate. So if there is evidence of a Jezebel spirit in operation, it should not be given any place of authority.

Godly authority needs to be demonstrated without fear, and a full-blown Jezebelic spirit can be frightening. It can cause leaders to become afraid and discouraged like Elijah. Somehow there needs to be a drawing of grace from God to show that when you lead, you lead without fear. If it is influencing the church, then those operating from this stronghold need to be firmly confronted. If they refuse to listen or become divisive, then discipline must be exercised. If it becomes a stronghold that blocks the advance of the church, there needs to be teaching on true spiritual authority and the effects of the stronghold. It needs to be named and the leadership need to pray with authority over the whole sphere of ministry. I deal with the issue of strongholds in the church in a later chapter.

• *Dealing with Jezebel in individuals*

There are several very sensitive areas that need to be faced when dealing with this problem in individuals. It usually involves family influences. These can often result from witchcraft or other demonic influences in families. (It is important to remember that we are dealing specifically with Jezebel here. I deal with issues such as rejection and parental dominance elsewhere.)

The danger here is that manipulation and control are easy to develop, easy to maintain, yet very difficult to remove when the problems occur in family life. Anger can be frequently used inappropriately in controlling children. A manipulative style of relating in families can be maintained from generation to generation, especially where there is a history of occult practice.

Children very quickly learn to manipulate their parents and will carry on those skills into adult life. So, for example, a woman who has learnt to manipulate her parents from childhood will insist that the pastor is the only person who can deal with her 'particular' problem. If not recognised and dealt with very quickly, this pressure can drain a pastor's emotional resources and can lead to emotional dependency or even immorality. Paul dealt with this sort of problem in the context of the 'younger widows' when writing to Timothy.[7] He was also careful to say that older mature godly women should handle problems in younger women – not the pastor.[8]

I remember early in my ministry that a woman with a very clear prophetic edge used to seek me out to discuss things that she felt God was saying to her. Unfortunately I did not notice at the time that she would never speak to my wife, Scilla, about these issues and even made her feel inadequate. As you can imagine, Scilla soon pointed this out to me and I began to see the danger. Just recently (many years later), I received a telephone call from the pastor of a church the woman now attends. He asked me whether we had any experience of this particular woman always wanting to gain influence and involvement with senior leaders and ignoring their wives! Obviously the pattern is still continuing.

If you are from a culture where there is 'behind the scenes' or overt matriarchy, Jezebel can be a particular cultural stronghold. It needs to be regularly taught about to help people to walk free.

• *Jezebel and the prophetic*

Last but not least, I have to clarify the issues about Jezebel and the prophetic. This brings us back to the beginning, back to Thyatira and also to Elijah.

There are considerable dangers to the prophetic ministry from the Jezebel spirit and it is very important that these are recognised. The attack on Elijah by Jezebel in 1 Kings was against one of God's true prophets, and the letter in Revelation describes Jezebel as a false prophetess. Jezebel can wreak havoc through super-spirituality and untested prophecy.

This is important because the way that a Jezebel undermines the prophetic role can have a devastating effect. Control, manipulation, false direction, a lack of accountability and the emasculation of men in close relationship to the so-called prophetess can all bring a church into danger very quickly.

There was one occasion I remember, for example, involving a woman who considered herself a prophetess and who actually used the words 'How dare you test my words when I am speaking as a prophetess?'

Although this was perhaps an extreme case, the amount of control that can be introduced through a lack of accountability in this situation can be awesome. The spirit can also infiltrate the very important and sensitive arena of intercession ministry. This can be powerful and prophetic when it functions according to the scriptural model, but there must not be independence or a retreat from accountability.

A person under the influence of Jezebel often appears very 'spiritual' as at Thyatira. As well as the danger of false prophecy, the example of Elijah demonstrates that it is clear that the demoralising anger that this Jezebel spirit releases is a great danger to prophetic people. Its effect on Elijah was painful, and could have destroyed so much.

John the Baptist is described as being one fulfilment[9] of Elijah coming again. He had to confront a Jezebel operating through Herodias, who was instrumental in causing John to lose his head. Her anger also demoralised John, causing him to question Jesus' ministry as the Messiah.[10]

The spirit of Elijah is said to precede the Second Coming of Jesus.[11] I believe there is to be a prophetic church which will rise to take the gospel to the ends of the earth. What will oppose it? What opposed Elijah? The spirit of Jezebel.

This aspect is of particular danger to charismatic churches, where the danger of super-spirituality and untested prophecies can wreak havoc.

Again, the key to dealing with this issue is to exercise discipline, bring in godly authority and ensure that true prophecy is identified and tested through biblical principles.

Biblical femininity

Jezebel can also be seen in the Scripture as a distortion of biblical femininity. The Bible does provide role models for us for both godly masculinity and femininity, though to be fair, it also very honestly reveals the weakness in the character of its heroes and heroines. Mary, the mother of Jesus, reveals the opposite characteristics to Jezebel in her willingness to receive the angel's message to her.[12] Abigail[13] and Deborah[14] are both biblical examples of godly femininity with real foresight, initiative and wisdom. They certainly took action; they were not quietly allowing the enemy to walk all over them. They provide alternative role models of which Jezebel is a distortion.

Effective Strategy Number 13: Recognise, but do not shrink from the reality of the spirit of Jezebel and seek to confront its effects whether in culture, individual lives or the church.

NOTES

[1]*The Three Battlegrounds*, Francis Frangipane, page 119; [2]Revelation 2:20; [3]2 Kings 9:35; [4]Revelation 2:14; [5]Frangipane, page 119; [6]*Sunday Times*, 19 June 1994; [7]1 Timothy 5:11; [8]Titus 2:3–5; [9]Matthew 17:10–13; [10]Luke 7:20; [11]Malachi 4:5; [12]Luke 1:38; [13]1 Samuel 25:14, 18–42; [14]Judges 4:4–14, 5:1–31.

Chapter 14

STRONGHOLDS CREATED THROUGH OUR EMOTIONS

Emotions are an important part of our personalities and therefore the enemy seeks to construct strongholds of wrong thinking in relation to our emotions. Sadly, many people still feel that they should not show their emotions. For us English it is fine at a football match, but the rest of time it is often not acceptable. Yet God created emotions; we are emotional people in His own image.

God has emotions; he feels and expresses love, anger, grief and joy. They are not, however, sinful emotions but perfection of emotion. Sometimes people complain about others being emotional in worship. How can you worship without being emotional? Worship is a demonstration of our love for God and it is impossible to show love without any emotion.

However, our emotions, which are God-given and created as a reflection of His nature and personality, need to come practically under the lordship of Christ. I have found through many years of pastoral ministry that when it comes to our emotions, many are governed by Satan's strongholds, erected in their past experiences, rather than expressing emotion under the Lordship of Christ. They need to be set free. Hurt is never to be an excuse for failing to do the will of God.

Rejection

Rejection is one example and is a major emotional stronghold that establishes a set of negative thought patterns and attitudes. It is a very common problem that I meet frequently in the context of pastoral care.

Satan is a rejected being – he was cast out of heaven – and the atmosphere of his kingdom is rejection. He seeks to undermine the atmosphere of the kingdom of God, which is acceptance through Christ. When Adam gave way to Satan and allowed him authority instead of obeying God, Adam was cast out of Eden and so became a rejected being himself.

There are many reasons why people experience rejection, but the end result is similar. Anyone in the grip of this stronghold will feel that they do not belong. They feel lost in a crowd and they feel unwanted. Rejection can also cause problems in pastoral care or any situation where correction or accountability is involved because the correction is simply interpreted as rejection.

Many people experiencing rejection try to hide their emotions, not letting people get too close. They may plunge themselves into work in the hope that being the hardest, best or most diligent worker will gain them recognition and respect and hence acceptance. The sad thing is that even when they gain respect, they still feel rejected. A similar problem is re-enacted in church situations, because a person suffering from rejection will sometimes try to be the hardest worker in the church. They feel that their involvement in good works, will encourage people to accept them, but then when, for example, they are not fully recognised or praised as they feel they should be, it has the opposite effect, reinforcing the symptoms of rejection still further.

A frequently unexpected response from someone with rejection symptoms is the tendency to gossip. Have you ever noticed that gossip is always something that someone else does? Gossip, according to Proverbs, is like the tastiest piece of meat,[1] but together with disloyalty is a common rejection response. The person suffering rejection will become involved in gossip as a way of feeling accepted by the person they are talking to, of becoming 'one of the crowd'. Gossip is horrible because it pulls other people down and the people doing it are usually too insecure to know that they are accepted for who they are and really do not need to undermine somebody else in order to boost their own acceptance.

We have looked at some of the characteristics of rejection; now we need to look at how it is created in people's lives. There are many reasons why this stronghold is established. Sometimes people are described as an 'accident', an 'unwanted child'. The child is likely to be aware of the emotions involved, and these emotions, while beyond his or her understanding, will affect them as they mature and become adults.

Often rejection is the result of unthinking remarks by authority figures such as parents, teachers or, frequently, by a child's peers or siblings. Bullying, being ignored, not wearing the right clothes, or being excluded for any reason can all lead to someone feeling rejected.

A stronghold of rejection is not usually established by a single event; most of us can handle that. The feelings are reinforced by repetition of the scenario, for example, always being the last picked for the football team, as if there is no one else left and they have to scrape the bottom of the barrel and you are it. One particular example I remember was someone whose father always shouted at her when she failed to get good marks in exams. When she did eventually get good marks, he would just tell her that it was no better than she ought to have done anyway.

Although dealing with this problem may involve the need for deliverance, which will be covered in a later chapter, demolishing the stronghold of rejection must be carried out through effective teaching from the Word of God.

For example, instilling an awareness that God does not create accidents helps to demolish the stronghold. I often encourage people in this situation to read and re-read Psalm 139 until they get it into their system: 'You are wonderfully made and I knitted you together in your mother's womb.'[2] That is what God says here and He means it. I get them to read these words until they are able to say 'Thank you Lord that I am wonderfully made,' or 'I'm here not because I look in a mirror, but because I look in the Word and say that I am one of the wonders of God!'

Sometimes during the course of a seminar I will get people to turn to the person next to them and say, 'Did you know that I am one of God's special and wonderful creations?' Some people find that difficult to say, but it is important that they do because that is what is said in the Scriptures.

Furthermore, the truth of the gospel is that God obviously has accepted Jesus and says that He is the Son who gives Him pleasure. He has placed us in Jesus and because we are in Him, God accepts us as well. It does not matter who we are or what we have done; when we come to Christ God accepts us in exactly the same way that He accepted Jesus – 'This is my beloved Son, in whom I am well pleased.'

We do not have to do anything else to be accepted by God. We have nothing to prove, Jesus has already done that. If we did nothing for the rest of our lives, God would still accept us because He has already accepted Jesus. Acceptance is to be the atmosphere of the church, the body of Christ. You could argue that all of Paul's wonderful theological teaching in the book of Romans is leading towards chapter 15 vs 7 – 'Accept one another, then, just as Christ accepted you, in order to bring praise to God.'

Responses to rejection are generally negative until the

stronghold is demolished because this personal negativity, this very strong feeling of failure is a fundamental outcome of the faulty thought patterns that have been established.

God says that He chooses the foolish things, the despised things, the rejected things of this world, those that do not count for anything, to shame the wise and the strong.[3] He told Paul that His power is made perfect in weakness and Paul says in response that he is able to do *everything* through Christ who strengthens him. As we help those who have been rejected to absorb this teaching, we are helping to build maturity into their lives and are demolishing, through our teaching, the stronghold of rejection.

Negativity

Sadly, many of the people of God have become bound by negative attitudes. They seem to be in the grip of strongholds of negativity. There are a number of different types and I want to deal with each separately.

Personal negativity

As a pastor I find this one cropping up frequently in people that I am ministering to and it needs to be confronted. The typical reactions are based on a personal sense of failure or a sense that even if something positive were to happen, it would not last. Common expressions of this stronghold are that we feel unable to overcome, or have been prayed for many times and 'it does not seem to work'.

Typical of this response was someone that I prayed for during a ministry time for healing. This person told me for my encouragement(!) that she had already been prayed for by Reinhard Bonnke and Yonggi Cho, but nothing had happened, so she now wanted *me* to pray for her. You can imagine what that did for my faith! It was strange because I was aware of such a sense of negativity in this person, yet she had a constant desire to be prayed for until something happened. I did not find it easy to understand how these two opposite reactions could co-exist, but they did. The strong feeling was that she had tried it before and it had never worked, and this seemed to reflect a deep-seated antipathy toward any healing.

Often when I am doing DIY I have been heard to say that I am a failure; I always make a mess of things. I even get angry about it sometimes, especially when I have to call out someone in the church to sort it out for me! DIY really tests my belief structures concerning my acceptance in Christ! 'Why is everybody else good at this and I am absolutely useless?' We say that, do we not?

Or perhaps we say something in a cell group and spend the next three months wishing that we had said it differently, or worrying whether we offended somebody! So we go around thinking that we are utterly useless, no good for anything, but this is all negativity and we need to turn it around. We can, you know. Instead of seeing one failure as a curse pronouncing the inevitability of future personal failure, we need to look at the situation as representing an opportunity for God to work through our weaknesses.

Refuse to look at it negatively. Refuse to say 'I'm no good' or 'I'll fail' or 'I'll get it wrong'. Instead, we can say, 'OK. I got this wrong, but I believe this . . ..'

My friend Philip Vogel used to visit our church often in the early days and recommended that whenever we were about to use the word 'problem', we should substitute the word 'opportunity' instead. I wonder how readers would have reacted if I had done that throughout this book? Yet it could really help to break this stronghold of negativity. Imagine considering every problem as an opportunity for prayer and for seeing God work through our situations.

So where there is a sense of failure, we need to turn it

around, to see it as an opportunity for God to change that failure to success. Maybe it all seems hopeless. What an opportunity for God to turn that hopelessness into a positive charge of hope! Take hold of that thought, 'It's no good me praying for someone, I'm no good, it needs a pastor to do that'. Turn it around. Take that thought captive and say '*I* can do everything through Him who gives *me* strength'.[4] Or maybe you are just about to say that God has not worked in your life like that. Take that thought captive. Say instead that you are enjoying the presence of God and you have faith that you can do anything through Christ who strengthens you. It is when we are feeling weak that God can move into our lives and make us strong.

National negativity

This really is a British disease. We always support the loser. There is something in our national consciousness so negative that it makes us extremely cynical. Our attitude is that even though our friends across the ocean might get taken in, we never will. It is a part of our national heritage. It appears in our humour as a constant setting up of people in order to pull them down. There is a cynicism and self-deprecation that really is a stronghold in our nation.

There is now a powerful cynicism amongst our young people towards politics and politicians, and while this might be considered justifiable in view of the lack of moral leadership that exists, it is evidence of this terrific stronghold of negativity. New ideas seem cynically to become just another confidence trick and the result can be an incredible sense of hopelessness.

Negativity in the church

This can cover several different areas:

- Inaccurate, exaggerated reporting can fuel cynicism and unbelief.

- When God's people were going through the wilderness, they constantly grumbled and complained in spite of all the wonderful things that God did, so they were called a disbelieving generation.[5] Many of us love to grumble and complain, don't we? If we do not want to be numbered as part of a disbelieving generation, we must not complain. Either take action to change things or accept them graciously.

- I sometimes encounter a level of cynicism about love, community and fellowship because of hurts, lack of friendship and breakdown of relationships that individuals may have experienced in their church life. The Scriptures tell us that love bears all things and believes all things. So even if some of your original vision for your church and the community it was going to be has not quite been fulfilled yet, do not let that create cynicism or negativity.

- Humility is distorted, and becomes self-deprecation. True humility comes with the recognition that I am weak without God, not that I am useless. We are told in the Scriptures that God created us for good works that He chose for us beforehand.[6]

Passivity

I have to be careful with the next stronghold because it is one of the rare occasions when I really *have* to make a sexist remark. You see, the stronghold of passivity is most common amongst *men*.

It is a fatalistic attitude that views problems as too difficult to solve and so does nothing. It is not a new problem. One of the Seven Deadly Sins preached against in the Middle Ages was 'accidie' or 'sloth', which was more than laziness; it meant a withdrawing into indifference and inaction – in other words passivity.

The *Book of Common Prayer* speaks not only of confessing the things that I have done that I ought not to have done, but also those things that I ought to have done but have not.[7] I believe that often we need to think about this and say with conviction, 'Lord, please forgive me for the things that I haven't done today', or 'Lord, please forgive me for the times when I haven't taken the initiative'. There are many men who need to confess this. Ask their wives! Passivity can be the Ahab antithesis of the Jezebel spirit that says it is all too much trouble. It is perhaps strange that some men who are ready to take on a lot of responsibility at work, just sit back and let it happen in other situations such as family or church. There are cultural gateways for this stronghold to affect men in many places. For example, in working class culture in parts of Britain, it would not be uncommon for a working man to hand over his pay to his wife (keeping back some for beer money) and let her take the strain of managing the family and its finances. In South Africa, the terribly ungodly system under apartheid of separating migrant workers from their homes and families had a similar effect.

Men were created to take responsibility and to initiate. It is not that women should not initiate; rather, that men need to ensure that they express their masculinity in this way. However, what can happen instead is the scenario that we find in Genesis when Eve gave Adam the fruit of the tree of knowledge. Rather than taking responsibility for the situation and endeavouring to sort it out, he lapsed into passivity and went along with what Eve was doing. Then when he was found out, he blamed God and his wife, and Eve in turn blamed the serpent! Where *was* Adam when Eve was being tempted? He was not out drinking with his mates, we do know that! According to the Scriptures he was actually *with* her when the serpent started talking to her.[8] So what *was* he doing?

I believe that passivity is a greater problem for leadership in the church, and initiatives for the kingdom, than over-ambition.

William Booth, the man who started the Salvation Army, was heard to say once that all his best men were women. Gladys Aylwood, a missionary in China, was reportedly once asked why she never married. She replied that God had a man for her, but that he hadn't the guts to go to China.

Fear

These strongholds are powerful, and the next one we have to look at is no exception. This is the stronghold of fear.

Many people live out their lives paralysed by fear of all kinds. One of the best examples in the Scriptures is in the life of King Saul. He was an anointed man of God, yet on three separate occasions he allowed fear to rule his decisions.

The first of these concerned the offering of a sacrifice. The people of Israel were about to go into battle against the Philistines, and the prophet Samuel was asked to prepare a sacrifice as usual before they went into battle. This time the sacrifice was delayed because Samuel was held up on the road. Saul waited seven days for Samuel to arrive and by that time, his men were quaking with fear because of the numbers of men and chariots in the Philistine army. Eventually Saul performed the sacrifice himself instead of waiting for Samuel, but Samuel arrived just as the burnt offering was being made.[9]

The next occasion was when Samuel told Saul to kill every one of the Amalekites when he overcame them. God gave Saul victory in the situation, but Saul spared the Amalekite king and kept the best of the spoils instead of destroying the whole lot. The weaker animals were killed, but the people wanted the best of the livestock. Again, Saul feared the response of his people and gave in to them instead of doing the will of God.[10]

Finally, there was the occasion when Saul went secretly to a spiritualist medium. Samuel was dead by this time, and without his mentor, Saul lacked courage to act on his own initiative. He felt he needed advice and so went to the medium to get an interview with Samuel. The reason given for his sin on this occasion was that when he saw the Philistine army 'terror filled his heart'.[11]

Do you see what happened here? In each case the initial fear built up to such proportions that it caused Saul to sin and thus lose his anointing. Fear almost always leads to sin because it stops us taking the initiative in doing God's will.

In the Scriptures we find that when Israel was preparing for war, they would tell all those who had got engaged to be married or had just bought a vineyard to go home, and all those who were *afraid* were also told to go home. We might think that is no way to run an army, but fear is very contagious and they knew that if they had men in the army who were afraid, the others would catch the scent of their fear and they would all become afraid.[12] This is what happened to Saul's army in the first situation described above.

There are many different kinds of fear.

The fear of man is a trap for many.[13] This is a fear of what other people might think. It is the sort of fear that says 'If I do this crazy thing for God – and I know that He told me to – what will everybody think?'

Sometimes it can be the fear of getting it wrong . . . again.

A common problem is the fear of being hurt. Life is hurtful because it is lived in Satan's domain and we do get hurt. This leaves us with situations that we feel we cannot face again and fear gets in the way. Most of us probably think that this is a reasonable excuse, but being hurt is never an excuse for a Christian not to do what is right. God can always heal hurts, and we can overcome their effect in our lives. We do this by personally taking responsibility for our reaction to the hurt. We are called to be overcomers of the enemy.[14]

Superstitious fear can come in many disguises. I know someone who said that if they did not have a 'quiet time' in the morning, something terrible would come to spoil their day. Their quiet time had become a superstition. When I used to take exams, I would work through a weird routine as a preparation. I would study as much as I could, then work out a set of exam questions based on all the things that I had not studied. I had to be careful I did not become paralysed with fear. Superstition is a legalistic fear concerned with 'What happens if . . . ?' and is another very powerful stronghold.

Anger

I remember praying with someone who had very strong anger; she was so full of it that a demon had attached itself to her anger. Before I prayed with her, I allowed this demon to manifest itself so that she would experience the full horror of the destructive nature of her anger. It started to churn up inside her, causing terrible pain, and she wanted to express this anger against me. I wanted her to see what had been motivating her life.

The stronghold of anger is a powerful motivator. I have known people who did not want me to cast out a spirit of anger because they thought that it was the strength of their whole personality. They felt that if it went they would become weak. Their anger was helping them to cope with life.

Ray Lowe, who leads Biggin Hill Christian Fellowship, told me how he was leading 'freedom from strongholds' meetings when the Holy Spirit first began to move in power in his church. On the way to one of these meetings, God convicted him about his anger. When he arrived at the meeting, he got the other leaders together and asked them to pray for him before it started. As they were praying he felt God remind him about his eighth birthday. He was an only child and on that particular birthday he had collected up all the cards and his mother had asked him to read them to her. He had got stuck on one of them, which he found impossible to read, and his mother had said that he was stupid and that he was old enough to read all of them now that he was eight. What was he learning at school, anyway, if he could not do a simple thing like that. He became so angry that he tore the card in two and stormed out of the room. At that point, a stronghold of anger had entered his life and had become a source of some of his motivation. God dealt with it that night and he was a different person afterwards. He told us that his wife could bear witness to the change that had occurred in him. God had revealed how a stronghold of anger had become established, so that it could be demolished.

Interestingly, I told this story in another place where I was ministering. Another pastor present found that the story came like a 'word of knowledge' to his own life. On his eighth birthday, his father had become furious because he had left some homework undone and this had reinforced in his life a sense of failure with which he had recently been struggling.

Anger is not necessarily a sin if it is expressed in a godly way, like Jesus did with the moneychangers in the temple. However, anger that is held on to is sinful and becomes bitterness; a place for the devil to have a foothold in our lives.[15]

Unforgiveness

Linked closely with the stronghold of anger is that of unforgiveness.

A lady came to me one day to ask for help. She was nearly eighty but had been ill-treated by her late father when she was nine or ten years old. A stronghold of unforgiveness had been established in her life, as she had never been able to forgive him. This had caused her a lot of pain and had affected other relationships. We prayed for her and she was wonderfully set free after nearly seventy years of having this stronghold of unfor-giveness in her life. She became a most joyful worshipper and would often complain because no one else was dancing!

The Bible compares holding on to unforgiveness with being in prison. Even though people may have been hurt many times, they are the ones who are in prison, until they release and forgive those who have hurt them. That is what unforgiveness does to people.[16] Forgiving someone means letting them off completely, cancelling all their debts against you, determining never to hold their offence against them in the future. This can be very hard to do, especially when something like abuse is involved. I have no desire to make light of abuse; I have coun-selled a large number of people in this situation and have taken time with them, helping them see release in the situation, but the fact remains that until they are able to forgive they remain tied to the hurt and also to the person who abused them. This link cannot be broken until forgiveness occurs.

We must remember too that forgiveness is not a feeling – it is a choice we make with our will.

The prison of abuse

The effect of any form of abuse is to cause the abused person to feel imprisoned. They become prisoners to their emotions, bound by the secrecy that is so often put upon them to prevent the perpetrators being found out. Emotional imprisonment is usually the result, with emotions such as rejection, particularly self-rejection, being common.

Abuse is still particularly difficult to discuss because of the secrecy and fear that is involved. It is made more difficult when a figure of authority is involved, such as a parent, teacher or minister. A vow of silence is often enforced upon them – 'This is our secret'; 'Don't let anybody know' – and this establishes a powerful control on someone's life. If the abuse is sexual, then an entry point for unclean spirits is sometimes established and soul ties can occur, establishing powerful links with the abuser. I remember counselling and praying for a young man because of sexual sin in his life. As we talked he opened up to the effect that he had been sexually abused by a priest he had trusted. I believe this was one way in which sexual strongholds had been created in his life.

Problems caused by abuse include deep resentment, which invariably results in bitterness that can disrupt relationships for the rest of a person's life unless healing comes.

Resolving a situation where abuse has occurred requires time, because there will invariably be what Proverbs calls a 'crushed' spirit.[17] Where a vow of silence has been taken, what happened will need to be spoken out (or written in diary format if that is more helpful). The most difficult part will almost certainly be the approach to forgiveness. A person who has been abused must reach the point where they are able to forgive their abuser, even though it may take a long time.

Effective Strategy Number 14: Recognise that strongholds can be created in emotions, from which people need to be set free, so that past wrong emotional experiences no longer govern present conduct.

NOTES

[1]Proverbs 18:8; [2]Psalm 139:13–14; [3]1 Corinthians 1:26–29; [4]Philippians 4:13; [5]Hebrews 3:10,19; [6]Ephesians 2:10; [7]*Book of Common Prayer – Order for Morning Prayer – A General Confession;* [8]Genesis 3:6; [9]1 Samuel 13:7–10; [10]1 Samuel 15:24; [11]1 Samuel 28:5; [12]Deuteronomy 20:8; [13]Proverbs 29:25; [14]1 John 2:13; [15]Ephesians 4:26–27; [16]Matthew 18:32–34; [17]Proverbs 15:13, 17:22.

Chapter 15

HELPING PEOPLE TO FREEDOM
DISCERNING THE PROBLEM

This chapter and the next deal more specifically with what is often called 'deliverance ministry'. Therefore, before going on to explain how to deal with demonic issues, it is important to be aware of some of the dangers.

It is tempting to start each chapter by saying that the most important job the Church has been given to do is to glorify Jesus and extend His kingdom in the world. The problem with talking about 'deliverance ministry' is that it can create an over-emphasis on the work of deliverance that causes us to lose sight of Jesus, and leads us to glorify our own ministry. I do *not* believe in a separate 'deliverance ministry'. I do not see it in Scripture in any of the lists of gifts or ministries. I believe it is part of our pastoral and evangelistic ministry (just as it was for Jesus and the apostles). Therefore we need to be equipped to do it as part of caring for people, discipling them and sharing the good news with unbelievers.

There have been situations in my ministry for example, when I have gone somewhere and the pre-meeting advertising has said that I am involved in 'deliverance ministry'. I have even seen handbills in some countries inviting people to 'deliverance meetings' with David Devenish. This just isn't true. I am quite

happy to do evangelistic meetings, teaching seminars or training courses, and if there is a ministry time, or if there is a
demonic manifestation as a result, then I am quite happy to
deal with it. I believe that is the way that we should work. I certainly do not advocate 'independent' deliverance ministries. I
believe that anybody involved in such ministry must be functioning well within a local church and accountable to the eldership (or equivalent) of that church. Otherwise, there is a danger
of a particular ministry specialising in these sort of problems
and becoming unbalanced.

Let us again remind ourselves who we are dealing with when
we face demonic issues. The dualistic image of spiritual
warfare, in which God and Satan are viewed as more or less
equal in power, with God just about winning by the narrowest
of margins, is not an accurate picture at all. Although I have
mentioned it earlier, it needs to be repeated again and again
until it is understood. Satan is not God's equal. Jesus has
already won the battle; it is not damage limitation we are
involved in, but the clean-up operation.

Another danger is treating every problem as demonic. For
example, some manifestations might appear to be demonic
when they are not at all. This is particularly important to
remember when dealing with emotional pain or deep trauma.
Often such situations can involve powerful emotional turmoil
coming to the surface, which can easily be misinterpreted as
demonic in origin when in fact it is purely the emotions of the
person being set free. When this happens, we should prayerfully
and sympathetically speak truth to the person from God's
Word, to bring reassurance and healing.

Paul told the Colossians that the evil of the flesh must be put
to death.[1] Our fight is not just against demonic power, but also
against the allure of the world and the temptations of the flesh.
Don Basham talks about this in his book *Deliver Us From Evil*.
He suggests the following:

A Test for an Evil Spirit

1. Treat your hang up first as a simple carnal sin and see what happens. Confess it, ask forgiveness, believe that forgiveness has been granted. Now apply will, discipline and prayer to the habit patterns that have entrenched themselves in this area. Whenever they reappear, put them 'under the crucifixion' of Jesus, knowing that He is able when we are not.
2. If all this produces no victory, you may be dealing with a demon – and you should seek deliverance.[2]

It is only when Basham's stage one has not worked and the problem is not resolved that we need to consider whether deliverance may be a solution. Demons are not a part of us, they have simply taken up residence, so they can be evicted. They have invaded our lives from outside like an enemy that infiltrates to disrupt and destroy. Evicting them, or 'casting them out', is sometimes a necessary process, but only when we are sure that it really is the problem.

Once the demonic influence has been driven out, teaching is always necessary in order to demolish thoroughly the strongholds that are left behind, the wrong thought patterns that have been set up during the period of demonic infestation. Renewing the mind should be seen as just as important a part of the solution as deliverance. For example, suppose someone is afflicted by a spirit of rebellion, and this is evicted. It is no good thinking that now the spirit has gone, there will not be any more rebellion. What has happened is that thought patterns have been established during the period of infestation, and these need to be changed. So although the spiritual strength of the problem has gone, some of the symptoms remain and still need to be dealt with. A person must therefore maintain a repentant attitude towards their rebellion and be willing to deal with it whenever it arises.

We must train the mind to think in a different way. As we know, strongholds are thought patterns, and re-training someone to think and respond in a different way helps us to destroy these faulty thought patterns by replacing them with godly ones.

If there is no re-training, no renewing of the mind, then an entry point will be left for the demonic force to return, perhaps with a few of its friends.[3] Often the battle to help someone walk free is harder than actually setting them free. Individualism is a typical example of this. I have taught on this subject many times and I have not seen it as an issue of demonic infestation. It is usually an entrenched cultural attitude, a thought pattern or stronghold that is just as important to deal with as any particular evil spirit.

I need to be careful here because I do not want to be critical of others engaged in this important ministry. However, I have found that when people concentrate on the deliverance only, and its associated manifestations, then people can almost subconsciously be trained to produce such manifestations whenever they have problems. I remember praying with someone, referred to me by the pastor of another church, for whom that was the case. I soon realised that I had to concentrate on helping the person to walk free of the influence that the evil spirit had had in her life. To use old-fashioned warfare parallels, we need to 'hold ground' as well as 'take ground'.

Healing of past hurts is also important. When someone has been seriously hurt, the pain will dominate their thinking. It is important that time is spent listening. As we do this, it helps them to take authority over the hurt, instead of letting it rule their lives. Often people are reacting out of the hurt and we need to help them to express what has happened so that they can deal with it from a perspective of truth instead of one of pain.

So 'deliverance' is not a quick-fix solution at all.

I want to go on now to deal with some of the common entry points that demons use to invade someone's life.

Sin

At one time, I thought that people could only be affected by demons if they had been involved in the occult. I then came across situations where this evidently was not the case. I then saw that this was true to Scripture.

Saul, for example, was a powerful man of God when he became king. Saul's sin of rebellion is described as being 'like the sin of divination' (or witchcraft).[4] Later he became afflicted with an evil spirit. It was not that the occult led Saul to have an evil spirit. His rebellion opened the door to the evil spirit and later drove him into occult practices.[5]

Of course, it is true that we have all sinned. It is equally true that most of us are not demon-infested. However, serious sin can provide an entry point for demons. Anger that is held on to, self-hatred and hatred of others are all sins that can create entry points. Others include pornography, sexual perversion and wrongdoing. I would also include abortion in this list. Abortion can be an entry point in the baby's mother, father, or anyone else involved in the decision to carry out the abortion. For example, I was once called round to a house where a new Christian was experiencing demonic manifestations. I sensed God saying to me that it was to do with abortion. The woman concerned had persuaded her teenage daughter to have an abortion and that had been the entry point for the demon.

Anger

We need to look at the entry point of anger in more detail. Paul told the church at Ephesus that it is all right to be angry providing we don't sin.[6] 'It's true! However, he doesn't stop there.

He goes on to explain that we must resolve the issues that are causing the problem before the sun sets in the evening, so that evil is not given a foothold. So, if we deal with anger in a biblical fashion, we prevent Satan from gaining a foothold.

I discovered the scriptural principles relating to anger through reading a missionary book about a Chinese Christian leader[7] during the last century. At the time I was reading this book, I had noticed that a lot of the people I was dealing with were having problems with anger, people who had been seriously hurt and subsequently demonised. It was difficult then for me to understand how this happened, but the book helped. You see, in the part of China where this leader was working, he was experiencing similar problems, and the reason for this soon became obvious. The cultural tradition there was that if you were offended, it was the expectation for you to spend many days in an angry rage. A footnote in the book led me to the verse in Ephesians referred to above and I saw the point.

Occult entry points

I have already mentioned the occult, in connection with strongholds through past sin, in Chapter 11. There are many varieties of occult practices that can afford entry points for demons and it is important to list some of these when ministering to people, since many do not recognise them as occult and need to do so. I repeat here the list of occult practices from Chapter 11 and stress that it is by no means exhaustive:

Fortune telling: Ouija boards, tarot cards and any kind of fortune telling such as tea leaves, palmistry or a crystal ball.

Spiritualism: Horoscopes, spiritualism, so-called Christian spiritualism, séances and mediums, automatic writing, spiritualist healing and clairvoyance.

Magic: Black and white magic, table lifting, levitation, casting spells and hexes.

Mystical: Transcendental meditation, astral projection, mind reading, mental telepathy, thought transference and mind expanding drugs.

Religious: Satanism, idol worship, eastern religions, new age.

Family demonisation

Initially I used to have misgivings about the concept of demons gaining access through past generations because I did not feel I could prove it biblically. Sometimes people refer to Scriptures such as God visiting the sins of the father to the third and fourth generation.[8] I came to see that this is probably a valid application, because it is the sin of idolatry that is involved. I have to say that I believe it is frequently a logical issue of lifestyle. Where people have been brought up in a family where demons are working, it is logically quite likely that the next generation will be affected. In experience, I have found this to be particularly true where very strong 'family control' is exerted.

Traumatic experiences

Another difficult area is that of traumatic experiences. As well as the necessity of preaching repentance and forgiveness to all, because we are all sinners, I also believe we are supposed to minister God's healing grace to those who are 'broken-hearted'.[9] This means those who have been sinned against. Obviously, they are still sinners themselves so they still need to take responsibility for their own sin and their reaction to hurt.

However, I believe demons can invade us through chinks in our natural armour caused by trauma. For example, I remember a young man whose mother had sought unsuccessfully to abort him. I met him during the early years of my involvement in this ministry, and it was quite unsettling praying for him because the trauma was so severe that he was temporarily struck dumb as we prayed. The emotions that were created when he had to come face to face with the rejection were so incredibly immense.

Symptoms of demonic infestation

Before going any further, I must issue a 'Devenish Public Health Warning', because the next part is like one of those family doctor books that most people have. You know the sort of thing – you get a slight stomach ache, look it up in the book and find that you have got every awful disease that was ever discovered.

You see, in this part I want to talk about symptoms of demonic infestation. The difficulty here is that it is not something that can be treated as an exact science; there really are not too many rules to be followed.

Sometimes, for example, I have prayed for someone to be released from a problem like ouija and a spirit has manifested; then, because the person has also been into astrology, I've prayed against that and there has been no demon there.

So this list is just for guidance. The presence of one or more of these symptoms indicates the *possibility* of demonic infestation:

- Distorted, unpleasant physical reactions, especially when the power of the Holy Spirit is present.
- Addiction to drugs or alcohol.
- A problem with compulsions such as lust, fornication, pornography, masturbation, homosexuality, stealing, murder, lying, suicide or eating disorders. (We need to remember

that many such compulsions stem from broken emotions –
past sins against the person – and a need for 'sexual healing'
rather than deliverance.)

- Bondage to emotions such as fear, depression, anxiety or
rage.
- Bondage to sinful attitudes such as self-hatred, unforgiveness, bitterness, resentment and contempt.
- Chronic physical sickness, especially those sicknesses that
have been in the family for generations.
- A history of occult involvement or idolatrous worship.
- A disturbed family history involving things such as incest,
alcoholism and various forms of child abuse.

Symptoms of rejection

This last condition is another tricky one, because rejection can
be either emotional or demonic and it is often impossible to tell
which until you actually start to pray it through.

When a person is suffering from rejection, I usually check out
as well whether there are spirits of 'self-rejection', 'fear of rejection' or a 'rejecting spirit' ie the person is very rejecting of
others – even of their own children.

Self-rejection, for example, can be either demonic or emotional and the symptoms are a general lack of self-care and a
deep lack of value. Generally, people in this situation are negative about everything, and there are sometimes thoughts of
suicide involved.

Symptoms of rejection usually include an inability to feel
love, to build relationships or even to trust people and this will
often result in an inability to receive correction. Where
someone is suffering from symptoms of rejection, any attempt
at correction will be seen as further rejection. It's important to
recognise this before any help can be given so that someone in
this situation can be supported until they are able to see that

they are not being rejected when faced with correction.

Another difficulty is that people with rejection problems often create barriers that will cause people to reject them. They believe that they are going to be rejected anyway and would rather be in control of the situation by causing it to occur in a way that they can handle. So they try to create situations where they will be rejected to make you lose interest in attempting to establish any form of relationship with them.

Discernment of spirits

The gift of discernment of spirits is obviously very important when assessing whether the demonic is involved. We need to ask God for that gift and not just 'have a go' at deliverance on the basis of 'if all else fails, let's give it a go'.

A few years ago, the Holy Spirit had fallen on a group of pastors and their wives when we were meeting together for a retreat. Many were lying on the floor, others 'drunk in the Spirit', others being filled with joy and laughter. As I walked around looking at what was going on, I looked at one man and felt God give me the discernment that what was happening to him was not entirely of the Holy Spirit. I went away for a few minutes therefore and asked God what was going on. He gave me a 'word of knowledge' about the person's situation, which I then went and shared with him. I told him I believed what was happening was not just a sign of the Holy Spirit's presence but rather that there was a spirit involved that had resulted from his background and his feelings of inadequacy in leadership. He looked surprised but at that very same moment his wife was struck with terrible pain she could hardly bear. I therefore prayed for them both, the pain left the wife and the husband was set free from this afflicting spirit. He has since told me that this has made a tremendous difference to his leadership and he is no longer suffering from any feelings of inadequacy in this respect.

It is very important that we learn how to discern when an evil spirit is present in a person's life and that we find out what the entry points were. This will help form the basis for setting the person free as we describe in the next chapter.

Effective Strategy Number 15: Learn to discern when an evil spirit is afflicting a person so that it can be expelled.

NOTES

[1]Colossians 3:5; [2]*Deliver us from Evil*, Don Basham, page 119 (Chosen Books LLC, Chappaqua, New York. Used with permission.); [3]Matthew 12:43–45; [4]1 Samuel 15:23; [5]1 Samuel 28:7; [6]Ephesians 4:26; [7]*Pastor Hsi*, Mrs Howard Taylor; [8]Exodus 20:5; [9]Psalm 109:16 (the opposite of what evil people did according to this verse), Isaiah 61:1.

Chapter 16

HELPING PEOPLE TO FREEDOM DELIVERANCE AND AFTERCARE

Before going on to the main subject of this chapter, there is an important aspect I need to deal with. Most of this book is concerned with setting Christians free from strongholds to function in the church in the way God intends. This chapter, however, is about deliverance ministry, that is, setting people free from demons, and we need to address one aspect that is not covered elsewhere in the book. That is the issue of praying with non-Christians for their deliverance. I am often asked whether we can or should do this.

According to Scripture, the answer is a qualified yes. In the gospels, most of the people set free from demons were the covenant people of God, the Jews. In the book of Acts, however, the picture changes: because of Paul's move to introduce the gospel to Gentiles (non-Jews), some of those who were set free were complete non-believers. For example, the servant girl with the fortune telling spirit at Philippi was set free[1] though there is no evidence that she ever came to know Jesus. Having said that, it is interesting that Paul did not deal with her immediately. She followed him around for 'many days' before he cast out the spirit, and I have often wondered why he delayed. My suggestion is that he did not act until it became clear that he would otherwise be unable to preach the gospel in peace. He seems to have been in no hurry to minister deliverance to an unbeliever.

This is important, because there are not the same guarantees of success when we minister to unbelievers. If they come to Christ and are born again and filled with the Holy Spirit, it is unlikely that the demons that are cast out will ever return. If, however, a non-believer is unwilling to accept Christ, there is little that can be done to protect him for the future, even if he is set free now. There is a risk that not only will the original demon return, but others may come, too. Jesus specifically warns of this.[2] This is because entry points are not being dealt with and the non-believer is not able to call on God's protection. To be assured of remaining clean, the person needs to come to Christ, be filled with the Holy Spirit and start dealing with issues of discipleship and any strongholds that could be entry points and footholds for the enemy.

One of the stories I told in Chapter 1 is an example of this kind of situation. In the very early days of our church in Bedford, we were invaded most Sundays by a much larger group of young teenagers who insisted on causing a disturbance most of the time. You may recall that one Sunday night the meeting ended and I returned home to find a large group of the missing teenagers on my front lawn, many in tears, most of them scared stiff. They had gone to a friend's house for a session with an ouija board. The trouble was, a demonic spirit had actually manifested and had chased them down the stairs and out of the house. I invited them into my home and explained the gospel to them. However, I had to warn them that although I was quite prepared to pray for them (which is what they expressed they wanted), I could not give them any guarantee of remaining free unless they came to know Jesus. I did pray for them, and they went away. I eventually lost touch with most of them, although one is now a member of our church. I have no

idea what happened to most of the others – I do not know that
any of them became Christians.

Moving on, now, I would like to give a few guidelines that I
have put together. You see there are no rules in this particular
ministry. Every situation that you meet is different, and you
have to make swift judgements sometimes.

I cannot prescribe a 'how to' concerning setting people free
from demons. It just doesn't work that way. Most of what
follows now is purely and simply a collection of things that I
have learned from experience. When teaching on practical 'how
to's' like this, I always point out that this comes with a different
authority than when I am expounding clear biblical truth.
These are just things I have found helpful, so I am passing them
on. They are not a 'blueprint' though I do not think that they
run contrary to any scriptural teaching.

Ensure that you are rooted in Biblical truth

Although this might sound obvious, it is important that
anyone who is likely to deal with deliverance must not only be
convinced of biblical truth about his or her authority in Christ
but also the validity biblically of this ministry. Because deliverance is an authority issue, if you are not persuaded theologically about this, you will not feel secure during a time of
ministry.

Make deliverance part of a lifestyle

As already pointed out, deliverance is not an isolated ministry.
There is no such thing as a separate deliverance ministry in
Scripture; it is simply part of both pastoral care and the evan-
gelistic ministry of the church.

This does not mean that only pastors can do this work,
either. In our own church, we have ministry teams of trained

workers and counsellors to handle these issues and I actually do very little deliverance there at all.

Work alongside other people wherever possible

Always try to work in a team. At our church there are teams for just about everything; all our healing prayer ministry is done in teams; much of our counselling is done in teams and while a team might only involve two people, it is still important to work this way in situations that are likely to involve deliverance.

Here are a few reasons why teamwork is the better way:

- It is good to work alongside someone else, especially when you are in a training situation. It is a good learning environment and you get the opportunity to learn from someone who is experienced.
- There is a strong spiritual benefit where each member of the team is able to support the other in prayer or in ministering spiritual gifts. It is important that in praying for people we are using the gifts of the Holy Spirit. There might be a word of prophecy ministered, for example, and that should not be permitted in a one to one situation because there would not be anyone to test it.
- Being part of a team helps us all to focus on Jesus, not on ourselves.
- It is essential that there is always someone present of the same sex as the person receiving prayer.
- In a purely natural sense, it helps sometimes to have a witness handy. Things may be going on that could appear a bit strange, and it might be useful to have someone for moral support. People receiving counselling and prayer ministry can be very manipulative. Having at least one witness provides a safeguard in this area.

There needs to be a willingness to be discipled

The disciples learnt from Jesus during His ministry on earth. They were a small team that He gathered together and there were times when they got it wrong. For example, they came back to Jesus after an unsuccessful ministry session and asked Him why they had been unable to deal with it, and what they had done wrong in the situation. When that happens, it helps to have someone you feel comfortable with to go and ask what went wrong and why it did not work the way you expected. You must not be afraid to ask questions like 'Why wouldn't it work this time? Was I doing something wrong?'

Don't feel pressurised by people or situations

This work is not something that should be rushed. Take it easy and do not feel pressurised by anything going on around you. If it cannot be fully dealt with in one session, do not be afraid to arrange another to finish the task. If you have only half an hour, do not be afraid to tell the person that you will pray for half an hour now and arrange a further session later. If there is a demon, do not feel that it has to be dealt with *now*; there may be issues of repentance and ungodly lifestyle that need to be discussed first.

When I first started doing this sort of thing, people would phone me up at all sorts of unearthly hours to tell me that they had a demon manifesting and would I go and pray for them. Then the person training me rebuked me severely. He asked me why I had not realised that I was running at the beck and call of demons. Usually, if someone calls at a difficult time, I put them off and arrange to go and see them later, at a time convenient to both of us.

If they complain, (and they do), that they have a demon manifesting, I try to calm them down and help them understand that it is not as urgent and immediate as they think it is. Obviously it would not be pastorally appropriate to tell them, (no matter how much you *feel* like saying it!), that the demon has already been there for maybe twenty-five years, so a few more hours or even days is not really going to make much difference – but this is still a valid point for your own security!

Sometimes things can get a bit public. Demons sometimes manifest in meetings, for example, and you may have to deal with them. The important thing to remember is not to get under pressure. If it cannot be dealt with there and then, arrange a time when it is convenient. If the demon keeps manifesting, command it to be quiet and arrange another time.

What about self-deliverance?

People do teach as a possible solution that we can set ourselves free. I do believe that some Christians have had valid experiences of 'self-deliverance'. It is certainly possible to deal with curses in this way, particularly related to a sphere where we have leadership responsibility, for example as a husband with responsibility for a family.

However, I believe this is an opportunity to serve one another in the body of Christ. It is good for us to receive from each other and, more importantly, to be accountable to one another.

Guidelines for teams

Deliverance is an authority issue and while I do not believe that elders should do it all, I do believe they should only give such responsibility to those in whom they have confidence. I cannot stress strongly enough that it is important for anyone working in this field to be rightly related to godly authority in the local church.

At one time at Christian conferences, it was not uncommon

to see a crowd of people gather when a demon manifested. They would all stand around shouting at the thing to leave, and there was so much confusion, no one knew what was going on. The devil loves confusion, and in that sort of situation we were actually *helping* him. Do not crowd around.

In our church, we usually handle it through the cell group system (provided those involved have been trained), although there is always a back-up team of more experienced people to provide support if the cell cannot cope.

There are guidelines for all our teams, and it is important to recognise that in a team situation, there should be a leader. It does not mean that the leader must dominate every ministry session, but there should be a sense of godly order.

• *Put the person at ease*

The person who is being ministered to needs to feel at ease, so it is important to take the mystery out of the situation, to explain to the person the truths from Scripture. It is also important to ascertain whether they really want to be set free. They may need to be told that their lifestyle will probably have to change, for example, and they might not want that. The key issue here is not to get 'spooky' about it, but to try to maintain as normal an atmosphere as possible.

Mention the word 'demonic' and all sorts of things tend to collect in the minds of ordinary people. One woman I remember, for example, had a demon manifesting and she kept trying to push it down. This went on for some time, until I said to her, 'Look. What is the matter here? You don't seem to want to let go of this thing.'

It turned out that she had seen the film *The Exorcist*, and although it is not something I would wish to see, apparently in the final scenes the child gets set free, but the demon goes into the priest who is ministering to her. So whenever the demon tried to manifest in the woman I was dealing with, she thought it would go into me when it left her. She didn't want that to happen, so she kept trying to push the thing down. So I explained to her carefully that it would not happen like that, and once she understood, we sorted the thing out and she was set free.

This illustrates the importance of maintaining a dialogue to put the person at their ease, make them feel as comfortable as possible and ensure that they know what is going on. Once you've done that, the next step is to pray asking the Holy Spirit into the situation. However, if things start to get emotionally excited, then calm things down and discuss the relevant issues.

• *Confession of sin*

It is important for the person to confess any sin that might have provided an entry point for demonic influence. This can some-times get quite personal. If the person I am ministering to is a woman, I will offer to leave the room and allow my wife to hear what the person has to say. I rarely ask my wife about the situation afterwards, unless it is something I really need to know for a future consultation. I am not interested in the details of people's past sins; I only want to help people get free of their problems.

The sort of sins involved here include any that could be a foothold for demonic activity (see Chapter 15). For example, we would be looking for occult activity, whether current or in their family. Where there are occult books or articles involved, the person will need to destroy them. It is very important that they themselves burn or otherwise dispose of such materials. It is they who are renouncing their involvement, and they need to take full responsibility for it. Having said that, I might go with them, but only to ensure that they have completed the task.

Renouncing the sins of the forefathers might be required where the problem is related to what might be called 'genera-tional' demonisation.

• *Forgiveness is often a key in deliverance*

Forgiveness is an important issue in any deliverance situation, whether seeking forgiveness from God for involvement in sin such as occult activity, or forgiving others.

One area where forgiveness can be a particular problem is self-rejection, and it is vital to seek forgiveness for this because to reject oneself is to reject something created by God. We are made in the image of God, and self-rejection challenges God as to whether He made a good job of it. It may be accompanied by deep anger against God. There needs to be confession and repentance for such anger, and for challenging or opposing God. I sometimes hear people speak of 'forgiving God' in this context. To me, this seems almost a blasphemous idea. He is the Potter, we are the clay.[3] Who are we to argue back at Him?

I will not minister deliverance to someone who is unable to forgive those who have hurt them. The problem of unforgiveness is frequently a bigger issue than the deliverance itself, and it can be a major battle to bring someone to the point of forgiveness. As soon as forgiveness has been achieved, however, the damaged emotions can be healed; this is yet another victory.

The same is true of getting someone to the point where they are able to receive forgiveness from God, especially in cases of self-rejection. Receiving forgiveness involves accepting God's Word that if we confess our sins, He is faithful and just to forgive us our sins and to purify us from all unrighteousness, because the blood of Jesus cleanses us from all sin, and 'there is therefore now no condemnation for those who are in Christ Jesus'.[4]

• *The releasing prayer*

Once these issues have been sorted out, and the person fully understands any changes that might have to occur in their lives, then they can be released in Jesus' name from any curses or, if appropriate, any family involvement with the demonic. Family issues are a sensitive area for some people, but they need to be dealt with because there might be control issues or demonic infestation that has been there for generations and they need to walk free of all the things in which their family has been involved.

Specific action might be needed to enable them to walk clear when more extreme situations of family domination are involved. We had one particular case, for example, where a woman was required by her mother to telephone regularly at (say) twenty past eight every Thursday night. It took us nearly a year to break that stronghold and for the woman concerned to stop telephoning her mother so regularly. It might seem inappropriate to counsel someone on when not to phone their mother! Specific, relatively small actions, however, can demonstrate an important bigger principle, and in this case, occult forces were at work in the family.

We command the demon to leave the person in the Name of Jesus. It is good to be a little creative in our use of relevant Scripture. Does that sound strange? Well, obviously it is important to command demons to go in Jesus' name, but we can use all that His name implies. For example, we can refer to the authority that the name of Jesus carries, like the words of Philippians 2:9–11, where it says that He is above every other authority and has been given a name above every name. We can talk about His authority being such that those below the earth, even in the demonic realm, have to submit to Him.

We can refer to the truth of the cross, or the empty tomb, or the truth of the blood of Jesus (demons cannot stand that). We can refer to the person as being the temple of the Holy Spirit. What all this does is to confront the demonic influence with the truth. The person that we are ministering to is a new creation in Christ and demonic forces have no place in their life; we can announce this powerfully, though it is important that we try to keep the emotional temperature reasonably stable. This process might take some time, but it should not be too prolonged.

It is good to get the person to co-operate by telling the demon to go, as well. They might say things like 'I don't want you any more'. There is no need to shout at this point. Demons are not deaf! They do not need to be shouted at. Speaking with authority does not involve shouting.

It is important to pray with our eyes open. We need to be able to see what is going on. We need to see if there has been any movement of expulsion. Listen to God while you are praying, and ask the person whether *they* feel that it has gone. We have to be careful here, and check our own spirit. If there is any doubt, if we have a gut feeling that it has not gone, or is hiding, we need to be honest. I do that, sometimes, when the demon has stopped manifesting, and things have gone quiet. I might say something like, 'In Jesus' name, if there is any demon there, I command you to manifest and go!' If it is hidden, the demon will then reveal itself again.

As well as keeping our own eyes open, it is important to watch the eyes of the person you are praying for, because you can sometimes see what is going on there. So I might say something like: 'Look at me. I know it's not very pleasant, but I would like you to look at me for a while.'

Sometimes, if the demon manifests in a particular part of the body, it might be helpful to place our hands on their body but, of course, it depends where. We have to be very sensitive about this. If I am praying with a woman, I will always have a woman helper and, maybe, if it is appropriate I will ask her to place her hands on the person's body. Again, that depends on what part of the body is involved and there may be cultural issues involved here, too.

People ask whether it is all right to use the gift of tongues during a deliverance session. It is fine for the people ministering; it helps to build them up spiritually and that is very useful.

However, I would not normally allow the person being prayed *for* to use tongues whilst we are commanding the spirit to go. Demons can imitate this gift and there have been occasions in my experience when a demon has answered me in the same tongue as I was using.

Generally, I make it a rule to stop praying after about five minutes. If the demonic force(s) haven't gone in that time, I might stop and ask whether there are any other issues that are preventing it happening and need to be resolved?

Naming of spirits

People also ask me whether it is important to name spirits in order to have authority over them. I am doubtful about this. There is some scriptural support for names of spirits eg lying spirit,[5] deaf and dumb spirit,[6] unclean spirit.[7] Whether it is really a 'name' or a revelation of what they are doing to the afflicted person, is a valid question to which I have no final answer. I would not make a rule about it. It can help the person concerned to define the area in which the spirit has been giving them trouble.

A good example is in cases involving rejection. Naming the spirit of rejection identifies the problem so that the person will be equipped to recognise rejection situations in the future, and will be able to respond appropriately, aware that they must not give in to unforgiveness and intense feelings of anger at the rejection, which the spirit could latch onto again. However, I do not ask a spirit for its name. It may well lie anyway!

What about 'manifestations'?

Manifestations are the various ways in which a demon is showing that it is present and affecting the person. They can take various forms and we need to distinguish between two main types. There are those which occur when the demon leaves the person and these might involve coughing or hard blowing, vomiting, or screaming. All these are manifestations of ejection and should not be stopped.

Other more showy examples of manifestations, sliding around the floor like snakes, for example, or shaking violently, or rolling around are just for show and I do not encourage them; if they occur, I usually tell the demon to stop.

If, for any reason, a demon does not go within a short period of time, I will generally ease things down a bit, to bring the emotional temperature to a more stable level. We should not encourage any build-up of emotions. I might stop for coffee, so that we can talk about what is happening and any entry points still remaining.

If the demon is not going, there has to be a reason and it may be that the person is hiding something. If there is sin they are unwilling to confess and repent of, then we cannot proceed further. We may counsel and arrange another time. The issue here is that we want to help Christians grow up in their faith, not just get rid of demons in their lives.

Post deliverance care

After the deliverance session, it is important to ensure that the person is taught how to walk in the freedom that they now have, free from the thoughts and influences of the past. This is an issue that is often forgotten and is the most common reason why there are further manifestations and deliverance seems to be repeatedly necessary. It is essential that people are taught how to handle their new freedom by renewing their mind instead of continuously asking for deliverance. Get rid of the demonic influence, but make sure that strongholds of thought life and/or emotions are demolished as well.

As part of this training period, they will need to understand that demons can come back. I believe that they can regain entry if the person persists in sin, allows bitterness or unforgiveness into their lives, or is not in close Christian fellowship.

This really is the key, because people who are walking free will find it easier to deal with demonic influences in their lives through prayer. An after-care programme should be maintained, ensuring that regular contact is kept with the person, building them up and standing by them to resist any further attacks from the enemy. They should be drawn into worship, fellowship and study of the Scriptures to help them come to terms with the changes in their lives. It is very important to see any deliverance from demonic power as part of the discipling process to which all Christians should be committed.

Effective Strategy Number 16: Be trained in how to set people free from demons and then get on with it without fear but with accountability.

NOTES
[1]Acts 16:16–18; [2]Luke 11: 24–26; [3]Romans 9:21; [4]1 John 1:7–9; Romans 8:1; [5]1 Kings 22:22–23; [6]Mark 9:25; [7]Mark 5:8.

Chapter 17

BUILDING THE CHURCH THE CONTEXT OF SPIRITUAL WARFARE

In an earlier chapter, I gave the following definition of spiritual warfare. '*Spiritual warfare is the reality that the advance of the gospel and the building of the church involve us in attacking and experiencing counter attacks in relation to real cosmic forces of darkness under the control of Satan.*' I have emphasised throughout this book the importance of not divorcing the issue of spiritual warfare from the pastoral and evangelistic ministry of the church.

I did a study of all the New Testament Scriptures relating to spiritual warfare and they were almost without exception in the context of the church. Let me give some examples.

The Church prevails against the Gates of Hades

Jesus himself affirmed the principle that the battle is about building the church, when He was talking to Peter one day. Jesus said that *He* would build His church and the gates of Hades would not prevail against it.[1] This puts spiritual warfare in the context of building the church. The gates of a city in the Old Testament were where the elders met, where the government of the city took place, where decisions were made, justice administered and counsel given to individual citizens. The gates of Hades (or hell) we understand to refer to the strategies and counsels of the enemy, Satan, the god of this world. It seems to suggest that the enemy's strategies are to prevent the church being built, but in this text Jesus gives us confidence that nothing will, in the end, stop the church; the enemy's strategies will fail.

I believe this teaches us two important applications of spiritual warfare:

Firstly, the whole counsels of hell stand against the church being built. I think we can see many ways in which this works out in practice. Imagine a major evangelistic effort is being made in your town. All the churches are mobilised, a gifted reaping evangelist is booked to come. Counsellors are trained to know how to lead people to Christ. Even more importantly, many prayer meetings are called to beseech God to work through the evangelistic mission so that many will be saved. As we pray, we will be consciously involved in warfare that the counsels of hell will be defeated and that the Lord will rebuke the efforts of Satan to keep people in bondage. Then the mission takes place. Usually, we are encouraged by seeing people 'make commitments to Jesus Christ'; in some parts of the world where there is more openness to the gospel, hundreds or thousands of people may flock to the front or fill in a response card. This is great; it is what we prayed for. We then take a break because of exhaustion and return to our normal lives.

However, there is a problem which in our excitement we may not even notice! Very few of those converts are added to any of our local churches. We organise follow-up but we are a bit too weary to put much effort into it. What has happened? The church is not being built. That was the enemy's strategy. In some parts of the world, we hear of huge evangelistic campaigns with virtually no impact on the subsequent size of local churches. Sometimes people have described the flow of an evangelistic awakening in parts of Africa as being like a river which is very broad (many get swept in), but also very shallow because there is insufficient discipling of new converts. Please do not misunderstand me. I rejoice in the way that God is moving in Africa; I wish it were happening in England. I have seen myself, with my limited personal experience, that building strong, accountable, discipling churches even in parts of the world where God is moving powerfully can be very difficult. The point is that God is committed to building His church: the enemy wants to stop it. Surely the focus of our prayer should not just be the success of the evangelistic mission. After it is over, our prayers and efforts should re-double. Warfare prayer does not end at the mission. Let us pray that churches are built as Jesus promised.

The early church understood this. In the book of Acts they did not even count people until they were 'added to their number'.[2] What counted was that people were added to the church, the corporate expression on earth of the life of God, the body of Christ, the new community, the one new man in Christ. This should be the focus of our prayers, our mission, and our warfare.

The second consequence is the flip side of all this. It means that what the counsels of hell fear is the building of the church. Satan knows the Scriptures. He knows that as the church is built, his schemes cannot prevail. So let us start churches in all the dark areas in our land! That is warfare. People often say such and such an estate, or town, or rural area is so dark. Let us start churches there or at least plant cells of God's people in these places. That, I would suggest, is a more biblical form of spiritual warfare than 'praying on the high places' around those towns or villages. Obviously, of course, church planting must proceed from, and be accompanied by, fervent prayer – but when you are in such a pioneering situation praying is what you will tend to do!

Spiritual warfare and the church in Ephesians

Another example of the context of spiritual warfare being the church is in the letter to the church at Ephesus. Paul speaks of the role of the church in the purposes of God. He gives the doctrinal background in the first half of this letter, where he describes the church as a family, the household of God, a temple where the presence of God is to dwell.[3] He speaks of it as one new man in Christ and as the 'fullness of Him who fills everything in every way'.[4] His prayers are for the church and he stresses that our power to understand the fullness of the love of Christ is to be for all of God's people.[5] There is a hint of spiritual warfare in the doctrinal part of this epistle when Paul declares that God's intention is to demonstrate His multi-coloured wisdom to the principalities and powers, and explains how that is to be done – yes, you've got it *through the church*.[6]

In the second half of the letter, Paul applies this doctrinal teaching to the actual life of the church. Chapter 4 describes how the church is to be brought to unity and maturity through the equipping ministry of its leaders, apostles, prophets, evangelists, pastors and teachers.[7] He then deals with the appropriate ethical behaviour necessary for the church to be what it is called to be in God's purposes. Even his teaching on marriage draws from the parallel of the relationship of Jesus to His bride, the church. It is in this context, that we come to the famous classic passage on spiritual warfare. 'Finally, be strong in the Lord and in His mighty power. Put on the full armour of God so that you can take your stand against the devil's schemes. For our struggle is not against flesh and blood, but against the rulers, against the authorities, against the powers of this dark world and against the spiritual forces of evil in the heavenly realms.'[8] This is a corporate command addressed to the church as a body; it explains what we should do *together* to stand firm against the efforts of the enemy to corrupt us and drive us off course.

When, he talks about the shield of faith he is talking about the large Roman shield. In the Roman army, two thirds of the shield itself covered the body of the man that carried it. The other third covered part of the man next to him. So, when a line of soldiers stood together and presented their shields, they formed an impenetrable barrier that not only protected the soldiers carrying the shields, but swept all before it as they moved forward. The image that Paul seems to be creating here is that though the shield of faith seems to be a defensive weapon, it is designed to be used corporately by the church to protect it while it attacks the enemy's lines. Sometimes it is claimed that this armour is only defensive. This can give the impression that Christians are sitting back waiting in the shelter of their fortress for Satan's attack. As Hendrickson comments, 'The context does not allow this rather common interpretation. The "standing" of which Paul speaks is not that of a brick wall that is waiting passively, as it were, for the assault of the battering ram. The soldiers referred to here are drawn up in battle array and rushing into the fight. They are both defending themselves and attacking. . . . It may be regarded as a trite saying, but it is true nevertheless, that the best defence is an offence. All of Paul's missionary journeys may be regarded as manifestations of offensive warfare. Paul was invading the territory which heretofore had been the devil's own.'[9]

Other warfare passages

Another familiar warfare passage is Peter's reference to the devil prowling round like a roaring lion seeking someone to devour.[10] This Scripture, too, is in the context of the church, specifically the relationship between elders of the church and young men. This relationship could be an easy prey to the devil seeking to destroy the church. Peter goes on to talk about the worldwide church suffering as it resists enemy attack. Again, he is talking about spiritual warfare in the context of building the church.

We have already looked at the Scripture about demolishing strongholds in 2 Corinthians 10. Again, Paul's concern is that the church should not be infiltrated by deceitful false teachers who look good on the surface, so-called super-apostles, who question and try to undermine Paul's authority and teaching. Here again, spiritual warfare is discussed in the context of Paul's concern for the church. He continues in the next chapter to speak about these false apostles, saying his only motive in withstanding them is that he has promised the church as a pure virgin to Christ.[11]

In the same letter Paul explains the need to be aware of the enemy's schemes and plans, telling the people of Corinth that they need to be ready to act to outwit the enemy and prevent him outwitting them.[12] The context is the issue of forgiveness in the church. One of Satan's strategies is to produce an atmosphere of unforgiveness in the church, which will undermine its effectiveness.

Spiritual warfare in Acts

I believe we also see the importance of the church as the context for spiritual warfare in the book of Acts. This book can be viewed from the perspective of describing the acts of the Holy Spirit in enabling the triumphant spread of the gospel across the Roman world and the establishment of the church in many cities, towns and rural areas as a radical alternative community of faith. Another perspective, however, is that it exposes the strategy of the enemy in seeking to undermine the church and thus hinder the spread of the gospel. It almost seems that when each tactic failed, Satan had another up his sleeve to throw at the young church.

First came outward opposition and persecution from the

Jewish authorities. This resulted in the believers turning to powerful prayer[13] and speaking the Word of God even more boldly. This enemy tactic misfired and the church grew.[14]

Next, the enemy tried the strategy of inward corruption. Ananias and Sapphira were enticed by Satan (indeed, as we have seen, filled by him) to lie.[15] Furthermore the issue on which they lied related to one of the greatest evidences of the grace of God on the early church, which demonstrated its credentials as a loving, radical community, caring for the poor. This was the willingness of richer members to sell land and goods so that there could be no needy person among them.[16] It was an insidious, demonically inspired attack on the church and its credibility.

When this failed the enemy tried division by causing grumbling between two groups of widows about who was being cared for best. This tactic had the side-benefit (from the devil's point of view) of diverting the leaders from their main task.[17] When this failed, again the church grew as the issue was handled with Holy Spirit inspired wisdom.

The enemy then threw wholesale persecution at them.[18] But far from destroying the church, this resulted in the believers scattering and the gospel spreading out of Jerusalem and Judea far and wide and eventually reaching the Gentiles.

This constitutes a blueprint of the enemy's strategies of which Paul reminds us we should not be ignorant, and which has been repeated many times in church history. Opposition, persecution, corruption, division and diversion of leaders from their main calling remain issues of warfare today. Let us face them as the early church did, and overcome our enemy.

Consequences of the link between spiritual warfare and the church

We need to take very seriously this scriptural emphasis that the context of spiritual warfare is the building of the church. I can see no scriptural support for separating spiritual warfare from this context and am concerned when I see this happening. The link between spiritual warfare and building the church has a number of consequences:

Firstly, it is important to have clear teaching on this, teaching that is supported by a clear authority structure, particularly when dealing with the demonic in people's lives. This should not be relegated to the work of a few specialists. It is sadly true that issues like spiritual warfare, intercession and dealing with the demonic tend to attract people who can only be described as 'weird'. If these issues are maintained as part of the corporate life of the church, appropriate training can be given and the situation managed to ensure that only those people best qualified to handle this task actually get involved. I am concerned that sometimes churches do not teach and train in this area because of concern about 'extremes'. The result can be that people in those particular churches then become so desperate for freedom, that they go elsewhere for help, sometimes to those very same specialists that the church leaders feel are 'extreme'!

Secondly, we can establish from all this that pioneering work in any situation will involve spiritual warfare. If you read through the life of the early church, there were counter-attacks in almost every situation where the gospel was being advanced.

So it should come as no surprise to us if we are confronted by demonic attack in any form of church pioneering work. Involvement in any of the following is almost guaranteed to bring a counter-attack:

- Winning the first converts
- Getting the first converts established in the church as disciples
- Winning the first converts in any new area of the church's expansion

- Establishing effective team leadership
- Developing new teaching and training courses.

Recognising this enables us to plan, pray and effectively counter the enemy's strategies.

Practical examples

Let me give a few examples of what I mean from my own experience.

I remember in the first years of our church, my friend John Callow and I used to meet every Saturday night. We prayed people into the service the next morning and battled for new converts. We did this virtually every Saturday night for about 2 years until we began to see the breakthrough described right at the beginning of this book.

As I mentioned in the first chapter, several years ago I developed a *Caring and Healing Course* that was designed to train people to do the regular work of deliverance and healing so that I could be set free to do other things. I had no idea at the time that the course would prove to be very effective both nationally and internationally. I explained how, in developing that course we received 'kickbacks' in our family life.

What I did not mention before was that we had a similar experience when I first initiated a Bible School at Woodside Church a little while later. This was not a course on which I was teaching about spiritual warfare or the demonic. My purpose was to ensure that all who so desired could be taught a basic systematic theology. 'Is that warfare?' you might ask. Yes, enabling people to have a clear understanding of truth is one of the best things we can do to help them stand against Satan's attacks. Furthermore, God had plans that I had no idea about. Soon afterwards, I was asked to put together the theological element of a training scheme for people in our New Frontiers

Churches who wanted to give a year to God to be trained. The Woodside Bible School became the basis of this training syllabus, which has now trained many young (and not so young!) people over many years.

Battle for team leadership

Another example concerns the issue of the team leadership. I have noticed that a number of leaders find that building a 'peer-level' leadership team is one of the biggest challenges of their leadership ability. (Sadly, it is also true for many others who do not actually notice it!). I believe the enemy is set against it because it is the divine pattern of church government (elders in the plural) and mission. Jesus sent out the twelve, two by two.[19] Paul would not take advantage of an open door for a mission in Troas because his team was not there.[20]

A friend of mine found himself confronted with such a situation. He had pioneered a new church but as he tried to establish a leadership team, deep tensions suddenly developed between those involved. I am sure there was fault on both sides, but we need to recognise in such situations that it is not against 'flesh and blood' (ie one another) that we are fighting. Eventually, the other potential team members left him. It was very sad but he started again to build a new team with people who had previously stood with him. To my amazement, the enemy got in again between people who had seemed so close and who shared a common vision. I am sure my friend had to learn things regarding his own character, but I warned him that it was now a real test to his leadership call and that it should take top priority in his praying and his leadership strategy. Praise God, he did then build a successful team, but the whole story illustrated spiritual warfare to me in a way that is not always popularly discerned.

Many Christians get negative about spiritual warfare and

complain that they are always under attack. But it is the church, not the enemy, which initiates spiritual warfare! The kingdom of God advances forcefully, and forceful people take hold of it.[21] So although Satan's reactions to that may involve us in spiritual warfare, he is responding to the advance of the gospel and the kingdom of God and building of the church. It is important that we grasp this. Let us free ourselves of a negative perspective of a church under attack and waiting with a 'hold the fort' siege mentality until Jesus rescues us at his second coming. No, the church is to be released to be the powerful agent of the kingdom, the kingdom that belongs to the One of whom it is said, 'Of the increase of His government . . . there will be no end.'[22]

The battle against legalism

There is one final battle in the context of building the church that we must cover. This is the battle for grace against legalism. Legalism has two aspects: it regards the keeping of certain laws as necessary for salvation, and also the means of our continued acceptance by God and one another. Many churches around the world today bind upon people all sorts of legalistic practices, which are not required in Scripture. These may relate to the way we dress, what jewellery we can wear, hairstyles, the way we take communion (eg insisting it is unleavened bread), and what we are allowed to do on Sundays. It may be accompanied by very inflexible church services, which do not allow the freedom of the Holy Spirit, and also the creation of an elite of 'approved' people who somehow manage (externally at least) to keep all the rules. I know; I was brought up in such a system.

The Bible makes it clear that there are evil spirits behind legalism. Paul refers to it as 'doctrines of demons' in the context of his opposition to food laws or forbidding people to marry.[23] Speaking of the cross, Paul writes, 'Having disarmed the powers and authorities [ie demonic forces], He made a public spectacle of them, triumphing over them by the cross. Therefore do not let anyone judge you by what you eat or drink. . . . Since you died with Christ to the basic principles of this world [these may be translated – 'elemental spirits'] why, as though you still belonged to it, do you submit to its rules?'[24] Paul thus moves straight from the truth of the triumph of the cross to the battle against legalism.

Paul develops this teaching particularly in the Epistle to Galatians. Galatians is a warfare epistle. Paul is endeavouring to wrest his converts back from the enemy, back onto grace from legalism. Notice his language. 'Who has bewitched you?'[25] 'Bewitched', 'Paul – what are you saying?' 'Witchcraft?' This is strong language, but appropriately so. Legalism robs us of our inheritance of enjoying God's grace now. The enemy binds us up. Christ sets us free for freedom.[26] We need today to wage war against legalism in the church and the enemy's strategies behind it, as strongly as Paul did.

Effective Strategy Number 17: Recognise that the most effective way of overcoming the enemy hold in an area is to build the church there, with the clear understanding, however, that the enemy will oppose such a venture, so we must be prepared.

NOTES

[1]Matthew 16:18; [2]Acts 2:47; [3]Ephesians 2:19–22; [4]Ephesians 2:15, Ephesians 1:23; [5]Ephesians 3:18; [6]Ephesians 3:10; [7]Ephesians 4:11–13; [8]Ephesians 6:10–12; [9]*New Testament Commentary on Galatians & Ephesians,* Hendrickson, page 273–274; [10]1 Peter 5:8; [11]2 Corinthians 11:2; [12]2 Corinthians 2:11; [13]Acts 4:24–30; [14]Acts 6:7; [15]Acts 5:3; [16]Acts 4:34; [17]Acts 6:2–4; [18]Acts 8:1; [19]Mark 6:7; [20]2 Corinthians 2:12–13; [21]Matthew 11:12; [22]Isaiah 9:7; [23]1 Timothy 4:1–3; [24]Colossians 2:15–20; [25]Galatians 3:1; [26]Galatians 5:1.

Chapter 18

STRONGHOLDS IN THE LOCAL CHURCH

For a church to be effective in spiritual warfare and in advancing the gospel it is important that its foundations are godly and that there are no footholds that the enemy can use as entry points into its corporate life. If this is not the situation, the church will find it almost impossible to progress towards its goal or fulfil its corporate vision. Footholds that the enemy can use as entry points are usually found in strongholds that have either been established in the foundations of the church, or have been introduced at a time of major change. Strongholds can exist in institutions and corporate bodies such as churches as well as in individuals. Our western mind-set does not always recognise this.

The importance of good foundations

Although we would like to think that a church is built on the basis of a godly vision, that is not always the case. When a new church is founded there can be strongholds in its foundation that become built into the corporate life of the church, and are sometimes not recognised until the church has already grown to a reasonable size. They may be related to the reason why the church's founders left their previous situations and started up the new work. Sometimes they are only identified after a number of years of inadequate corporate church life.

The foundations of any building determine the character of the building, so if a church is founded on ungodly issues, these issues can become a seat of wrong spiritual power there. The effect is usually that as people join the church, the particular spiritual force in its life also influences them.

Earlier in the book I told the story of a pastor in Haiti.[1] This story was about a literal building and its foundation but it illustrates what can happen in the spiritual foundation of a spiritual building, a local church. They cleared an ungodly altar out of the way, before God told them that they could erect the building. It is just the same with any work that we build in Jesus' name. God does not want any work built on an ungodly foundation

A similar thing can happen at a point of major change in the life of the church. If a change is made for ungodly reasons, strongholds can be established that will become entry points for the enemy. Similarly, if a change is strongly resisted so that a church does not move forward in the purposes of God, further entry points can occur and new strongholds can be established.

It is important that anyone involved in pioneering leadership is building on godly foundations with a God-given vision for the work. Their record under the leadership of others should be examined, because this can be an area where pioneers have difficulty. If they have been unable to submit to godly authority, they will find it difficult to build team values and mutual submission into the leadership of the work they are pioneering.

There are a number of issues that might be identified as strongholds or entry points for the enemy and it is not unusual to find that more than one exists in a particular church. The following examples are all based on situations I have been asked to deal with on a number of occasions.

• *Bitterness*

This is often a foundational issue and is usually the result of some sort of enmity. Bitterness can affect the character of a church if it has come into existence in reaction to hurt in other situations. When the hurt has not been dealt with and leaders have not repented of their wrong reactions before the church is started, a stronghold may develop. This bitterness can grow and becomes a characteristic of the church, affecting everyone who becomes involved in it. We have to be careful to start churches out of positive vision and not out of reaction to something of which we do not approve.

The author of the book of Hebrews tells us to ensure that no-one misses the grace of God and that no bitter root grows up that will defile many.[2] It is my experience that when bitterness has infected the foundations of a church (or creeps into a group of people at a time of major change or advance), it gives such a strong foothold for the enemy that it can lead to almost any sin. It hinders both the unity of the church and the advance of the gospel.

• *Rebellion*

Again, this is often a foundational issue where there is a leader who is not able to work things out in the church that he came from because of a problem with submission. The leader starts a new work and the church grows because of his charismatic leadership skills, but it is founded in rebellion and this will keep appearing in the new work because it has formed an entry point for a source of wrong spiritual power.

I believe in many new churches being started. Our nation and all the nations need more churches for the sake of those who do not know Jesus. I do not have too many problems with people coming out of an existing church to start another. A lot of churches start this way when the existing church refuses to accept the moving of the Holy Spirit, for example. However, if the church has been started from a place of rebellion and not from a call to start a new church, this can lead to problems. These can involve frequent splits occurring, a lack of respect for leadership and a lack of clarity in leadership.

• *Division*

Another foundational issue is where churches are based on division, because the leaders could not get on in their previous churches or perhaps had ambitions for 'ministry' that others did not recognise. I do not know what the situation is in other countries, but in the UK there are small charismatic groups that keep splintering instead of growing because division is in their foundations. I want to see lots of churches started, but on the basis of vision, not *di*vision, because where they are founded in division, they will just divide and divide. Sometimes the division can be perceived by the founders as a positive step. A church may have been planted out because the four elders in the parent church were not able to agree, so they thought that the best way to resolve the situation would be to plant out a new church and divide the elders between the two. They believed that this would resolve all the problems and that they would be seen to be a forward looking 'church planting' church! Needless to say, the church that was planted out would be very insecure on such an unstable foundation.

• *Domineering or manipulating leadership*

This is often the result of a particularly dominant leader, where there is little delegation and people are not released into their ministry. A leader could be good at gathering people but unable to train and release them into service. The leader may be insecure and unwilling for others to 'overtake' him in God.

As we have said before, the essence of witchcraft is control and where this occurs in a church, there will be a foundation of control and manipulation. It sometimes amazes me that Paul included witchcraft amongst the works of the flesh when writing to Christians.[3] In a situation like this, hardly anyone is ever released to do anything. The extreme form of this is a Jezebel spirit and this can be exercised either by a leader who leads manipulatively, or by a group within the church manipulating the leadership. I have already dealt with this in Chapter 12.

• *Humanistic teaching*

In some churches there may be good teaching on basic theology but there can be humanistic teaching in relation to other issues, such as family life or counselling. The result of this is a church where everyone has their own opinion, and it is impossible to challenge or confront people on personal issues.

• *Democratic or committee-based leadership*

I do not believe democracy to be an appropriate foundation for the exercise of spiritual authority. It is the Holy Spirit who appoints people to leadership.[4] It is Jesus who gives leaders to His church.[5]

Committee based leadership is not a team, but a gathering of people who represent specific interest groups within the church or specific departments of church life. If democracy is in the foundation of the church, it becomes very difficult for leaders to lead and each major step forward may be challenged. Some churches may not be democratic by constitution, but may have insidious spiritual forces at work whereby leaders are constantly challenged by 'special interest' groups or 'family connections'.

• *Sexual Immorality*

It concerns me deeply that there are churches that have sexual immorality in their foundations, often in the leadership. It is always deceitful, and usually works through manipulation. The Jezebel spirit is often influential in this situation, which may take two or three years to identify. Sometimes it only comes to light when we look into the background of a church and it is possible to see the effects of the manipulation.

I have found that sexual immorality frequently leads to a spate of similar incidents in a church before it is identified in the leadership. So where there is a leader who is involved in homosexual activity, there is likely to be an outbreak of homosexual or lesbian activity in the church before it is identified in the leader.

Similarly, if a leader is in an adulterous relationship then the church can be characterised by a spate of adultery, flirtatious behaviour, a lack of clarity relating to boundaries in relationships between the sexes and no guidelines for cross-sex counselling, with the result that unclean spirits can be at work.

I remember a situation where there was a breakout of sexual immorality amongst the young people of a church. The situation was finally resolved through the discovery of uncleanness in some of the young people's leaders which was not found out until later.

• *Relationship breakdown*

Sometimes there may be a close emotional dependency occurring within a group of people who are significant in the life of the church. This dependency can result in people becoming so close that they have an almost exclusive relationship. They become such good friends that the relationship is no longer a healthy one. Something goes wrong and the people fall out with each other.

Relationship breakdown like this arises from a work of the flesh, but the enemy may exploit it so that it occupies a lot of leadership time to the exclusion of other work. It is very hard to deal with and can involve a lot of people, drawing them in to take sides. This situation requires prayer to resolve it and a determination not to let the situation become all consuming.

Dealing with strongholds in the local church

As with all other strongholds, several options may be appropriate in handling the situation. I have become involved with helping churches to sort out such issues a number of times.

Basically, what I do is to discuss the situation with the leaders and often with the people in the church as well. I look out for patterns of church life and problems that keep repeating themselves. Obviously a prophetic gift of discernment is necessary and it is good for more than one person from outside the church to be involved. Any leader in sin who is still in position (or even around on the scene somewhere) will need to be confronted and appropriately disciplined.

The church should then be taught on the principles of strongholds in the life of the church and on the relevant issues in their own church life. It would be a mistake to confront without first giving clear teaching. The church should then be called together and invited to join in renouncing the strongholds. We would then pray for them to be released and again teach on what it means to live out corporate church life in freedom. What we are actually looking for here is for the church to agree to no longer go down that path but to see the stronghold broken in the power of the name of Jesus.

I have to say this will only be necessary in more serious cases. In other cases all that is required is a leadership which understands the issues and which gives relevant teaching on the specific issues involved. In all cases, it is important that after the issues are dealt with, the leaders should lead firmly but gently, confronting in love any further manifestations of the former stronghold as they may arise.

Effective Strategy Number 18: Recognise that there can be corporate strongholds in church life which need to be discerned and overcome in order for our churches to be effective against the enemy.

NOTES

[1]Chapter 2; [2]Hebrews 12:15; [3]Galatians 5:19–20; [4]Acts 20:28; [5]Ephesians 4:11–13.

Chapter 19

SPIRITUAL WARFARE AND CHURCH LEADERSHIP

A survey carried out by *Christianity Today* a few years ago, amongst leaders in the church, indicated that, of those who replied, 12% had had sexual intercourse with people who they related to in ministry, and 18% had indulged in fondling, passionate kissing or mutual masturbation.[1] This was in the USA, but the same story can be repeated all over the world, though the exact statistics may differ.

I have already referred twice in this book to the first letter of Peter, where he talks to leaders and to the young men who are working with them and warns them that the devil prowls around like a roaring lion, seeking someone to devour.[2] This is a warning that all leaders should take seriously. In particular, those involved in pioneering work of any kind, need to watch out for the enemy redoubling his efforts to undermine what they are doing.

Leaders may face a number of problems that will cause pain, heartache and apparent delay, absorb a lot of time and energy and cause us to experience frustration. When we are facing frustration we need to watch our vulnerabilities. In extreme cases they could lead to sin. I do not want to exaggerate the spiritual warfare dimension of a leader's work. It is important that we keep in balance the three factors referred to in Chapter 3, namely submission to the sovereignty of God and recognition of our personal responsibility as well as being aware of the work of the enemy. Having said that, we face an implacable foe, who is determined to undermine our leadership if at all possible.

Christian leadership is a glorious privilege, but also an awesome responsibility for which we have to give an account to God.[3] It is by anointing and appointing leaders that God ensures His purposes are fulfilled. Throughout Scripture, nothing much happens unless an anointed leader is appointed to lead God's people. The people of God in Egypt, for example, though they were crying out to God to be rescued, did not just decide to leave. It required a leader, Moses, to be trained and commissioned. The book of Judges illustrates how the people of God declined into spiritual lethargy and even idolatry, except for those times when God intervened and raised up leaders to save them from their enemies and bring them back to dependence on God. So obviously the devil will target leaders.

Paul might be thought today to be somewhat extreme when he says, 'Therefore I do not run like a man running aimlessly; I do not fight like a man beating the air. No, I beat my body and make it my slave'.[4] His reason however is clear, 'So that after I have preached to others, I myself will not be disqualified for the prize.' I suggest that we leaders now need to have the same determination not to let the enemy trip us up.

It is often said that the enemy particularly targets leaders in three main areas: sex, money and power. To deal with all the challenges to leaders would take a book in itself! But I must cover a number of areas.

1. The challenge of sexual purity

Are leaders not aware that they are in a battle? Is Satan going to turn round on Sunday and say, 'Poor guy, he's worked so hard preaching all morning and evening as well, we'll give him a break tonight'? Of course he's not. So how can a leader presume to worship God and preach on a Sunday morning and then go home to watch an immoral film on Sunday evening?

Look at what happened to Elijah after he overcame the prophets of Baal and slaughtered four hundred of them. Did Jezebel hold back for a while? Did she say, 'Oh dear. Let's give Elijah a break. He's destroyed all those priests and worked so hard praying to his God to see fire descend on the sacrifice'? Of course she didn't. Her anger consumed her, and she attacked Elijah straight away before he had a chance to rest and recover.

We are in a battle here, just as Elijah was then, and we cannot afford to drop our guard for one moment. The dangers are too great. Leaders are particularly vulnerable when they have been doing well like Elijah. If we have preached on Sunday evenings, we need to wind down. We can then be vulnerable. I remember meeting a pastor who was seeing God work very powerfully, transforming people's lives and the worship and ministry in the church. The Sunday evenings were particularly good times, when God was evidently present in their gatherings. After Sunday evening, he felt so 'high', that he regularly went round to visit a particular lady rather than go home to the routine of family life. You can guess what happened. He fell into immorality and had to step down from his leadership at such a crucial time in the life of the church.

I have already referred to Jezebel and sexual strongholds earlier, so I will not go back over that ground now. However, I keep hearing of leaders in trouble or having to stand down from ministry as a result of these problems and it hurts when people say, 'There goes another one!' 'Another one bites the dust.' It is painful. We *have* to walk with integrity on this issue. How can leaders demolish strongholds in other people's lives if they are walking dishonestly in their own?

As I travel around, I never cease to be amazed at the numbers of church leaders who confess to me personal bondages involving pornography, particularly when I preach on sexual strongholds. I have had to handle it in my own church too. This is a serious issue. Francis Frangipane writes, 'There are respectable men who love God and seek to serve him, yet secretly in their hearts they are prisoners of Jezebel. Even now they are usually deeply ashamed of their bondage to pornography; and they can barely control their desires for women. Ask them to pray and their spirits are awash with guilt and shame. Their prayers are but the whimpers of Jezebel's eunuchs.'[5] These are strong words.

Leaders need to have clear guidance for their lives including the following:

- Avoidance of one-to-one situations with anyone who is influenced by a Jezebel spirit.
- Avoidance of one-to-one cross-sex counselling.
- Accountability times with the leadership team, where full and frank questions are asked about temptations, how things are going in their marriages – both generally and in the sexual area. The book of Proverbs is quite blunt about the necessity for good sexual relationships in our marriages as preservation against temptation.[6] Accountability structures must be in place in any leadership team, and will require open and honest participation if they are to be effective.
- Try to avoid travelling to distant venues and other nations on your own.
- Have times when husband and wife can share openly about their relationship, with somebody in whom they both have confidence.
- Speak in tongues and/or invoke the name of Jesus when you are facing temptation.

- Learn where the 'off' button is on the TV set and use it!
- Ensure your computer has a program which screens out sexual references and images from the Internet.

I recognise that I have focused up to now on leaders who have 'full-time' or preaching ministries. Before I was in 'full-time' Christian ministry, I was serving the kingdom as a senior manager in international banking. I spent seventy to eighty days per year overseas and I understand the temptations found in these circumstances. A couple of stories may be helpful to illustrate what I am talking about for those who are facing similar pressures.

I was with a group of men in a part of Africa where it is quite dangerous to go out at night – certainly alone. I was not leading the party and the leader of the party, who was from another company, had responsibility for the car and its driver. After we had been out for a meal, he laughed and said that we were going to visit a particular brothel where he had been for a drink before. I protested and asked to be taken back to the hotel first. My protests were unavailing as everybody in the car thought it was a good joke to take me there. They were obviously aware of my Christian stance. In the car I prayed like mad. When we got to the venue, the 'madam' said that there was a party for air force officers at the airport and all the girls had gone there. I still do not know exactly what I would have done but I know that God would have found a way out for me, as I prayed and really did engage in spiritual warfare.

Now for a very different illustration. I remember picking up a book at Heathrow airport on my way out to Algeria. The book was a thriller about high finance and therefore interested me. I was staying in a Soviet built hotel in Algeria with huge bedrooms. I came to a point in the book where I realised that the unexpected sexual detail on that page was not going to do me any good. I remember throwing the book with all my force as far as I could to the other side of this massive bedroom. I never picked it up again. You do have to be drastic in resisting temptation.

2. *The challenge of power*

When Jesus sent out the seventy-two, they returned to him full of stories of how they had authority over demons. His response was that they should not rejoice in that, but instead they should rejoice that their names were written in heaven.[7] In other words, they were to rejoice in the work of God's grace in saving them, rather than in anything they themselves had achieved in terms of warfare victory.

Just occasionally, I have been speaking in a meeting when I have known such an anointing that I have been able to prophesy and pray over each person in the room. At such times, I felt that I could do or say anything and it would just happen. It does not happen to me that often, however, because I do not normally work at that sort of level; but this is dangerous territory. You can get such a buzz under the anointing that you start going for that, and not for the glory of God. It is important that we learn how to handle the anointing. Accountability is a strong antidote, so is team ministry instead of one-man ministry.

In new churches today, considerably more trust is given to leaders. Thank God, they are given freedom to lead. Peter Wagner records the worldwide phenomenon of this new style of churches in his book *Churchquake*.[8] This is a very positive development. However, the corollary is that we must learn to handle authority and power in a godly way. We may no longer have diaconates or church committees whose attitude is 'Lord you keep him humble, we'll keep him poor!' We therefore have to build in new safeguards, remembering that a crucial part of Satan's original fall, and therefore a prime weapon of his armoury, which he has had millennia of practice in using, is the temptation to pride and misuse of authority. Safeguards we need to build in against this temptation include:

- Genuine servant leadership. Paul's wonderful description of Jesus taking the form of a servant, not seeing power and glory as something to be held onto,[9] is used as a lesson for the church but is even more applicable to leaders.
- Again, teamwork and not one-man ministry. However, this must be where team is genuine peer level relationship and accountability, rather than the dictatorial school of team leadership that says, 'I decide – my team do it'.
- A passion for the well-being of those you serve and a willingness to suffer for them.

3. The challenge of Jesus' wilderness temptations

Jesus faced three challenges from the enemy when He was tempted in the wilderness. Obviously there is much about that story which is unique to Jesus. He was the second Adam, coming to overcome where the first Adam fell. Nevertheless, there are lessons in the temptations for us:

- The temptation to turn stones into bread illustrates the danger of using our anointing for our own advantage, when God has not given permission. In using our anointing we must ensure that we live by 'every word that comes from God's mouth'.[10]
- Satan took Jesus onto a high mountain and showed Him all the nations of the world.[11] Jesus had been promised the nations. This is spoken of prophetically in Psalm 2. The temptation here, however, was to achieve the promise without the cross. For our part, we can be tempted to try to achieve God's promises for our lives and ministries without the cost.

- Jesus was also tempted to jump from the top of the temple to see whether the angels caught Him. It is a temptation in the charismatic movement to use anointing for entertainment and the spectacular. Power ministry is particularly vulnerable to this testing.

4. The challenge of pioneering

As I have pointed out repeatedly in this book, pioneering work of any kind is usually met by a high level of enemy resistance. The enemy always resists *any* advance into his territory, but we tend as leaders to forget that, and are often surprised when we meet resistance.

Yet, as we read through the gospels or the book of Acts, we see that it happens all the time. From the start of Jesus' ministry, when He was faced with the devil's personal challenges, through to Paul's ministry, whenever he went anywhere new, the attacks occurred. As we have seen, when Paul went to Cyprus, he was met by a sorcerer; when he went to Philippi, it was a slave girl with a fortune telling spirit; and in Corinth he seems to have fallen into a demoralising depression until God appeared to him in a vision to explain that He had a large number of people in the city.

I have also known many examples in my own church life, as I have already related. The first time ever I gave teaching on strongholds was at Stoneleigh Bible Week in 1994. We went on holiday immediately afterwards to a campsite in Italy. At around midnight one night, our daughter, Justine, suffered a burst appendix and had to be rushed to hospital. Furthermore, Scilla and I had been married for nearly twenty-five years, but following my teaching on sexual strongholds and Jezebel, we experienced an attack in the sexual area of our marriage relationship, an area in which we had never had any problems before. After a few weeks, we asked some other couples in leadership to pray for us and things were fine again.

I do not want us to indulge in self-fulfilling prophecy, so that we expect the worst and consequently find it! However, I do want to urge that we are aware of the enemy's strategies and are prepared to take remedial action.

5. *The challenge of diversionary tactics*

This can occur at whatever leadership level we are functioning and is a particular ploy against the leaders of a church. For example, where a new corporate strategy for the church has been planned by the elders for the next year, they will have a vision for the strategy, God will have spoken prophetically to them concerning the venture, and they will be ready to start planning. Or, at another level of leadership, it might be a venture like a new cell group being planted out from an existing cell. The enemy loves to divert people right at this strategic moment, to absorb all the leaders' time and energies into dead-end situations. A common problem here is a difficult pastoral situation designed to drain all the leader's energies (whether pastor or cell leader).

In the elders' meetings at our church, we try to ensure that pastoral issues are left to the end of the meeting, because if we start on them at the beginning, we will not get anything else done.

In a cell group situation, it might be a member who has a particularly demanding set of problems. It is important in this situation to be aware of two sorts of people. These are:

- *The person with problems,* who will want to get their problems dealt with so that they can get on with their lives. This will be time well spent, even though it might be demanding, because as soon as the problems are resolved, they will not need so much support.
- *The problem person,* who will absorb all the leader's time, energy and attention, but nothing will ever be resolved.

It is important that these two different situations are recognised and dealt with appropriately. It is also noticeable that demanding pastoral issues often come in 'waves', rather than occasional single events. It is important then that the leadership stand firm, deal carefully with each situation without panic but also call each other to prayer so that Satan's disruptive efforts are frustrated. We need to call upon the Lord to rebuke Satan to stop his attacks on the church in this way.

A similar problem occurs with interpersonal disputes. These occur when two close friends fall out with each other. It always occurs suddenly, without warning, and can involve the two people we were planning to rely on for the venture that we are pioneering!

Another issue that can absorb a lot of time and energy is special interest groups with their own personal agendas. They want their particular interests to become the focus of the church and a lot of time can be wasted by leaders attempting to justify their refusal to adopt the group's agenda.

6. The challenge of busyness

A difficult issue to resolve is that of excessive busyness, because sometimes the reasons seem to be outside our control. This is characterised by everything exploding all at once, perhaps in our secular jobs, just as we are about to do something significant for the Lord, like starting a new cell. Invariably this sort of thing just 'happens' because the enemy wants to divert our attention. We do need to cover these situations in prayer as well if the busyness is undermining the will of God for us and our family life. We may also need to take specific action in our jobs, because sometimes the amount of time required of us can become an ungodly demand.

7. Issues from the past

Perhaps the most painful attacks occur when things in our personal background, family upbringing or culture suddenly rise to the surface just as we are about to take on new responsibilities.

We have had to deal with this on a number of occasions recently in our own church, with people who were moving into leadership situations. Just at that moment an unresolved issue in their lives rose to the surface and the enemy got hold of it.

What tends to happen is that the attack is not recognised as such because it just presents itself as an overwhelming problem that happens to have arisen. It needs to be recognised as the enemy's strategy, then time needs to be taken to resolve it, linked with a determination not to allow it to affect the advance of the work of the kingdom. The trouble is that when this happens, the person concerned so often feels demoralised, unable to continue or unworthy. In this sort of situation, I have learnt to encourage them to look behind it and see what is really happening, and we try to resolve the issue without taking them out of the battle. Some do want to take a break, but my feeling is that, if God has allowed it to come to the surface, His timing should be respected and the experience used in order to help the person mature, rather than retreat from responsibility and allow the enemy, to that extent, to gain the advantage.

8. Personal attacks

Other direct personal attacks at crucial times can include sickness (sometimes mysterious, without an obvious medical diagnosis); sickness in children; a child being bullied at school, falling out with a teacher, or being treated unfairly. Sometimes it might be that a child suddenly feels very insecure. The difficulty is that these kinds of issues so often occur at a vulnerable time, when we are seeking to advance the kingdom.

Personal criticisms against our own integrity can be particularly difficult to handle, because they can bring to light our own insecurities. I have known situations where a really effective leader has been criticised, or even has absorbed perceived criticism that has not actually occurred, and it has put them out of action for months.

We need to learn how to handle criticism, especially as it usually occurs during a time of vulnerability, and learn to recognise that we are not fighting flesh and blood. We are not fighting the person making the stupid, untimely remarks. We are fighting an enemy who is out to stop us building the church.

There is a proverb that says silver is tested in a crucible, gold is tested in a furnace but man is tested through praise.[12] Sometimes praise can lead to pride and an assumption that everything will be okay because 'we can handle it'.

9. Warfare challenges facing general church leadership

* All-absorbing pastoral situations
* Internal tensions in the eldership team (sometimes these can come very suddenly and unexpectedly, a clear sign that Satan is at work to bring about dissension)
* Seemingly insoluble practical situations
* People with their own agendas and cliques
* Situations requiring the exercise of firm overcoming faith
* General communication problems and misunderstandings

Persistent prayer is needed when leadership is faced with any of these problems. Some we have already addressed.

In our church, the eldership team decided to set aside two faith issues that we planned to pray through at every elders' prayer meeting during 1998. These involved finance and the need for more leadership. The first issue was a desire to see a 25% increase in funding over the year, and we achieved 28%. In the second issue we began to see a change as we prayed against passivity; but we still need to keep battling, particularly when people show the potential for leadership, but one of the issues referred to above knocks them back for a while.

Communication is always a difficult area. Somebody was once asked about the best way to communicate in a larger church and he just said one word – 'Often!' Communication becomes more difficult as churches grow, and the enemy exploits the situation because people tend to get offended so easily. So many leaders think that because they have *said it*, everybody has *got it*. However, on any Sunday morning, about 30% will not be there, a percentage will be involved with the children's work, another percentage will choose that moment to switch off, and another percentage will have heard the words, 'Here are the notices' and immediately switched off anyway. We tell them, but so often the person who needs to be told is the one person who does not get to hear about it! We must always seek to improve communication; it is a mark of respect for one another. However, when things go wrong, we must not allow the enemy an advantage by taking offence at any lack of communication.

10. Warfare challenges in small groups

I have already mentioned demanding pastoral situations, but here are some other issues that can be just as demanding.

Do not let the work in small groups be dictated by the greatest need. The direction for any small group should be defined by the vision for the group, and by giving attention to those who want to move forward.

Do not let petty relationship problems get blown out of all proportion. They should be dealt with quickly. People tend to forget the simple instruction given in Matthew 18. If you know someone has done something wrong, go and talk to him or her alone. Instead, what usually happens is that the person will tell the cell group leader, a pastor, their prayer partner, or someone they think should sort it out because they are afraid to do so themselves. The problem in trying to sort it out this way is that the enemy uses these situations to cause offence. The instructions of Matthew 18 were given, I believe, so that the enemy does not gain an advantage from such situations. Once major offence has been taken, the enemy can have a field day in causing relationship breakdown. As the book of Proverbs wisely puts it 'An offended brother is more unyielding than a fortified city, and disputes are like the barred gates of a citadel'.[13] Talk about strongholds that need taking! My experience is, sadly, that the Matthew 18 procedure is often forgotten in disputes within the church.

Be careful of gossip, of people who 'control' others, or display anger within the group. People who are gossips, who need to control, or who are very angry can dictate the agenda, and the enemy uses this sort of thing to divide the group.

If all I have written in this chapter is true, then prayer support for leaders is vitally important. Many of you who are not in leadership will have noticed some of the issues I have written about. You will have also observed real deficiencies in leadership. I would like to recommend therefore that you redouble your efforts to support your leaders in prayer.

I believe that leaders, particularly those who are pioneering new ventures, need specific supporting prayer groups. I now have people praying regularly for me, to whom I send a monthly letter. We also need specific prayer on a wider scale when we are encountering particular difficulties or, as in my case, taking seminars on spiritual warfare, or indeed writing this book!

Effective Strategy Number 19: Recognise that the enemy particularly targets church leaders so we need to pray for them with greater diligence and fervour.

NOTES

[1]'How Common Is Pastoral Indiscretion?', *Leadership 9, no 1* (Winter 1998), page 12; [2]1 Peter 5:8; [3]Hebrews 13:17; [4]1 Corinthians 9:26–27; [5]*The Three Battlegrounds*, Francis Frangipane, page 122; [6]Proverbs 5:18–20; [7]Luke 10:20; [8]*Churchquake*, C Peter Wagner; [9]Philippians 2:6; [10]Deuteronomy 8:3; [11]Luke 4:5; [12]Proverbs 27:21; [13]Proverbs 18:19.

Chapter 20

THE BATTLE FOR THE
SUPERNATURAL AND THE PROPHETIC

In Western Christianity, the battle for the supernatural is immense, chiefly because of a cynicism that is as powerful as idol worship is in some other parts of the world. We really have to battle this one through to enable the church to advance. The difficulty here, as we have already seen, is that people's minds tend to be dominated by a rational Western worldview.

The effect of this is to undervalue miracles, so that whenever one occurs, it either tends to be rationalised out of existence or its reality is questioned or doubted and its permanence debated. We suggest that it might be 'just coincidence', or ask 'Will the healing last?'

Our whole educational system is designed to train us to think in rational terms. I am not against that. God in His providence acts, generally speaking, rationally and consistently, as He has always done in sustaining the universe. This is, theologically, the basis for scientific research and endeavour. The petrol that enabled your car to run yesterday will also enable it to run tomorrow, not just because of some scientific law, but because God, the Sustainer of the universe, has arranged in His providence for that to happen.

However, in the West, it is not God's providence that we

stress, but human knowledge and understanding. We have been brought up to think that knowledge is power and that we *know* how things work. Because the Western worldview is so rational, we understand what medical problems are but can tend to exclude the supernatural dimension. For example, we are taught that sickness is either caused by bacteria or a virus, but this knowledge can prevent us from accepting the possibility that God *can* actually heal supernaturally.

This is again a battle concerning right thinking. It is a battle in our minds, which Satan is influencing through our culture and education system to try and ensure that people do not turn to God. In Western thinking we can easily fall into the trap of wrongly dividing between 'natural' and 'supernatural', 'material' and 'spiritual'. That is not the 'worldview' of the Bible, which views both natural and supernatural as equally real, and created and sustained by the same Almighty God. The biblical worldview leads us to believe that if we pray for a sick person and they are healed through medicine or an operation, then God is at work and has answered our prayers. If they are healed through a miraculous intervention of God, which we cannot account for rationally, then again they have been healed by God.

We are to expect both. As in Bible times, in the ministry of Jesus and the early church, we are to expect God to intervene miraculously. We are to battle against cynicism and against our historic lack of experience of healing miracles, for the truth as revealed in God's Word. We want it to be demonstrably true that our preaching of the gospel is not in word only, but in a demonstration of the Holy Spirit and power so that the converts' faith stands not on human wisdom but on *God's power.*[1]

We must battle against discouragement and passivity in this context. Otherwise, when we eventually do pray for people to be healed and nothing happens, we get discouraged; we believe that we have failed, and do not do it any more, instead of being forceful people who take the kingdom forcefully[2] and therefore keep on praying for the sick until we see breakthrough.

The Word of God about the supernatural

How then are we to engage in spiritual warfare to break through in the supernatural power of God for healing?

- First let us go to the Word of God. The Word of God, not our present experience, must govern our thinking. So Jesus said, 'I tell you the truth, anyone who has faith in Me will do what I have been doing. He will do even greater things that these, because I am going to the Father.'[3] The context of this verse is the miracles that Jesus has been doing.

  James describes normal church life. 'Is anyone in trouble?' he asks. 'He should pray.' Of course. 'Is anyone happy? Let him sing songs of praise.' Naturally. Then James goes on to say something he clearly regarded as equally obvious: 'Is anyone of you sick? He should call the elders of the church to pray over him and anoint him with oil in the name of the Lord. And the prayer offered in faith will make the sick person well; the Lord will raise him up. If he has sinned, he will be forgiven.'[4]

  My experience up to now does not measure up to the Scripture. But this is no excuse to give up! Rather, I will take the Word of God, go on believing it and continue to ask and pray. I will, with determination, preach and call the sick to come forward for healing until we break through (although I am not saying that all will be healed – the kingdom does not come in all its fullness until after Jesus returns).

- Second, it is very important that we do not let the legitimate task of organising the church squeeze out the anointing and the expectation of God's felt presence. In organising our churches into cell groups, for example, it is not just so the elders are less bothered by pastoral problems. Cells are there so that there are *more* places where the anointing can flow freely and effectively, so that there is *more* prayer for healing and *more* effective moving in the prophetic. Then when there is a special meeting for healing, for example, there will be a rise of faith and expectancy that enables even greater miracles to occur. Our cell group systems should develop our expectation in the spiritual dimension because, built into our cells, is the regular expectation of God moving.

I was encouraged that in the very week I was writing this chapter, we had a relevant experience in the cell group I attend. A visitor from another church was staying with two of our members. During the cell group meeting, he brought a number of very accurate prophetic words for people present, about things which he, as a visitor, could not have known. The result was that one person present was born again.

One Sunday in our church, I received a strange picture of a bowl of custard. For those from a different cultural background, I had better explain that custard is a thick, sweet, milk-based sauce that, if left to stand, forms a skin on top. If a hole is made in the skin and left for a few minutes, the skin will re-form.

In my vision, we were under the custard skin, and in our prayers were punching holes up through it. The trouble was, not enough holes were being made, so the skin kept re-forming. It may not have been a very elevated vision, but it was an analogy of how things tend to be in Western churches as far as the supernatural power of God is concerned. We are under a cultural skin of unbelief. Every so often, we pray for the sick and someone is healed. We have punched a hole in the skin and rejoice for a short time. Then we do not pray any more for the sick for a while, disillusionment and cynicism set in again and the skin re-forms.

Let us be aggressive in breaking the skin, let us push enough holes, so the skin cannot re-form.

The prophetic and spiritual warfare

This brings me to the issue of the prophetic and its key role in spiritual warfare. Prophets hear from God on current issues, and can discern strongholds in cultures and in churches. Because of this, it is important that our prophetic people are open in prayer in the same way that Daniel was, so that they can receive revelations concerning the nature of the battle, just as he did.[5]

Daniel prayed as he did because he was hearing from God prophetically; the devil hates it when this happens and seeks to undermine and distort prophetic vision. It is my belief that although there are prophetic advances today in understanding the battle (for example, through books like Rick Joyner's, *The Final Quest*[6]), prophetic people have never been so vulnerable in the charismatic church; so much at risk of moving off safe biblical ground into speculation.

The Jezebel spirit is out to destroy genuine prophets just as the original Jezebel did.[7] A friend of mine inadvertently let into his church a prophet who was not accountable to any leaders. The problem was that though there was accuracy in the prophetic words, they bound people up rather than releasing them into service. There was a tendency to create loyalty to the visiting prophet rather than to the local leadership. Although it was overcome by prayer, sickness affected families of leaders who sought to confront the manipulative prophesying.

This is spiritual warfare and the genuine prophet is a key resource. There is an inherent danger here; that the enemy will isolate and undermine genuine prophetic anointing because it exposes him and his work. Prophetic people are also to encourage God's people and provoke them into action, and if the devil can slow that down, he will. Often he will do this through diversionary tactics and a story in 1 Kings 13, (that I have to admit I don't fully understand), demonstrates this. The story concerns an old prophet who was used to divert the attention of a man of God and cause his death. It is a strange story but it does show the enemy's strategy to divert a prophet of God, and thus rob the people of God of a genuine prophetic voice.

Prophetic symbolism

Stereotyped actions can be an unhelpful diversion of the prophetic if they are allowed to become a model for spiritual warfare. There is a story in the book of Kings that describes how Elisha was on his deathbed and the people of Israel were about to go into battle. Jehoash, who was king at that time, went to see the prophet and was told to get a number of arrows. He was told to fire one out of the window, and to bang the others on the ground. However, because he only banged them on the ground three times instead of six or seven times, he was told that he would not completely destroy his enemies.[8] Now that did not become a model for future battles. They did not go out and bang arrows on the ground every time that they went into battle! It was a specific prophetic action for that occasion. It is true that Jehoash's failure to keep on banging the ground was a sign of lack of persistence. Our calling therefore is to persist in prayer for God to move, not to persist in prophetic symbolism such as regularly banging sticks on the ground in our prayer meetings!

I believe that God can and does, from time to time today, give a specific action to be done by people at a particular time, but I am very concerned if that symbolic action becomes a regular pattern. I heard about one group of people who tied white bandages around their heads, and danced around the room in a clockwise direction to demonstrate that they were 'flowing in the Spirit'. Any who weren't flowing in the Spirit had to dance around the room in an anti-clockwise direction!

Now while I can just about accept that this might have been a prophetic demonstration originally, it seems that it had become a model, a way of doing things that they thought would work for them. It becomes almost like magic. It is this sort of thing that gives prophetic people a bad name. I am not saying that it is wrong to perform a prophetic action – I have done some strange things myself in the prophetic. However, we do need to recognise that they are nearly always for that one occasion and not intended to be constantly re-enacted. This becomes particularly pertinent in the field of spiritual warfare.

In order to take the city of Jericho, Joshua and the Israelite army were told to march around Jericho for seven days and blow trumpets.[9] However, this did not become a pattern for taking all the cities in Canaan. I do not see that example ever being repeated in the whole Old Testament. David is indeed commended for not following a precedent in attacking and defeating the Philistines. On one occasion, he was to go straight on up and attack; on the next occasion, he was to wait for a mysterious noise in the balsam trees.[10]

A set pattern is dangerous, because it can lead people into an 'if we do this, then the enemy will be defeated in this situation' frame of mind. Then if it doesn't work, they become disillusioned. It can cause all of us to be diverted from our main focus – advancing the kingdom, winning the lost, making disciples and building the church. There is plenty of warfare involved in each of these, as we have seen. A set pattern is also dangerous because it can take our eyes off God and our total dependence on Him and put them on the method we are using instead.

The people of God are specifically warned against taking prophetic symbols and honouring them. Whilst going through the wilderness, Moses was told on one occasion to hold up a bronze snake so that all who had been bitten by snakes would live if they gazed on the bronze snake.[11] In later years, this very bronze snake became a snare for idolatry for God's people when they venerated it.[12]

There is a danger, too, that prophetic demonstrations like these can cause prophetic people to be marginalised when they need to be centre-stage, fulfilling a true New Testament prophetic calling.

The prophetic calling in the church today

What is the prophet called to in our day? To go into this in detail would require a book in itself, and a number of good ones have been written.[13] However, it is helpful to give a brief summary of some of the functions involved in the prophetic calling so that we see their priority and do not let the enemy divert us from them.

- In New Testament times, the prophet as well as the apostle was foundational to the building of the church.[14] This is to be a prime role today as well, to ensure churches are built on foundations that follow the prophetic vision revealed in Scripture.
- Haggai and Zechariah helped encourage the people to rebuild the temple and the walls.[15] Encouragement to build is an important aspect of the prophetic role, and one which is much needed today. Prophecy is for the edifying (building up) of the church.[16]
- Giving specific key words to people within the body of Christ as Agabus did for Paul[17] and as Timothy received over his life when the elders prayed for him.[18]
- Warning the church as to what is to come so that the church can take action in advance, as when Agabus predicted the famine.[19]
- Bringing vision to God's people of the wonderful prophetic purposes that are laid out in Scripture.

- Bringing discernment about issues including strongholds in the church generally, in local churches or in individual lives, which will hinder the spread of the gospel and the building of the church. I believe that the letters to the seven churches in Revelation[20] were specific prophetic words to those churches. They involved words that gave encouragement to them, but also identified issues, which would hinder them in their progress if they were not dealt with. I believe there is a strong spiritual warfare dimension to this aspect of the prophetic gift.
- Encouraging the development of charismatic life and the expression of all the gifts of the Holy Spirit in the local church. Just like the other ministries of Ephesians 4 vs 11, prophets are to equip the saints for their ministry. They encourage all our churches to be prophetic communities.

All these functions are greatly needed in the church today. Let us not allow the prophets to be diverted from their task through unbiblical spiritual warfare.

Marginalising the prophetic

The promotion of pastoral care and organisational development at the cost of recognition of the supernatural dimension also tends to marginalise the prophetic. Tested prophetic words from God really should have a major bearing on the agenda of leaders' meetings and on any decisions that are made. The enemy can use legitimate pastoral concerns to divert attention from the prophetic when, in fact, anointed prophetic insight could assist in resolving problems.

The prophetic can also be marginalised by pushing it to unbiblical extremes, by treating it as weird, or by enthusiastic but *untested* prophesying.

One last danger in the battle for the prophetic is that of

'one-to-one' prophesying. By this I mean one person giving another a prophecy without witnesses present. Again this, by definition, gives no opportunity for testing and is without accountability.

How then do we ensure that the enemy does not get an advantage concerning this very important issue? A few hints:

- Ensure that anybody who claims to be a prophet or prophetess is genuinely accountable to a local church and its leadership.
- If functioning on a broader level, prophetic ministry should also be working in team with, and be accountable to, recognised apostolic ministry.
- Ensure that the main burden of the prophetic is to enable and equip the people of God to fulfil their prime calling in this world – to advance the kingdom, win the lost, make disciples and build the church.
- Ensure there is good teaching in our local churches about the role of the prophet and the importance of prophesying.
- Try to make sure that the prophetic gifting is released to function in our churches. Prophets need encouragement. If the gift becomes frustrated, it is more liable to be diverted into unhelpful channels. To be frank, pastors often do not know how rightly to release and work with the prophetic; it often tends to be a low priority for those with a pastoral gift. This is very unhelpful. It robs the church of an important ministry and can frustrate and therefore divert the prophetic.
- Do not allow one-to-one prophesying within the church.
- Ensure as best we can that church members do not run after independent prophets who, though they may be exciting, could end up in putting people in bondage to untested expectations rather than releasing them to God-given service.

Effective Strategy Number 20: Overcome the enemy by believing for God's supernatural power in our day and by making room for the prophetic ministry in our churches.

NOTES

[1] 1 Corinthians 2:4–5; [2] Matthew 11:12; [3] John 14:12; [4] James 5:13–15; [5] Daniel 10:10–14; [6] *The Final Quest,* Rick Joyner; [7] 1 Kings 19:1–2; [8] 2 Kings 13:14–19; [9] Joshua 6:2–5; [10] 2 Samuel 5:23–25; [11] Numbers 21:8–9; [12] 2 Kings 18:4; [13] Some I have found helpful include: *Growing in the Prophetic*, Mike Bickle, *Developing Your Prophetic Gifting*, Graham Cooke, and *Prophecy in the Local Church*, David Pytches; [14] Ephesians 2:20; 4:11–13; [15] Ezra 5:1–2, Haggai 1:3–4, 7–8, 13–15, Zechariah 1:16; 8:9–11; [16] 1 Corinthians 14:4; [17] Acts 21:10–11; [18] 1 Timothy 4:14; [19] Acts 11:27–30; [20] Revelation 2 and 3.

Chapter 21

WHAT ARE OUR WEAPONS?

We must approach the issue of spiritual warfare from a positive perspective. It is not something to be feared, nor to be too pre-occupied about. We must not overestimate Satan and his power. Our focus must be to glorify Jesus and to do His work in the world. Our priority is to seek first His kingdom, His rule in everything, in our homes, our churches and our places of work.

However, we must not underestimate Satan either, and need to recognise that as we do the work of the kingdom we will be opposed by Satan and his demons. We do have an active foe. To deny this is to expose ourselves even more to his subtle attacks. He loves to persuade people that he does not exist. Dr D Martyn Lloyd-Jones put it like this, 'I am certain that one of the main causes of the ill state of the church today is the fact that the devil is being forgotten. All is attributed to us; we have all become so psychological in our attitude and thinking. We are ignorant of this great objective fact, the being, the existence of the devil, the adversary, the accuser, and his fiery darts.'[1]

Satan, though, was defeated at the cross, and we need to remember that, especially if we are actively involved in demolishing strongholds. He was defeated once and for all. That is why we are to carry the effects of that victory at the cross to every nation.

Ultimately we can never be defeated. We are more than conquerors through Him who loves us.[2] We are told in the Scriptures that we overcome by the blood of the Lamb, by the word of our testimony and by not loving our lives so much as to shrink from death.[3] Even death, the enemy's ultimate weapon, is for Christians an entry into eternal life, so we cannot lose. The enemy's ultimate weapon against us brings us the victory. That is our provision in Christ.

God has provided weapons for us for use in this battle.

The Word of God

We are told in the Scriptures that the sword of the Spirit is the Word of God.[4] We need to use it when the enemy is trying to sow the seeds of discouragement.

The Word of God is given to expose the strongholds and bring them to the light. The enemy is a liar and a deceiver and we need to expose his works. As we have seen, the word 'occult' means hidden and we have to expose strongholds so that we can deal with them. It may not be something we often think about, but God exposes. 'What you have said in the dark will be heard in the daylight, and what you have whispered in the ear in the inner rooms will be proclaimed from the roofs'.[5]

His Word is given to help our discernment, 'For the Word of God is living and active. Sharper than any double-edged sword, it penetrates even to dividing soul and spirit, joints and marrow; it judges the thoughts and attitudes of the heart'.[6] I have found that as I have taught around the world on the subject of strongholds, all sorts of things have been exposed so that people can be released. Many have realised for the first time in Western countries that they tend to think individualistically, or assess church from a consumer mentality. Exposing the strongholds is half the battle; the other half – dealing with them – is just as vital! I remember when I taught on the stronghold of individualism at our Warrensburg Summer Camp in the USA, many people told me afterwards that they had never even thought of that issue before. It was just the way that they had been brought up. They had been conditioned by their culture (and sadly, church culture as well) to think individualistically. Exposure of strongholds, therefore, by the Word of God is important.

The Word of God is also given to equip us to battle against the strongholds and to renew our minds. Because our minds have been wrongly conditioned by the strongholds that dominate our society, they need to be exposed to Scripture. My friend, David Holden, has written an excellent book on this subject which my wife, Scilla, has used several times to disciple new Christians.[7] I don't know whether David thinks about it this way, but writing to help Christians renew their minds is spiritual warfare.

I, therefore, learn to confront the enemy with God's truth. So when the enemy says we are failures, in faith we can say that we are more than conquerors through Him who loves us. When the enemy says that such and such a person is against us and is saying all sorts of things, we can take the Word of God and say that we are not fighting against that person, but against principalities and powers. We are going to respond according to our renewed mind. We do not *have* to respond in anger. In this way, we take the Word of God and allow it both to expose the works of darkness and to enable us to react in a godly manner.

Perseverance

Spiritual warfare has more to do with perseverance than shouting at the enemy or demonic forces. As we have seen, James tells us that, as we submit to God, we can resist the devil and he will flee away from us.[8] Perseverance is not a popular quality in the culture of the Western World. We want everything instantly; fast food, instant access; we can even get impatient with our fast-moving computers because they seem so slow.

For God, a day is as a thousand years and a thousand years as one day.[9] He is not ruled by the tyranny of time and urgency, and neither must we be. Faith involves perseverance and endurance, which are qualities God honours. He enables us to receive what He has promised as we exercise these qualities.[10] As we submit to God and hold on in patience to what is right, we can see the enemy defeated. As he did with Jesus,[11] the enemy retreats for a while when we persevere in not giving way to his devices.

Faith

The faith that I am referring to here is active faith. Rather than going through life complaining about the attacks of the enemy, God says that active faith is about choosing to believe His words instead of the enemy's lies.

So faith is not about weighing up all the probabilities and assuming, on balance, that everything will be OK. It is about choosing to believe what God has said, even if circumstances seem to contradict it. Faith looks realistically at the circumstances but makes the choice to believe God's Word rather than be ruled by the present situation. For example, Paul reminds us that even though Abraham was about one hundred years old and that his body was as good as dead when he was promised a son, and Sarah's womb was also as good as dead, his faith never weakened.[12] Even though the circumstances were against him, he believed God had promised him a son. Even though he looked at his own body and said 'Impossible', then looked at his wife's body and said 'Even though I love my wife, it's doubly impossible', he believed God.

Though doctrinally I may disagree with some of the emphases in what are called 'faith' churches, I still want to emulate their aggressive faith. I can so easily give in to rationalisation instead of holding onto God.

Active faith is in contrast to passivity. There is a sense of waiting for God's time but it is active waiting, not passive. The Scripture raises the challenge, 'However, when the Son of Man comes, will He find faith on the earth?'[13] Let our answer be a resounding 'Yes'. As servants we are to be busy while our Lord is away.[14]

Understanding authority

All authority has been given to Jesus. We are sent out in His name. We have authority and divine power to demolish the strongholds. It is true we need both authority and power. Both are from God. Authority is in the command of the One who sent us. It is us going out in His name. Power is what He dynamically supplies to us as we step out in that authority. As we step out in the authority He has given, He releases surges of power to enable us to do His will.

Authority is for releasing and not controlling. True biblical authority exercised within the Christian church releases us to walk in freedom and minister with authority, but protects us and retains accountability. One of the main characteristics of the new covenant is that we can *all* receive grace and exercise spiritual gifts. So we are *all* 'taught by God'.[15] 'You can *all* prophesy one by one.'[16] Scripture speaks of the new covenant as 'I will pour out my Spirit on *all* flesh.'[17] True spiritual authority in the church therefore enables the working out of these new covenant promises as we all get involved. It is important to remember, however, that if we are under authority, we can minister with authority. An answer to the Jezebelic spirit is to have godly authority, which releases others to serve with authority as well.

Paul clarifies the manner in which we should move in this authority and power. He says it is in the meekness and gentleness of Christ that we are able to demolish strongholds. That might seem to be a strange way of moving in authority and power, but we do not fight using the world's weapons, but with divine power.[18]

Prayer

This is linked to faith and the secret here is to pray *for* the positive, not primarily *against* the negative. The prayers that Jesus taught us *deal* with negative issues but are primarily positive. He did not pray about how terrible it was that the reign of Satan was around, He prayed that God's kingdom would come and His will would be done on earth as it is in heaven.[19]

• *Intercession*

This is where I speak the word of God on behalf of someone else. This was the sort of prayer that Daniel prayed. He was devoted to a life of prayer. He prayed according to the prophetic word that he received, then found out afterwards that he had been engaging in spiritual warfare at a cosmic level against the prince of Persia. He did not deliberately engage the forces of darkness, but as he interceded, it was revealed to him that that was what had been happening. It is noteworthy that Daniel's response to the prophetic word of God was to call on God to fulfil what He had already promised. The natural response might have been as follows: 'I see from Jeremiah that in seventy years we will return from exile to our own land. Seventy years is nearly up, so look out for it everyone – it's about to happen.' That was not Daniel's reaction. He prayed even more fervently than he did the rest of the time, if that were possible. His prayer was desperate: 'We do not make requests of you because we are righteous, but because of your great mercy. O Lord, listen! O Lord, forgive! O Lord, hear and act! For your sake, O my God, do not delay, because your city and your people bear your Name.'[20]

I am so glad that so many are rediscovering this sort of persistent urgent prayer. Churches (or at least intercessors within our churches) are having more regular prayer and also special seasons of prayer, sometimes accompanied by fasting. Much of the church, in parts of the world where God is moving in greater power like China, Korea, Latin America and parts of Africa, is, of course, even more devoted to this persistent inter-cessory prayer. I remember hearing Colin Dye of Kensington Temple at one of our conferences attributing much of the growth of that church to a group of African ladies interceding for it. Colin said he liked to have the intercessors in the front row while he was preaching and sometimes as a result he could feel the power of God getting too strong for him.

• *Warfare praying*

Much has been written about this and it is usually in the context of what is called strategic level spiritual warfare. As I said in Chapter 4, I have grave misgivings about this as a methodology. However, I do believe there are times when the Holy Spirit stirs up what can only be called 'holy indignation' and we start praying militantly. This is not a model for all prayer but is used during particular situations as the Holy Spirit specifically and prophetically directs. We might even feel that it is *not* the way to pray, but when it happens, we need to run with it and not try to quench the experience. I remember one particular occasion during our NFI elders' prayer and fasting days we heard that a pastor in India had been rushed to hospital with a life-threat-ening illness; it was as if I received a gift of faith for that moment and I asked to lead the prayer. I was conscious of God saying, 'Yes! Yes!' and I asked everybody to raise their hands and we prayed in a warfare fashion, in tongues and in English. We heard later that the pastor was well again.

• *Praying in the Spirit*

Paul tells us to pray in the Spirit with all kinds of prayers and requests. Furthermore, he tells us to do so on all occasions.[21] I believe that this refers to a great variety of prayers as God's Holy Spirit leads us. However, there is particular value in the use of the gift of tongues which I am sure is included in praying in the Spirit. After all, Paul said that he spoke in tongues more than anyone![22] I wonder sometimes if this is how Paul kept going with everything the enemy threw at him. He suffered shipwrecks, persecutions, opposition, stoning. On one occasion he gave a whole catalogue of the sufferings he had to face.[23] Was it because he spoke in tongues more than anyone, that he was able to overcome the efforts of the enemy to dislodge him and divert him from his task?

I recognise that I do not know how to pray as I ought.[24] Praise God, that when I am not sure how to pray, the Holy Spirit prays through my spirit in tongues. I sense the need even more as we engage in warfare issues that we do not fully understand, to use this wonderful gift that God makes available to us as we are filled with His Holy Spirit.

Worship

When Jehoshaphat was involved in one particular battle, he sent out his musicians and singers first and they sang the psalm, 'Give thanks to the Lord for His love endures forever.'[25] Worship thus preceded the battle. Concentration on God leads to faith growing in us, and worship that magnifies God concentrates our vision on Him. Increasing our faith should never be a motive for worship; our motive should always be simply to glorify God. Nevertheless we know that to focus on God in praise and worship does strengthen our faith in His ability to act. We used to sing a song where the words of the chorus began, 'With the high praises of God in our mouth and a two-edged sword in our hand'.[26] We seem to have lost sight of this aspect of worship to an extent today.

Teamwork

We have already stressed many times in this book the need for working in teams when confronting the demonic. The enemy can attack us more effectively when we are isolated. However, I want to re-emphasise it in this chapter because teamwork – working well with others – is not only for our protection but is a positive force for overcoming.

When Elijah got depressed because of the onslaughts of Jezebel, the first thing he was told to do was to anoint Elisha. Elijah had been on his own for a long time. Now for a while he was able to experience the benefits of teamwork, even though his team member was like a trainee.[27] A team, however small, can be very effective. Jonathan was an example of a man who would take bold initiatives for God against the enemy. However, he did so with his armour bearer, who was prepared to back him up heart and soul.[28] When the seventy-two saw such victory in their evangelism, they had been sent out by Jesus two by two. It is amazing that so often as Christians we forget this principle. We forget the importance of having somebody with us when we are engaging the enemy in battle. We try to soldier on by ourselves. If you are facing an onslaught from the devil, if you are about to enter into an issue where you know the enemy will resist you, then take somebody else with you. Do it together. Teamwork is one of our weapons and it is, conversely, why the enemy seeks to undermine relationships between brothers and sisters in Christ.

Godly role models

In Chapter 11, we noted the fact that in today's society in the West there is increased confusion of masculinity and femininity. In his book *Eros Redeemed*,[29] John White emphasises that there is a desperate need for godly role models to enable people to come out of this confusion. As a role model for masculinity, he suggests that men obviously need to look to Jesus. As far as women are concerned, their biblical role models should be Mary the mother of Jesus, as she received in faith the words of the angel, and also the woman in Proverbs 31. It is true that we need to refocus on biblical role models. It is also true that for an emerging generation, an aspect of spiritual warfare against the confusion in our culture is to present godly role models within the life of the church.

There are many characteristics of the life of Jesus, which demonstrate godly masculinity in contrast to what is presented today:

- He initiated, but in clear submission to God His Father. It is a prime masculine quality to be able to initiate. We see in Jesus that even from the age of twelve He was determined to be on His Father's business. He took clear decisions; He had clear objectives, He knew why He had come into the world. He could speak of a completed task.
- He did not give way to fear. He stood up to the enemies of truth, whether they were Pharisees, Sadducees or the moneychangers in the temple.
- He was comfortable in the company of women. I have noticed that some men who are very conscious of male authority do not actually know how to be relaxed in their authority in the company of women. Jesus, on the other hand, flouted social conventions when they denigrated women.[30] He even appeared first in His resurrection body to a woman. Women felt very comfortable with Him. He never patronised them, but did not come wrongly under their authority at all. He did not allow His mother to manipulate Him into changing the water into wine, though He did initiate that miracle.
- He demonstrated servant leadership, showing that authority and servanthood are not contradictory.

- He knew how to express emotions in a godly way; He wept at Lazarus's tomb; He showed anger at the commercialisation of temple worship.

John White goes on to say, 'Men and women need one another *as* men and women. They need real men and women, *healed* men and women. And the day has come for manliness and womanliness to be restored. Yet I shall talk more about manliness than about womanliness. Why? Because I believe that when men are men, women will find much less difficulty entering into their own identity.'[31] As I said, godly role models are needed today as a contrast to the confusion of our culture. They are needed for the sake of the next generation, to help them out of the stronghold of sexual confusion. They are also needed in order to release the next generation in power to take the gospel to the whole world.

The whole armour of God

We have spoken many times in this book of Ephesians 6 and the battle against the evil forces of darkness referred to there. It seems somewhat trite, therefore, to include just a few short comments on the weapons described in that chapter, particularly as Dr D Martyn Lloyd-Jones has written two volumes on just these 11 verses, totalling 736 pages![32]

However, some remarks are necessary to help us in the battle, though I believe the principles contained in this section have already been referred to in this book.

• *Be strong*

This is an appeal to develop a robust faith not a namby-pamby, surface only 'believism'. Christianity is not for wimps. It is for people who can be strong. Strong in affirming God's truth when all around them are giving up. Strong in maintaining standards of godliness. Strong in holding one's body in purity, not engaging in sexual relationships until marriage. It takes strength to be a Christian today. But it is strength, not in our own efforts to grit our teeth and keep going, but in the grace supplied to us of supernatural power from God. We are to stand in His mighty power. Put on the full armour of God. It is not that we put it on each morning, but rather that the characteristic of our lives is that we are living continuously in the good of the truths that are symbolised by the weapons Paul describes here. Practise living by the truth now so that when the evil day comes, the day when it seems that the whole fury of hell and the subtle seduction of the devil's lies are thrown at you, you will still be standing. Times like that come for all of us; be prepared.

• *Standing*

At a time when so many are tossed to-and-fro by the latest paperback (hopefully, not this one!), or the latest warfare conference attended, it is important to see the emphasis in this section on standing firm. There is a desperate cry in our hearts in these days for God to send revival. I share that desperation and cry for it too. However, I am concerned lest we are deceived into unbiblical practices on the basis of 'if we only did such and such, then revival would come'. Our responsibility is to stand; stand against the wiles of the devil; stand firm in the midst of a society which is giving up on so many godly standards; stand true to the Word of God, which is our only anchor. Do not give up as so many seem to, when their exciting introduction to the Christian faith turns into days of difficulty, when it perhaps seems even more difficult and pressurised than before they came to Christ. Then is the time to stand.

• *Belt of truth*

Commentators differ as to whether this refers to the truth as revealed in Scripture or the idea of our being truthful or sincere.

When in doubt, apply both. Both are relevant. Truth is essential if we are not to be deceived in spiritual warfare. We need the body of sound doctrine revealed in Scripture. I would encourage you to be strong in understanding the Bible; get yourself well-versed in systematic theology. A friend of mine was somewhat cynical about 'dry, doctrinal teaching'. He felt that what the church needed was greater demonstration of power. He was on a training course I was running. I taught him and the other trainees for two days on 'the doctrine of God'. I talked about who God is, His attributes, His sovereignty, divine providence and what it means and the glorious mystery of the doctrine of the Trinity. He began to find it interesting but was then amazed when I asked the whole class to stand and invited God to move on us in power by the Holy Spirit. He saw that doctrine and the demonstration of God's power went together, as students whose hearts had been touched with the glory of biblical truth then experienced a powerful encounter with the Holy Spirit. We need the belt of truth. It is also true that we need to wear the belt of genuine sincerity, without mixed motives, without selfish ambition.

- ### *Breastplate of righteousness*

Again, this can mean two things. It could refer to the free gift of righteousness in Christ and also to our leading a righteous and godly life. Again, both need to be laid hold of by us. I am glad that my life is protected by the free gift of Christ's righteousness. God looks at us and sees the righteousness of Christ; we are righteous as Christ is righteous. We are justified freely. We must also be concerned to live righteous lives, free from any of the strongholds of Satan that may still grip us from our past pre-conversion lives.

- ### *Boots of the gospel*

Be willing to share good news, willing to run from town to town, from nation to nation if God so calls with the good news of Jesus Christ. If God does not call you anywhere else, then take every opportunity where you are now to share your faith. Make friends with unbelievers as Jesus did. This is warfare; warfare for the salvation of men, women and children for whom Christ died. As we are positively engaged in sharing good news, there is a greater motivation to live godly lives and resist the attacks of the devil.

• *The shield of faith*

We have already covered the shield of faith in an earlier section. Remember that the enemy is firing darts of unbelief, repeating the temptation of 'has God said?'[33] regularly at us. Is your shield ready?

• *Helmet of salvation*

Rejoice in the fact that God loves you and has saved you. Keep hold of that joy and look forward to the fullness of your final salvation when you will be with Christ which is far better,[34] when you will be set free from all this conflict and receive a new body, like His glorious body.[35]

• *The sword of the Spirit*

We have commented on this already in this chapter so I will not repeat myself here.

Joy

The Bible says that the joy of the Lord is our strength.[36] The context of this was when Nehemiah had rebuilt the walls of Jerusalem despite being surrounded by the enemies of Israel. The book of Nehemiah is an interesting study in spiritual warfare. The people rebuilt the walls with a sword in one hand and a trowel in another. God's call upon us is similar, to fight for the kingdom, *and* build the church. In that new pioneering venture when the people of God were returning from exile to rebuild their city, the joy of the Lord was to be their strength. I often pray with people about pain from their past. It is important for them to express that pain. It is equally important to ensure they move from pain to joy, so that they can stand against the enemy strongholds that brought that pain.

We looked in an earlier chapter at how as the disciples moved out with authority, Jesus saw Satan falling. It is interesting that in that warfare situation Jesus is described as being full of joy through the Holy Spirit.[37] He delighted in the fact that God had hidden things from all the clever people on earth and had revealed them to people who were just like little children. It was those who were childlike in their faith that had seen demons come out of people, had seen strongholds falling. Jesus rejoiced in that.

Something more challenging to us, particularly in the Western world, is that joy is to be the defence against the attacks of the enemy through trials brought upon us. James says, 'Consider it pure joy, my brothers, whenever you face trials of many kinds.'[38]

It is joy and laughter that accompany the release of captives from things that have held them in bondage for years. As the people of God were released from their captivity in the Old Testament, it was said, 'Our mouths were filled with laughter, our tongues with songs of joy. Then it was said among the nations, "The Lord has done great things for them".'[39]

One of the most amazing Scriptures concerning laughter is that the Lord himself laughs in derision at the mere princes and rulers of men, empowered by all the demonic strongholds, seeking to come against the anointed One of God. It says in this context 'The One enthroned in heaven laughs; the Lord scoffs at them.'[40] That Psalm speaks about the inevitability of the final victory of God. It trumpets the absolute certainty of the victory of Jesus Christ. On the basis of the promises of this

Psalm, we can have confidence that the nations will be won for Christ. Whatever strongholds, whatever 'territorial spirits' hold the nations in bondage, they will be defeated. Loud voices in heaven will shout 'The kingdom of the world has become the kingdom of our Lord and of His Christ.'[41]

Effective Strategy Number 21: Know your weapons and use them!

It is appropriate that a book on spiritual warfare should end on a note of joy. It is even more appropriate that this note of joy should be in the final certain triumph of our Lord Jesus Christ.

NOTES

[1]*The Christian Warfare*, Lloyd-Jones, page 292 (The Banner of Truth Trust, The Grey House, 3 Murrayfield Rd, Edinburgh, EH12 6EL. Used with permission.); [2]Romans 8:37; [3]Revelation 12:11; [4]Ephesians 6:17; [5]Luke 12:3; [6]Hebrews 4:12; [7]*Battle for the Mind*, David Holden; [8]James 4:7; [9]2 Peter 3:8; [10]Hebrews 10:36; [11]Luke 4:13; [12]Romans 4:19–21; [13]Luke 18:8; [14]Luke 12:35–44; [15]John 6:45; [16]1 Corinthians 14:31 (RSV); [17]Acts 2:17; [18]2 Corinthians 10:3–4; [19]Matthew 6:10; [20]Daniel 9:18–19; [21]Ephesians 6:18; [22]1 Corinthians 14:18; [23]2 Corinthians 11:23–29; [24]Romans 8:26–27; [25]2 Chronicles 20:21; [26]*Songs of Fellowship* (1991) no. 543, based on Psalm 149, author unknown; [27]1 Kings 19:16–21; [28]1 Samuel 14:12–14; [29]*Eros Redeemed*– John White, page 186–212; [30]John 4:7, Matthew 26:10–13; [31]John White, page 194 (Eagle, 6–7 Leapale Rd, Guildford, Surrey, GU1 4JX. Used with permission.); [32]*The Christian Warfare* and *The Christian Soldier* – D M Lloyd-Jones; [33]Genesis 3:1; [34]Philippians 1:23; [35]Philippians 3:20–21; [36]Nehemiah 8:10; [37]Luke 10:21; [38]James 1:2; [39]Psalm 126:1–3; [40]Psalm 2:4; [41]Revelation 11:15.

BIBLIOGRAPHY

Randy Alcorn, *Money, Possessions and Eternity* (0-8423-8731-5, Tyndale House, 1989)

Neil T Anderson, *The Bondage Breaker* (1-85424-184-2, Monarch, 1990)

Clinton Arnold, *Spiritual Warfare – What Does the Bible Really Teach?* (0-551-03215-4, Marshall Pickering, 1999)

Kenneth E Bailey, *Poet and Peasant and Through Peasant Eyes* (0-8028-1947-8, Eerdmans, 1983)

Don Basham, *Deliver Us From Evil* (0-8007-9069-3, Chosen, 1972)

Mike Bickle, *Growing in the Prophetic* (0-85476-554-9, Kingsway, 1995)

David Burnett, *Clash of Worlds* (1-85424-107-9, Monarch,1990/1995)

David Burnett, *The Healing of the Nations* (0-85364-742-9, Paternoster, 1996)

David Burnett, *The Spirit of Hinduism* (1-85424-194-X, Monarch, 1992)

David Burnett, *Unearthly Powers* (1-85424-055-2, Monarch, 1988)

Rodney Clapp, *Families at the Crossroads* (0-85110-994-2, IVP, 1993)

Graham Cooke, *Developing Your Prophetic Gifting* (1-85240-144-3, Sovereign World, 1994)

Douglas Coupland, *Generation X* (0-349-10839-0, Abacus, 1996)

Eileen Crossman, *Mountain Rain* (0-85363-146-8, OMF Books, 1982)

Paul Daykin, *Crossing Cultures* (0-85009-736-3, Word, 1994)

Frank Damazio, *Seasons of Revival* (1886849-04-8, BT Publishing, 1996)

Dr Jack Deere, *Surprised by the Power of the Spirit* (0-85476-494-1, Kingsway, 1993)

Dr Jack Deere, *Surprised by the Voice of God* (0-85476-649-9, Kingsway, 1996)

Dr Patrick Dixon, *Signs of Revival* (0-85476-539-5, Kingsway, 1994)

Elisabeth Elliot, *Shadow of the Almighty* (0-340-02643-X, Hodder & Stoughton, 1958)

Francis Frangipane, *The Three Battlegrounds* (1-874367-26-4, New Wine Press, 1994)

Michael Green, *I Believe in Satan's Downfall* (0-3406-3034-5, Hodder & Stoughton)

Wayne Grudem, *Systematic Theology* (0-85110-652-8, Inter Varsity Press, 1994)

William Hendrickson, *New Testament Commentary on Galatians and Ephesians* (0-85151-333-6, Banner of Truth, 1968)

William Hendrickson, *New Testament Commentary on Luke* (0-85151-292-5, Banner of Truth, 1978)

William Hendrickson, *New Testament Commentary on Matthew* (0-85151-192-9, Banner of Truth, 1973)

Rodney L Henry, *Filipino Spirit World – A Challenge to the Church* (971-511-088-6, OMF Literature, 1986)

David Holden, *Battle for the Mind* (0 85476-787-8, Kingsway, 1999)

Dewi Hughes, *God of the Poor* (1-85078-297-0, OM Publishing, 1997)

John Paul Jackson, *Needless Casualties of War* (1-58483-000-X, Streams Publications, 1999)

Rick Joyner, *The Final Quest* (0-88368-478-0, Whitaker House, 1996)

Charles H Kraft, *Christianity in Culture* (0-88344-763-0, Orbis Books, 1979)

George Eldon Ladd, *The Presence of the Future* (0-8028-1531-6, SPCK, 1974)

Bob Larson, *Larson's Book of Spiritual Warfare* (0-7852-6985-1, Thomas Nelson, 1994)

Dr D Martin Lloyd-Jones, *The Christian Soldier* (0-85151-258-5, Banner of Truth Trust, 1977)

Dr D Martin Lloyd-Jones, *The Christian Warfare* (0-85151-243-7, Banner of Truth Trust, 1976)

Chuck Lowe, *Territorial Spirits and World Evangelisation?* (Mentor/OMF, 1-8579-299-5, 1998)

Vishal Mangalwadi, *Missionary Conspiracy – Letters to a Post-modern Hindu* (81-86701-03-6, Good Books, 1996)

Marvyn K Mayers, *Christianity Confronts Culture* (0-310-28891-6, Zondervan, 1974)

Elizabeth Moberly, *Homosexuality, A New Christian Ethic* (0-227-67850-3, James Clarke & Co, 1983)

Dr Ed Murphy, *The Handbook for Spiritual Warfare* (0-7852-1151-9, Nelson, 1997)

George Otis Jnr, *The Twilight Labyrinth – Why Does Spiritual Darkness Linger Where it Does?* (0-8007-9255-6, Chosen Books, 1997)

John Piper & Wayne Grudem, *Recovering Biblical Manhood and Womanhood* (089107-586-0, Crossway Books, 1991)

Graham & Shirley Powell, *Christian Set Yourself Free* (0-947852-17-4, New Wine Press, 1983)

Graham Powell, *Fear Free* (1-85240-015-3, Sovereign World, 1987)

David Pytches, *Come Holy Spirit* (0-340-38513-8, Hodder & Stoughton, 1985)

David Pytches, *Prophecy in the Local Church* (0-340-59566-3, Hodder & Stoughton, 1993)

John Richards, *But Deliver Us From Evil* (0-232-51250-7, Darton, Longman & Todd, 1974)

Don Richardson, *Peace Child* (0-8307-0415-9, Regal, 1974)

Dean Sherman, *Spiritual Warfare for Every Christian* (0-927545-05-5, YWAM Publishing, 1990)

Valerie Sinason, *Treating of Survivors of Satanist Abuse* (0-415-10543-9, Routledge, 1994)

Tom Sine, *Mustard Seed Versus McWorld* (1-85424-435-3, Monarch, 1999)

James W Sire, *The Universe Next Door* (0-8308-1220-2, IVP, 1976/1988)

Charles R Solomon, *The Ins and Outs of Rejection* (0-9622110-0-1, Solomon Publications, 1991)

John R W Stott, *The Message of Ephesians – God's New Society* (0-85110-963-2, IVP)

Philippa Stroud, *God's Heart for the Poor* (0-85476-825-4, Kingsway, 1999)

Mrs Howard Taylor, *Pastor Hsi* (0-85792-159-3, OMF, 1997)

C Peter Wagner, *Breaking Strongholds* (1-85424-218-0, Monarch, 1993)

C Peter Wagner, *Churchquake* (0-8307-1918-0, Regal Books, 1999)

C Peter Wagner, *Confronting the Powers* (0-8307-1817-6, Regal Books,1996)

C Peter Wagner, *Confronting the Queen of Heaven* (Wagner Institute for Practical Ministry, 1998)

C Peter Wagner, *Wrestling With Dark Angels* (1-85424-128-1, Monarch, 1990)

David C K Watson, *God's Freedom Fighters* (Movement Books, 1966)

John White, *Eros Redeemed* (0-86347-112-9, Eagle, 1993)

John White, *When The Spirit Comes With Power* (0-340-50340-8, Hodder & Stoughton, 1988)

Walter Wink, *Engaging the Powers* (0-8006-2646-X, Fortress Press, 1992)

John Wimber, *Power Healing* (0-340-39090-5, Hodder & Stoughton, 1986)

Nigel Wright, *The Fair Face of Evil* (0-551-01786-4, Marshall Pickering, 1989)

Ravi Zacharias, *A Shattered Visage* (0-943497-20-5, Wolgemuth & Hyatt, 1990)